Democratising Leadership in the Early Years

D0845722

Bringing together valuable insights from research and practice undertaken at the world-famous Pen Green Centre, *Democratising Leadership in the Early Years* illustrates how settings and practitioners can develop and maintain forms of leadership which foster collaborative practices across and within settings and services.

Effective leadership is key to establishing socially inclusive and democratic practices and as such, it has become a key concern for policy-makers, researchers and practitioners in the field of Early Childhood Education and Care. Drawing on authors' first-hand experiences on systems theory, psychological theory and neuroscience, chapters in this book illustrate the role of highly effective leadership in ensuring that services are accessible, inclusive and innovative. Practical advice will support professionals in overcoming destructive systemic and psychological dynamics to flatten hierarchies and improve relationships, learning and educational outcomes, and to encourage staff, parents and children to contribute creatively to collaborative enterprises.

Accessible and insightful, *Democratising Leadership in the Early Years* will improve understanding of approaches to leadership and support early years practitioners, students and managers as they develop their leadership skills and build capacity within settings and the wider community.

Margy Whalley, CBE, was Founder and former Director of Pen Green Centre for Children & Families, Nursery School and Teaching School, UK, and now works as a Research Associate and Education Consultant.

Karen John is a Development Pyschologist and works as a consultant and mentor of early years leaders.

Patrick Whitaker was Educational Leadership Consultant and Co Developer of the National Professional Qualification in Integrated Centre Leadership Pilot.

Elizabeth Klavins was Headteacher of an integrated, multi-functional Children's Centre for 25 years. She now works as an Education Adviser in schools.

Christine Parker is a former primary school Headteacher and currently works at the Pen Green Research Base, UK, leading on the Initial Teacher Training programme.

Julie Vaggers is a former nursery school Headteacher and now works as an Educational Consultant.

Pen Green Books for Early Years Educators

Titles in this series include:

Improving Your Reflective Practice through Stories of Practitioner Research
Edited by Cath Arnold

Young Children Learning Through Schemas
Deepening the Dialogue About Learning in the Home and in the Nursery
Katey Mairs and the Pen Green Team, edited by Cath Arnold

Using Evidence for Advocacy and Resistance in Early Years Services
Exploring the Pen Green Research Approach
Edited by Eddie McKinnon

Working with Children aged 0–3 and their Families
The Pen Green Approach
Edited by Tracy Gallagher and Cath Arnold

Democratising Leadership in the Early Years
A Systemic Approach
Margy Whalley, Karen John, Patrick Whitaker, Elizabeth Klavins, Christine Parker and Julie Vaggers

For more information about this series, please visit: www.routledge.com/Pen-Green-Books-for-Early-Years-Educators/book-series/PENGREEN

Democratising Leadership in the Early Years

A Systemic Approach

Margy Whalley, Karen John,
Patrick Whitaker, Elizabeth Klavins,
Christine Parker and
Julie Vaggers

 Routledge
Taylor & Francis Group

LONDON AND NEW YORK

3020

KH

First published 2019
by Routledge
2 Park Square, Milton Park, Abingdon, Oxon OX14 4RN

and by Routledge
711 Third Avenue, New York, NY 10017

Routledge is an imprint of the Taylor & Francis Group, an informa business

British Library Cataloguing-in-Publication Data
A catalogue record for this book is available from the British Library

Library of Congress Cataloging-in-Publication Data
A catalog record for this book has been requested

ISBN: 978-1-138-33796-1 (hbk)
ISBN: 978-1-138-33798-5 (pbk)
ISBN: 978-0-429-44204-9 (ebk)

Typeset in Garamond
by Apex CoVantage, LLC

Printed and bound in Great Britain by
TJ International Ltd, Padstow, Cornwall

8/23/19

Contents

Acknowledgements   vi
Notes on the authors   vii
Rationale: growing resilient leaders   x
MARGY WHALLEY

Introduction   1
KAREN JOHN

1   **Applying systems theory to early years leadership**   14
    PATRICK WHITAKER

2   **Holding the baby: leadership that inspires and contains ambition and anxiety**   38
    KAREN JOHN

3   **Leadership as activism**   87
    MARGY WHALLEY

4   **Who is taking responsibility? Becoming an authoritative leader**   115
    ELIZABETH KLAVINS

5   **We all have the potential to lead because we all have responsibilities**   139
    CHRISTINE PARKER

6   **Working together or pulling apart? How early years leaders and practitioners can encourage collaborative practice to flourish**   171
    JULIE VAGGERS

Index   203

Acknowledgements

> We are social creatures to the inmost centre of our being. The notion that one can begin anything at all from scratch, free from the past, or unindebted to others, could not conceivably be more wrong.
>
> Karl R. Popper (1902–1994)

At Pen Green we have worked within a 'democratic paradigm' which in Colin Fletcher's words (2014, xvii) 'opposes the injustices of inequalities'. As practitioners and writers we are aware of standing on the shoulders of giants and we want to acknowledge our debt to those that paved the way; the children, their parents and carers, the staff and the ever-increasing alumni that have participated in adult learning and continuous professional development programmes at Pen Green over 35 years.

Most of all in these acknowledgements we want to honour the work of Patrick Whitaker (1942–2010). Patrick was a gentle-man, unassuming, generous hearted, and a powerful thinker and writer. Patrick was a great friend to all of us at Pen Green and without his encouragement we would not have been able to articulate the democratic approach to leadership that underpins this book and all of our work. His contribution was immense and the impact of his writing and thinking informs both our day-to-day practice and our contribution to policy making, and policy transfer.

We all want to thank Dr Karen John for her powerful role in supporting the authors to drill down into their doctoral theses to produce these powerful chapters.

We want to appreciate the diplomatic skills of Tracy Gallagher (Joint Head of Pen Green) and Felicity Dewsbery (Deputy Head of Pen Green Integrated Centre with lead responsibility for Pen Green Research, Training and Development Base and Pen Green Teaching School) who acted as 'midwives' to ensure this book moved from preparation to publication.

Finally we want to thank Rebecca Elliott at the Pen Green Research Base for her consistent enthusiasm and meticulous efforts to ensure the manuscript got to the publishers on time and in good order.

Notes on the authors

Dr Karen John. Karen is a Developmental Psychologist who works as a researcher, trainer, psychotherapist and supervisor of therapeutic and leadership practice. With 46 years of leading, managing, consulting and teaching within academic research, mental health, social care and educational settings, her abiding aim is to help individuals, families, organisations and a range of professionals to reflect upon, identify and work to overcome internal and external obstacles that interfere with their healthy functioning and development. Over the past 20 years she has supported organisations, leaders and staff involved in providing and improving services for children, young people and families.

Dr Elizabeth Klavins. Elizabeth worked as Headteacher of an integrated, multi-functional Children's Centre for 27 years and came to view leadership as a continuous process of learning. She held a commitment to developing a sustainable learning organisation in which staff from different disciplines and with different levels of qualification were encouraged and supported to reflect individually and co-operatively about their work with children and families. Her intent remains to develop curious practitioners interested in deepening their understanding of their jobs in order to transform their practice. She continues in her role as a school adviser, supporting other school leaders since 2010.

Dr Christine Parker. Christine was a Teacher and Headteacher in primary and nursery schools in England for over 35 years. She is currently working as a tutor at the Pen Green Research Base, Corby, supporting students going into teaching and on the MA course. Her specialist interests are early childhood education, school leadership and multilingual childhoods. Christine spent a number of years working in Karachi, Pakistan. She found early years teachers to be very receptive to ideas of experiential learning and this experience made a significant impression on how she approached working with children and their families in multi-ethnic contexts in the UK. Christine studied for her PhD at Pen Green and developed primary school leadership through a systemic approach that was responsive to children's, families' and staff needs. She is currently developing her interest in psychoanalytic observational approaches.

Dr Julie Vaggers. Julie is fascinated by the challenges of leading in the early years, particularly sustaining the emotional wellbeing of leaders. Julie undertook the National Professional Qualification in Integrated Early Years Leadership (NPQICL) and subsequently established an Early Years Training consortium developing leadership capacity and working across Haringey. In her PhD she explored how leaders can encourage cross sector collaboration and the development of sustainable professional networks that benefit children and families. As Headteacher of a large integrated nursery school and Children's Centre, she encouraged a cohesive approach to integration and inclusion within her school and across the Local Authority. Julie has lobbied for recognition of the importance of early years education and was a member of the All-Party Parliamentary Group secretariat for Nursery Schools and has given evidence for the Education Select Committee and the Committee of Public Accounts. She taught in the early years for over 30 years.

Dr Margy Whalley CBE. Margy has an amazing daughter, Natasha, and three gorgeous grandchildren, Molly, Tom and Harriet. She has worked for over 44 years in education and community development projects in England, Brazil and Papua New Guinea. She was a Primary Teacher in a stunning primary school in Kent but has spent most of her professional life working in the early

years phase. She loves community work and is committed to engaging families to co-design, develop and run public services which need to be a lot more responsive to those that use them and pay for them in their taxes. She has an MA in Community Education and a PhD in Leadership within early years settings. Margy recently retired from her post as Founder-Director of the Pen Green Integrated Centre for Children and Families and although semi-retired is currently working as a Research Associate for the Pen Green Research Training and Development Centre, which she set up in 1997. Margy continues to be a passionate advocate for children and families and for the amazing, but generally underpaid, staff, who work with them in ECEC settings.

Patrick Whitaker. Patrick died after a short illness in 2010 and this book is dedicated to him. After a powerful career as a Headteacher and author he subsequently built a career as an Education Leadership Consultant working across the UK with schools and local authorities. The Pen Green Leadership team met him, unforgettably, at a residential weekend conference and he immediately embraced the world of ECEC. We were attracted to his brightly coloured ties in the sea of grey and black and brown coated primary heads of that period but even more to his powerful rhetoric which celebrated the voice of the child.

"If you want to know whether it's a wet playtime", he said "ask a nursery child! They are still autonomous, unafraid and able to speak truth to power. The dinner ladies don't want to be outside in the cold and wet but don't like to say it, the teachers don't want the children inside (because they wreck their classrooms) but are ashamed to think it and nobody can make a decision".

For the next 25 years we had the privilege of working with Patrick as a compassionate and wise mentor and tutor, co-developer of powerful and far reaching leadership courses and materials, an erudite and yet accessible trainer and writer. He has left an enormous legacy to the field of early childhood education and his contribution will never be forgotten.

Rationale: growing resilient leaders

Margy Whalley

Leadership in early years settings and services has become a key concern for policy makers, academics and practitioners. With few exceptions early years' education and care settings in this country were small-scale 'Cinderella' services in the '60s, '70s and '80s in this country. Under the Labour government in 1997 Early Childhood Education and Care (ECEC) became pivotal as a critical arm of Labour's social inclusion agenda. In Blair's terms, these services and settings were both the 'frontier of the welfare state' *and* the first and most critical phase of the education system. As each of Labour's national programmes – the Early Excellence Centres programme, Sure Start Local Programmes, the Neighbourhood Nurseries and Children's Centres – rolled out, the complex challenges of coalescing education, health and social work interventions within a single institution (or closely interrelated organisations) became a central concern for both government and for local authorities.

Leaders in what I will consistently refer to as integrated (ECEC) settings working with children *and* their families are required to:

- Balance the demands of sustaining outstanding practice across all aspects of their service, consistently reviewing the effectiveness of their interventions and developing innovative ways of working
- Ensure services are accessible to all parents and children, particularly to those parents who find it hardest to access public services
- Co-construct services with parents and engage actively with parents as services users
- Develop partnerships with the public, private and voluntary sector and negotiate radically new ways of collaborating – despite extreme cuts to budgets
- Build capacity within the community and within their staff teams and support staff who are often struggling with constant change

As Labour rolled out each new model of ECEC provision it became increasingly apparent that the major challenge for the ECEC system was to produce the leaders it needed to run these services.

As pioneering organisations, integrated centres for children and family under the remit of the Early Excellence Centres programme, Sure Start local programme, Neighbourhood Nurseries or the Children's Centres programme, all had to forge their own unique pathways working with multi-professional teams within different social, political and economic constraints. From small sites concerned with the education and childcare needs of very young children with small staff groups and fairly narrow remits, centre leaders were soon working with 500–800 local children and families on one site. By 2006 some settings were engaging with 3000+ families across newly emerging locality networks. All centres were under increasing external pressures and were working in a complex and fast-changing environment. Leadership capacity and the need to rapidly develop new leaders capable of running these new services became one of the critical factors in the success of the government's Early Childhood Education and Care initiatives over the decade from 1997 to 2007. Naomi Eisenstadt, the senior civil servant who ran the government's Sure Start Unit for its first seven years identified the leadership issue in this way,

> What I now believe we failed to understand at the time is how difficult the task of running a Sure Start programme would be. Bringing together local providers in different agencies, developing programme plans with local parents, commissioning major capital projects and an in-depth understanding of early childhood development were all essential skills and activities for SSLP managers. There were extraordinary people who were active in advising on the design of Sure Start. Among these were Gillian Pugh, who was then running Coram Family, Bernadette Duffy, head of early education at Coram Family and Margy Whalley, who had established Pen Green, perhaps the most internationally well-known Children's Centre. *These individuals were the exception, not the rule, and they could not be cloned.* Norman Glass believed that their energy, enthusiasm and creativity would be replicated across the country if we freed up local areas to design their own programmes, albeit with a clear set of outcome requirements set out in the Public Service Agreement (PSA). *I believe a major failure was to underestimate the skill set required to deliver a high-quality Sure Start programme.*
>
> (Eisenstadt, 2011:144)

Those of us already leading and managing well-established integrated centres shared a very different perspective. Most of the existing ECEC leaders had previously focused primarily on the learning and development needs of very young children. Now they were taking on a very different role requiring far more than Eisenstadt's rather reductionist notion of a 'leadership skill set'. The Dutch economist Ben Boog writes about the need to understand the powerful nature of the work we are engaging in if we are to make the kind of difference that the government was envisaging. 'If there is no explicit emanci-patory or empowering vision guiding the project from the onset, it will prove difficult to realise any emancipatory effects' (Boog, 2003: 434). For some of the most experienced leaders of small settings and for those currently being trained in universities and colleges what we were undertaking was 'much big-ger' than simply early education and childcare. What they were being asked to lead and manage was a completely new construct. Moreover the focus on a 'delivery' model was unhelpful. At Pen Green, a Centre that was founded in the teeth of local opposition we are aware that you can 'deliver pizzas but not public services' (Whalley, 2013:3). Public services that are funded through tax payers' money need to be driven and developed by the people who want to use them. A major failure in the development of all Labour's ECEC initiatives was the rather simplistic idea that the elements of services in integrated cen-tres for children and their families were like the ingredients of a cake which when mixed together would have the desired effect; a child's life chances would be transformed, a family would climb out of the poverty gap (21st Century Children's Centres Whalley and Riddell: Pen Green Publications).

'What' actually goes on in ECEC services is less important than 'how' the services engage with the community and work with the families that want to use the services. It was also true that 'off the shelf' packages of leader-ship or management training from existing university departments, or from the now defunct National College for Leadership did not fit the bill and equip these 21st-century leaders to face the complex pressures of running an integrated ECEC setting. What was required was a distinctive and specialist model of leadership development which would help new leaders to develop a deeper understanding of systemic thinking, community capacity building and the co-construction of services with potential users. The leaders of these new ECEC provisions also needed professional support and supervision out-side their traditional local authority line management arrangements because they were undertaking challenging work with complex families and working in a multi-agency context, not just within the education system. This new approach to leadership and management of integrated services and settings was fundamentally about developing leaders from many different disciplines, not just those from traditional early education routes.

Pen Green was contracted and supported by DfE from 1997 to develop alternative academic and professional leadership programmes to support all four major ECEC interventions. In this book we describe how these leader-ship programmes developed and what was significant about the leadership practice that emerged. We also identify the theoretical and conceptual frame-works that underpin this particular approach; an approach that has inspired huge interest across New Zealand, Australia, Germany, Scandinavia, Portugal and most recently the United States of America. What this book uniquely offers are the experiences of lead professionals in some of the most successful ECEC organisations that operated throughout this period. The centre leaders who have written chapters worked in Corby, Haringey, Accrington, Peterborough and all had first-hand experience of Labour's new initiatives and experienced the subsequent cuts and radical policy shifts under the coalition government. They have documented how these changes impacted on specific communities facing serious social and economic challenges. As 'studies of cases' (Fletcher, 2014, p. xviii) they show what has really made a difference for children, their careers and their communities. They illustrate the democratic intent, the democratic process and democratic implications of this extraordinary paradigm of 'system conscious leadership' that has emerged in the early years' sector in the UK.

References

Boog, B. (2003) The Emancipatory Character of Action Research, Its History and the Present State of the Art. *Journal of Community and Applied Psychology*, 13, 426–438.

Boog, B. W., Keune, L. & Tromp, C. (2003), Action research and emancipation. *J. Community. Appl. Soc. Psychol.*, 13, 419–425. doi:10.1002/casp.747

Eisenstadt, N. (2011) *Providing a Sure Start: How government discovered early childhood*, Bristol: Bristol University Press.

Fletcher, C. in McKinnon, E. (2014) *Using Evidence for Advocacy and Resistance in Early Years Services*, London: Routledge.

McDowall, A. & Fletcher, C. (2004) "Employee development: An Organizational Justice Perspective", Personnel Review, 33 (1), pp. 8–29, https://doi.org/10.1108/00483480410510606

Pen Green Publications Whalley, M and Riddell, B. (2010) *Critical Issues in 21st Century Children's Centres: Emergent Issues from a Series of Think Tanks*. Corby, UK: Pen Green Publications.

Whalley, M., Arnold, C. & Orr, R. (2013). *Working with families in children's centres and early years settings. 2nd ed.* London: Hodder & Stoughton.

Introduction

Karen John

The authors of the chapters in this book have devoted their professional lives to promoting social equality and wellbeing, with the explicit aim that the children and families they serve, and the colleagues with whom they work, feel they belong, feel they are of equal value to others and feel themselves to be creative problem solvers with something valuable to contribute to their communities. Our aspirations are ambitious but as we demonstrate in our research we are neither naïve nor unrealistic. Contrary to persistent perceptions in educational circles regarding the relative simplicity of working with young children, those who work in early years settings regularly encounter and engage with complexity. Complexity is manifest whenever we seek to understand a child, a parent, ourselves, our colleagues or relationships in families or teams, when we work across professional boundaries and when we attempt to negotiate the disparate systems involved in providing high-quality integrated services for young children, their families and communities.

This book is about the authors' individual and joint efforts to democratise early years leadership. However, by no means have we been alone in our endeavours. Unlike those who maintain strong boundaries around their organisations and disciplines, early years professionals and settings have worked hard to provide seamless and inclusive access to integrated services for children and families. It has not been unusual for an early years setting to offer nursery education, childcare, family support and health checks, inclusion of children with special needs, and adult education, training and employment advice and support. What is more, integrated early years settings have promoted strong and deeply respectful relationships with parents and carers, acknowledging them as their children's first teachers, and working in partnership with them to plan and evaluate the services provided.

Unprecedented early years funding to increase the life chances of children and families

Soon after the New Labour Government came to power in 1997, through the initiatives of Early Excellence, Sure Start, Neighbourhood Nurseries and eventually Sure Start Children's Centres, the early years received a long-overdue injection of funding, which was sustained through 2010. First, as a means of broadening access to high-quality nursery education and de-stigmatising social care for children and families 'in need', the Department of Education and Skills supported the development and piloting of 29 Early Excellence Centres, which numbered 100 by 2003. These settings as well as other community-based provision for young children and their families received considerably more capital and revenue funding when in 1998 the UK Treasury began to sponsor Sure Start local programmes to reduce child poverty by providing a range of support services to families with children from 0 to 4 years living in economically deprived areas. These initiatives acknowledged the early years as a time when social investment can have a significant impact on individual children, families and society (HM Treasury & DfES, 2007, p. 9), and sought to reduce inequalities in the quality of early education, childcare and support that both poor and better-off families could expect (ibid., pp. 18 & 35).

Pen Green and the early years leadership qualification, the NPQICL

Part of the funding was earmarked for early years staff and leaders, who were encouraged to gain vocational and professional qualifications and higher degrees as part of improving their settings and practice. The Pen Green Centre for Children and Families and Pen Green Research, Training and Development Base and Leadership Centre in Corby Northamptonshire was in the avant-garde of those educational and training efforts. Alongside innovations in integrated early years provision, Pen Green founder and Director Margy Whalley worked with the Department for Education and Skills (DfES) to produce learning opportunities and experiences tailored to the needs of enthusiastic and often overwhelmed leaders facing the challenges of change and complexity inherent in efforts to integrate and de-stigmatise services and meet the needs of all young children and families within local communities. In 1998, Pen Green Research was funded by the DfES for a new building to expand training facilities, to continue their work in designing, supporting and evaluating developments in integrated early years provision and to offer intensive work-focused training opportunities for the leaders of integrated early years centres. Between 1999 and 2003, 87 early years centre heads and deputies completed Pen Green post-graduate leadership courses and earned a post-graduate diploma in leadership. This work-focused, experiential course evolved and formed the basis of the year-long National Professional Qualification in Integrated Centre Leadership (NPQICL). The highly experiential NPQICL course, which conferred a third of an MA degree in early years leadership, was piloted in 2004–05 with 41 participants and then rolled out across nine regions, with over 700 participants completing the course nationally in 2005–06 and 2006–07 (Whalley et al., 2008).

Fittingly, the team that developed the NPQICL was multi-disciplinary, comprised of individuals from diverse backgrounds, all *boundary spanners*. The lead architect of the NPQICL was Margy Whalley CBE (1994, 2000), a community educator, visionary leader and innovator, who founded the Pen Green Centre for Children and Families in 1983, after working with communities in Brazil and Papua New Guinea, and went on to establish the Pen Green Research, Training and Development Base and Leadership Centre in 1994. She and her colleague of 20 years, former primary head teacher and influential consultant and author of educational, leadership and management texts, Patrick Whitaker (1983, 1993), developed and honed programmes made up of individual and group experiential learning opportunities and team tasks, as well as academic studies that challenged participant-leaders to be deeply reflective and authentically themselves.

Other developers were: Sheila Thorpe OBE (Thorpe & Gasper, 2003), former Head of one of the earliest and most significant integrated early years and family centres, Hillfields in Coventry, and a key government advisor on developing centres of excellence, supporting leaders and the NPQICL; Colin Fletcher (1993), professor of sociology and community development and avid proponent of practitioner-led action research; and Karen John (2000, 2008, 2011, 2012), developmental psychology researcher in psychiatry, former director of human resources and training for a UK-wide community mental health services organisation and Adlerian psychotherapist, psychotherapy and leadership supervisor, trainer and organisation consultant. From our diverse heritages and experiences, each of us had come to believe in developing and sustaining egalitarian and supportive leadership and environments. Leadership that promotes reflexivity, open dialogue and shared vision, values and standards for practice and relating. Leadership that invites challenge and seeks to unlock the creativity of individuals and groups – children, families and communities – in order to maximise their potential for lifelong growth, development and resilience.

NPQICL philosophy

Implicit within the NPQICL course, which was offered continuously across the nine government regions in England from 2005 through 2015, was that by the time participants enrolled in the programme, they already had acquired considerable knowledge about leadership through family life, through schooling, through education and work experiences and through observations of the world around them. They had developed their own particular ways of leading, based on their values and beliefs about how people need to be treated if they are to work effectively. The NPQICL programme invited participants to share their experiences, values and perspectives and to see learning leadership as a lifelong endeavour, one that requires regular and deep reflection, dialogue and cycles of evaluation and research.

Theoretical sources of NPQICL approaches to 'learning leadership' can be traced back to the Greeks. For example, *democracy*, like most concepts and theories, has been forgotten, re-discovered and refined time and again. Constructivist educationalist John Dewey (1916/1966) and social psychologist Kurt Lewin (1948) agreed that democracy must be learned anew in each generation, and that it is far more difficult to attain and to maintain than autocracy. Such is the challenge of applying and sustaining complex ideals. Through experience, each person and generation find their own truths. It is no wonder that governments, organisations and groups are attracted to pat answers and simple solutions, even though they do little more than reassure and relieve their immediate anxieties.

The NPQICL programme was designed to address the *complexity* and *turbulence* that the leaders and staff of integrated Children's Centres face and to encourage them to be ever mindful of issues of *sustainability*. It invited participants to challenge themselves and each other, to question their own and others' practice and motivation and to support others to do the same. Rather than ask participants to compromise their values and principles, they were encouraged to ask questions that begin: 'How can we. . . . ?'

Theoretical underpinnings of NPQICL

Andragogy is an approach to learning that places the needs, feelings, thoughts and experiences of participants at the heart of any educational programme. Andragogy is based on the belief that individuals achieve a self-concept of essential self-direction when they psychologically become adults (Knowles, 1970). This self-concept includes a deep need to be regarded by *others* as self-directing (Ryan, 1995). Adults tend to experience internal tension and display resentment or resistance in situations that do not allow or acknowledge their need for self-direction (ibid.). Interestingly, those working in the early years tend to appreciate that even small children respond in much the same way. Respecting and valuing the learners and the led – and recognising and developing their instrumental roles in learning and leading – were the concepts most often at the head of NPQICL participants' lists of the principles and practices underpinning effective approaches across *pedagogy, andragogy* and *leadership*.

The andragogic model asserts that five issues be considered and addressed in formal learning. Educators need to: 1) let learners know why something is important to learn; 2) show learners how to direct themselves through information; 3) relate the topic to the learners' experiences; 4) remember that people will not learn until they are ready and motivated to learn, which requires 5) helping them overcome inhibitions, unhelpful behaviours and beliefs about learning.

Democracy and equality – For there to be *equality*, which is a necessary condition of *democracy*, every human being – regardless of age, gender, sexual orientation, race, ethnicity, religion, family background, social class or status – needs to be seen to have equal value, needs to be entitled to equal rights and opportunities and needs to be treated with respect. Government guidance and officials regularly refer directly or indirectly to these principles. The principles of democracy and equality – that every human being feels at home on this earth – are at the heart of children's centres. Yet we inevitably grapple with how we can realise these ideals, both in light of gross material inequalities and within organisational and professional hierarchies.

One of the earliest depth psychologists, Alfred Adler (1938) observed that feeling equal to others is an essential element of mental health – and that for the principles of democracy and egalitarianism to be realised, a deeper understanding of *human psychology* is needed – one in which *compensatory* striving for power and superiority is balanced by developing and expressing our innate *interest in – and need for –* others. In other words, we need to be aware of how our sense of smallness, inadequacy and vulnerability can lead to defensiveness, false bravado and useless competitive striving for power *over* others, rather than cooperating *with* others and contributing our talents to creatively solve our common problems and improve our own and others' quality of life.

At the beginning of the 20th century, Alfred Adler (1956/1964) argued that social equality is a prerequisite for social living, without which there can be no stability (Dreikurs, 1971/1994, p. x). Adler was concerned with equality in terms of being of equal value and equally entitled to be taken into account and respected in all relationships, private and public. Privately, between partners and between parents and children – as well as at work and in other public domains – so-called feminine values are often missing (Marshall, 1994). Wilkinson and Pickett's (2009), *The Spirit Level: Why Equality Is Better for Everyone*, brings together data from several large-scale research studies on health and wellbeing from around the world, which show that people are much healthier and happier in countries and states with the smallest gap between rich and poor. Ideas about democracy and equality lead naturally to another main source of inspiration to the NPQICL architects: *humanism* and *humanistic psychology*.

Humanism and ***humanistic psychologies*** – An emphasis on the importance of *self-concept* and *self-actualisation* provide a natural link between humanism as a philosophy and as a theory of psychology. Humanism as a philosophy attaches prime importance to human, rather than divine matters, and stresses the potential goodness of human beings, emphasising common human needs and seeking rational ways of solving human problems. Humanistic psychologies focus on each individual's potential to be good, with the belief that mental and social problems result from deviations from a natural striving for growth and self-actualisation. Humanistic therapies, most notably the person-centred approach developed by Carl Rogers (1961), posit that growth and self-actualisation require the therapist's unconditional positive regard for the person, deep empathy and belief in the person's ability to grow and change within an encouraging or therapeutic environment that provides space and time for self-reflection and growing self-awareness that lead to self-actualisation.

Educationalist Jack Mezirow (1978, 1981, 1991) developed the notion of *transformational learning*, which describes a process of engaging in self-reflection and increasing self-knowledge, which while a rational exercise in some ways, also involves a profound emotional or spiritual transformation not unlike that which occurs in successful psychotherapy. For example, the experience of undoing racist, sexist and other elitist and oppressive attitudes can be painful and emotional, as these attitudes often are developed as ways to cope with and make sense of a world in which we tend to feel small and insignificant. This type of deeply self-reflective learning requires taking risks and a willingness to be vulnerable and have one's attitudes and assumptions challenged.

The other well-known humanistic psychologist Abraham Maslow developed a *theory of human motivation* in which our many varying human needs are seen to arise hierarchically (Maslow, 1954/1970). Maslow held that in order to attend to our 'higher' needs, each of our *basic* needs must be met. The first of our basic needs is the *physiological* requirement for food and shelter; the second is the need for *safety*; the third is the need for *love, belonging and identification*; and the fourth is the need for *respect and self-esteem*. The basic needs are regarded as *deficiency needs*, but the crowning need is a different type, that is, the need for *growth and self-actualisation*. According to Maslow's theory, the basic needs predominate when they are unsatisfied, but the higher ones predominate when the lower needs are satisfied. Maslow's hierarchy of needs offers a useful framework within which to account for *regression* in adaptation and functioning, particularly when *basic needs* are not being met, are threatened – or the individual *believes* them to be threatened.

Economist and well-being researcher, Richard Layard (2005) found that 'People are deeply attached to the status quo. They hate loss of any kind, and they care less about gains than losses' (p. 227). Impending change generally threatens loss and tends to evoke fear that our basic needs will not be met. This is particularly important for early years leaders to remember when leading change – particularly across professional boundaries and encountering defensive and less-than-generative behaviour amongst those involved.

Depth psychologies – Humanistic psychologies grew out of depth psychologies, and while the NPQICL did not major on them, ideas offered by such theoretical formulations as *iceberg theory* and *group dynamics* were vital in helping participants to appreciate that there is more going on within and between individuals and groups or teams than can be seen and that much of human behaviour is motivated by needs, which if not met, are expressed in unhelpful, uncooperative or even dysfunctional ways (e.g. Huffington et al., 2004; Obholzer & Roberts, 1994).

Experience-based, reflective learning and action research – Practitioner-led action research (Fletcher, 1993; Heron, 1971; McNiff, 2002; Reason, 1988; Reason & Bradbury, 2001; Schön, 1983) extends the reflective process of grappling with the experience of leading by offering a dynamic method of learning leadership through inquiry and investigation. *Action research*, also called *collaborative inquiry*, offers a powerful tool to help leaders to involve others in managing change. NPQICL participants were asked to involve their staff teams, other agencies and professionals, as well as members of the communities they serve, in 'spirals' of *participative enquiry* in order to study, reflect upon, lead and make progress towards shared goals. As in all reflective, experience-based learning, the process is likely to be at least as important as the outcome.

Community development and community action – The National Standards for Leaders of Children's Centres document (HM Treasury & DfES, 2007) stated that:

> Children's centres have the potential to transform the way in which families gain access to and can benefit from local services . . . raise expectations and aspirations so that families and the local community are encouraged to enjoy new opportunities for learning and better health.

> (p. 9)

Communities can only take responsibility and action when they achieve critical awareness of what affects their lives and gain the confidence to change what oppresses them. When communities are downtrodden, they are unable to credit their perceptions, experiences and skills. The same is true for children's centre leaders and staff members. Community development and action begin when those in power meet members of the community as equals, respecting, valuing and trusting them to identify and build on their individual and collective strengths and to exercise choice about things that really matter to them. To quote from the Pilot NPQICL Study Programme booklet, which draws on Paulo Freire's (1970/1986) work:

> it is not enough that we reflect in order to know or understand, it is necessary to reflect in order to make a difference – to bring about change. Praxis is a self-directed process springing from our core professional values, demanding that we continuously consider the impact and effect of our own actions. Praxis involves honouring our experience and relating it to theory, and thinking deeply about future action. Sometimes this deepening of awareness and reflexivity will result in us feeling uncomfortable, and realising it is our *own* actions rather than the actions of others that need attention. This may be particularly difficult in our leadership

roles, since we have grown up being encouraged to believe our leaders are superior, with inherently powerful capacities and qualities.

(Whalley et al., 2004, p. 38)

This book is very much about how early years leadership has, and can, make a difference in the lives of children, families and communities.

PhD studies in leadership

Twenty-three of the 41 NPQICL pilot participants went on to complete their Leadership MA at Pen Green in collaboration with Middlesex University. Then in February 2008, three of those pilot NPQICL and MA graduates embarked upon the newly established Pen Green/University of Leicester part-time doctoral programme, 'Leadership of Integrated Provision for Children and Families'. Those three were joined by a fourth person who had completed the Pen Green Post-Graduate Diploma in Leadership, a fifth who had completed the Pen Green/University of Leicester MA, Integrated Provision for Children and Families, and a sixth who was an M-level Pen Green Research staff member. Each proposed to study their own leadership more closely as they intensified their efforts to democratise the leadership and provision of early years settings.

Margy Whalley and Karen John developed the PhD programme and co-facilitated and provided tutorial support with Patrick Whitaker, until his death in 2010. The PhD extended the NPQICL philosophy and methods, and over six years offered a minimum of ten full-day face-to-face sessions annually, and somewhat less frequently for a further year. The sessions took the form of an action-learning set, known as the Doctoral Study Group. Because of work demands, one member of the Group withdrew after 12 months, with the remaining five participating fully in the Group for seven years. Two of the Group members decided not to finish their PhD theses, but each of the three who completed their studies and earned their PhDs have contributed a chapter to this book.

Precis of chapters

Chapter 1, 'Applying systems theory to early years leadership' is reproduced, with very minor updates and corrections, from a 2009 paper by Patrick Whitaker, which was produced for Pen Green staff and students but never published. In his words, Patrick's intention was 'to examine the implications of the somewhat sudden and insistent introduction of a systems theory perspective into the discourse about leadership and management in services for children, families and schools'. He highlights the confusion in terms and proffered application of systems theory for school leadership and delineates the inconsistencies within National College for School Leadership (NCSL) documents. He helpfully juxtaposes this critique with an introduction to the development and import of systems theory, along with the disciplines and intentions of its pioneers. He concludes with recommendations drawing on systems theory itself to identify and discuss six possible and powerfully inter-related areas of leadership development, namely: 1) *systems consciousness* – as a way of being, e.g. recognising challenges of confusion, uncertainty, ambiguity and being alert to subtleties and nuances and unafraid to adopt multi-perspective approaches; 2) *collaboration* – that is energetic and creative; 3) *emancipation* – particularly through reflective practice and practitioner-led action research; 4) *theory and practice* – that is iterative, with practice develop-ing new theory and new theory extending practice, and so on; 5) *research* – especially qualitative and practitioner-led; and 6) *organisation* – or dynamic organisational forms that offer opportunities for leadership, collaboration and research that routinely involve staff, children and families across the organisation.

In Chapter 2, 'Holding the baby: leadership that inspires and contains ambition and anxiety', Karen John focuses on 'what it takes to survive intact the challenges inherent in democratising early years leadership and provi-sion, keeping the baby safe and thriving'. She begins by reviewing the chal-lenges of leading integrated early years provision for children and families, and the need for both leadership and management, with evidence from the neurosciences that we are 'wired' to expect and undertake each of these func-tions. She notes the parallels between leading and parenting, especially that the same key dispositions are required for each within democratic societies. Karen also observes that neither children nor staff come with instructions, that from observing our parents and leaders we learn more about how *not* to parent and lead than about how to do so effectively. She then introduces a wide range of psychological understandings from theory and research that converge to provide strong evidence that effective leaders empathise, encour-age, hold and contain those they lead. That is, theory and research confirm that throughout our lives health and wellbeing depend upon love, under-standing and caring relationships with others – feeling that we belong, are competent and significant members of our communities, have the ability to recover from losses and disappointments, and that these psychological needs are supported by trusted and reliable authorities who help us to understand and contain both our ambitions and our anxieties. Karen contends that regu-lar work-based supervision needs to be provided for all staff members as a reliable means of offering leadership support, management and professional guidance and containment. She concludes with a summary of factors that undermine and factors that strengthen good authority and democracy, which is conceptualised as an ecological system that promotes and sustains good authority and democratic leadership.

Chapter 3, 'Leadership as activism' by founder-director of Pen Green, Margy Whalley, provides an account of leadership and development of the

Pen Green Centre for Children and Families and the Pen Green Research, Training and Development Base and Leadership Centre. She focuses on the crucial role of developing future leaders who are committed to transforming the life chances of children and their families by harnessing the energy for change and social solidarity in communities. Regarding leadership in early years as emancipatory practice, she argues that early years leaders need to conceptualise and construct their practice as part of a struggle for social justice and social change.

In Chapter 4, Elizabeth Klavins asks, 'Who is taking responsibility? Becoming an authoritative leader' and tells the story of being Head Teacher of Fairfield Nursery School and Children's Centre in Accrington Lancashire for 25 years. She came to realise that she was overfunctioning as a leader but 'that working hard is not the same as taking responsibility'. As part of the NPQICL Pilot programme, visiting innovative kindergarten settings in New Zealand was what awakened Liz's 'passionate belief in systemic, democratic leadership'. Recounting her six-and-a-half-year journey as a leader-researcher in undertaking her doctoral research, Liz candidly describes the challenges she encountered in attempting to put theory into practice. Placing practitioner-led action research at the centre of her efforts to flatten Fairfield's leadership hierarchy, encouraging staff to interrogate practice and potentially lead change, Liz discovered that what she wanted for others was not necessarily what they wanted for themselves. While initially feeling disheartened by ructions within the staff team regarding the first joint research project undertaken by staff members studying for qualifications or higher degrees, Liz remained committed to understanding the effects of her leader-researcher actions. She engaged an external consultant to facilitate the first of two focus group sessions to which all staff were invited in order to feedback formally but anonymously their views and suggestions about developments in the setting. The feedback revealed that a significant minority were feeling left out and undervalued for not being clever or academic enough to take part in researching practice. Liz courageously took the feedback on board, continued to consult with staff and revised her strategy, though she remained determined to offer children and families the best possible provision through encouraging practitioner-led action research. She not only survived the discouragement and distress expressed by discouraged staff, in the end she managed to engage all members of the team in identifying, collaborating and undertaking practitioner-led action research over a one-year period, with impressive results.

In her title of Chapter 5, Christine Parker declares, 'We all have the potential to lead because we all have responsibilities'. A head teacher of early years and primary schools for 16 years, Christine describes how during a focused six-year period she shared her leadership vision and learning with colleagues, children and parents at Gladstone Primary in Peterborough. A large, socio-economically disadvantaged inner-city school, Gladstone accommodates approximately 450 multi-lingual children, and during the time of Christine's study, the children spoke 20 different languages, although 90% were Muslim. Christine led school-vision and action-learning groups, professional development and community projects and a girls' chat group, encouraging active dialogue, collaboration, deep reflection and systems thinking throughout the Gladstone community. She was helped to make meaning of her leadership journey within the Pen Green Doctoral Study Group and a regional head teachers' learning set. Together with Christine's reflections on the phases of her core 'lead-learner' study and staff members' action research groups, she includes the powerful reflective narratives of one of the mothers who participated with their children in a Gladstone arts project 'Connecting Communities' and of a 10-year-old pupil who was a member of the girls' chat group. These narratives served to deepen Christine's understanding of life and perceptions in the wider community. The mother told of the significance of her old front door key and created a graphic representation of the locality. Her deep attachment to the area and its diversity was undiminished by the realities of drug abuse, physical attacks and burglaries. The girls' chat group followed from concern about underachievement among girls and a racist incident initiated by three girls. After being given time out of class to reflect upon their actions and writing letters of apology, the three girls met with Christine regularly throughout the school year, writing reflective journals and responding to the questions 'What is racism?' and 'What is bullying?' One 10-year-old girl's leadership story is a moving account of acknowledging past wrongs, taking responsibility, developing a systems consciousness and a deep sense of restorative social justice. This moving narrative culminates in the girl's reflections about leading a school assembly on racism, bullying, social equality and social justice.

In Chapter 6, 'Working together or pulling apart? How early years leaders and practitioners can encourage collaborative practice to flourish', Julie Vaggers explores 'the challenges of leading and supporting people from different professional backgrounds to work together collaboratively'. She identifies four leadership processes that encourage integrated working, as well as the barriers to integration, and describes a series of activities 'designed to allow thoughtful action and to build trust. Building trust requires a shared commitment to getting to know and under each other's life history, professional experience and heritage'. For more than 20 years Julie was Head Teacher of Rowland Hill Nursery and Children's Centre in Haringey, London, the tenth most deprived borough in England, and for five years she was a tutor, mentor and assessor for the NPQICL. In those roles she was persuaded that cooperation among professionals and successful integration of services were hugely advantageous for children and families, providing ready access to the services they need, and a sense of belonging, significance and efficacy within a welcoming and responsive setting. Wishing to maximise the impact of children's centres, Julie invited ten other children's centre leaders in Haringey to collaborate, learn from one another and seek transformation through participation in a practitioner-led action-research study. Over a one-year period group members met regularly and undertook parallel reflections and studies within their own settings. Together they critically analysed the state of their relationships with partner agencies, developed a critical discourse of multi-disciplinary and interagency working and a systems consciousness, and deepened the level of debate between professionals providing locality-based services. Julie and her colleagues' efforts provide a rich resource for early years and other professionals wishing to work effectively across agencies and disciplines.

References

Adler, A. (1938). *Social Interest: A Challenge to Mankind*. London: Faber & Faber.

Adler, A. (1956/1964). In H.L. Ansbacher & R.R. Ansbacher (eds.), *The Individual Psychology of Alfred Adler*. New York: Harper Torchbooks.

Dewey, J. (1916/1966). *Democracy and Education. An Introduction to the Philosophy of Education*. New York: Free Press.

Dreikurs, R. (1971/1994). *Social Equality: The Challenge of Today*. Chicago: Adler School of Professional Psychology.

Fletcher, C. (1993). An analysis of practitioner research. In B. Broad & C. Fletcher (eds.), *Practitioner Social Work Research in Action*. London: Whiting and Birch.

Freire, P. (1970/1986). *Pedagogy of the Oppressed*. (Translated by M.B. Ramos). New York: Continuum.

Heron, J. (1971). *Experience and Method: An Inquiry into the Concept of Experiential Research: Human Potential Research Project*. Guildford, UK: University of Surrey.

HM Treasury & DfES (2007). *Aiming High for Children: Supporting Families*. London: HM Treasury & DfES.

Huffington, C., Armstrong, D., Halton, W., Hoyle, L. & Pooley, J. (2004). *Working Below the Surface: The Emotional Life of Contemporary Organizations*. London: Karnac.

John, K. (2000). Basic needs, conflict and dynamics in groups. *Journal of Individual Psychology*, 56, 4, 419–434.

John, K. (2008). Sustaining the leaders of children's centres: The role of leadership mentoring. *European Early Childhood Education Research Journal*, 16, 53–66.

John, K. (2011). Theoretical underpinnings of the NPQICL: Inspiration and grounding. In L. Trodd & L. Chivers (eds.), *Interprofessional Working in Practice: Learning & Working Together for Children & Families*, pp. 145–153. Milton Keynes: Open University Press.

John, K. (2012). Authority and democracy 100 years on. In *ASIIP Year Book 2012*. London: The Adlerian Society UK and Institute of Individual Psychology (ASIIP).

Knowles, M. (1970). *Modern Practice of Adult Education: Andragogy Versus Pedagogy*. Englewood Cliffs, NJ: Prentice Hall/Cambridge.

Layard, R. (2005). *Happiness*. London: Penguin Books.

Lewin, K. (1948). In G.W. Lewin (ed.), *Resolving Social Conflicts – Selected Papers on Group Dynamics*. New York: Harper & Row.

Marshall, J. (1994). Revisioning organizations by developing female values. In J. Boot, J. Lawrence & J. Morris (eds.), *Managing the Unknown by Creating New Futures*, pp. 165–183. London: McGraw-Hill.

Maslow, A.H. (1954/1970). *Motivation and Personality*. New York: Harper & Row.

McNiff, J. (2002). *Action Research Principles and Practice*. London: Routledge.

Mezirow, J. (1978). Perspective transformation. *Adult Education Quarterly, 28*, 2, 100–110.

Mezirow, J. (1981). A critical theory of adult learning and education. *Adult Education, 32*, 3–23.

Mezirow, J. (1991). *Transformative Dimensions of Adult Learning.* San Francisco, CA: Jossey-Bass.

Obholzer, A. & Roberts, V.Z. (1994). *The Unconscious at Work: Individual and Organizational Stress in Human Services.* London: Routledge.

Reason, P. (ed.) (1988). *Human Inquiry in Action: Developments in New Paradigm Research.* London: Sage.

Reason, P. & Bradbury, H. (2001). *Handbook of Action Research: Participative Inquiry and Practice.* London: Sage.

Rogers, C.R. (1961). *On Becoming a Person: A Therapist's View of Psychotherapy.* London: Allen & Unwin.

Ryan, R.M. (1995): Psychological needs and the facilitation of integrative processes. *Journal of Personality, 63*, 397–427.

Schön, D. (1983). *The Reflective Practitioner.* New York: Basic Books.

Thorpe, S. & Gasper, M. (2003). Who Cares for the Carers? An Exploration of Support Provided for Leaders of Integrated Early Years Centres. *Leadership & Management Bursary Report*, October 2003. London: DfES.

Whalley, M. (1994). *Learning to be Strong: Setting Up a Neighbourhood Service for Under-Fives and Their Families.* London: Hodder & Stoughton.

Whalley, M. (ed.) (2000). *Involving Parents in Their Children's Learning.* London: Paul Chapman.

Whalley, M., Chandler, R., John, K., Thorpe, S., Reid, L. & Everitt, J. (2008). Developing and sustaining leadership learning communities: Implications of NPQICL rollout for public policy local praxis. *European Early Childhood Education Research Journal, 16*, 1, 5–38.

Whalley, M., Whitaker, P., Fletcher, C., Thorpe, S., John, K. & Leisten, R. (2004). *NPQICL Study Programme.* Nottingham: NCSL.

Whitaker, P. (1983). *The Primary Head.* London: Heinemann.

Whitaker, P. (1993). *Managing Change in Schools.* Buckingham: Open University Press.

Wilkinson, R. & Pickett, K. (2009). *The Spirit Level: Why Equality Is Better for Everyone.* London: Penguin Books.

Chapter 1

Applying systems theory to early years leadership

Patrick Whitaker[1]

The purpose of the paper, commissioned in 2009 by the Pen Green Research, Training and Leadership team, from which this chapter is reproduced was to examine the implications of the somewhat sudden and insistent introduction of a systems theory perspective into the discourse about leadership and management in services for children, families and schools (e.g. Collarbone & West-Burnham, 2008). This discourse was official, rather than academic, exemplified in a range of government publications and through documents produced by the National College for School Leadership (2004, 2006).

The New Labour Government elected in 1997 showed an early interest in leadership, believing that if school leaders could be well trained, then standards of attainment would rise. For this reason the National College for School Leadership[2] (NCSL) was established with the remit to develop world-class schools by providing a range of leadership development activities, publications and resources to suit the needs of leaders at different stages in their careers, and in a wide range of contexts. The NCSL also worked with schools and others to identify and grow future leaders and develop leadership within and beyond schools by enabling excellent leaders to share expertise (NCSL website, 2009).

The research for this chapter consisted of literature searches in the following areas: 1) the origin and development of systems theory; 2) the pioneers of systems theory and their contributions; 3) systems theory in the literature of the education service in England; 4) documents published by NCSL; and 5) the wider literature of leadership and management.

This chapter consists of the following sections:

- The confusion of terms
- The development of systems theory
- Some significant pioneers of systems theory
- Applying a systems approach to management and leadership
- The current systems leadership approach: some inconsistencies
- New directions in leadership development

The confusion of terms

The words system, systemic, systematic and systematically, are in common use by native English speakers. It is useful to make a distinction between general meanings and specific meanings. General usage may include comments such as, 'It's the system', or 'We need a better system'. Invariably, this is a convenient way of referring to current arrangements, sets of procedures or organisational structures. The term 'systematic' usually means a consistent and ordered way of doing things. As generally used, references to system rarely imply a connection with theories of systems developed in the 1940s. A great deal of confusion can be created when general meanings are intermingled with more specific meanings as they seem to be in much of the current documentation.

The development of systems theory

Systems theory was proposed in the 1940s by the biologist Ludwig von Bertalanffy (1968) and furthered by Ross Ashby (1956), an English psychiatrist. Von Bertalanffy was both reacting against reductionism and attempting to revive the unity of science. He emphasised that real systems are open to, and interact with, their environments, and that they can acquire qualitatively new properties through emergence, resulting in continual evolution.

Rather than enquiry based on the continuous reduction of an entity into its constituent parts, systems theory sets out to explore the characteristics of the whole by striving to identify the patterns established by the parts, and the dynamic nature of the relationships between them. Systems theory is more concerned with how things work, than with what they are like.

Systems theory takes a view of the world from two key perspectives: 1) the interrelatedness of all phenomena, and 2) the interdependence of all phenomena. The specialist and precise meaning of a system is 'an integrated whole whose properties cannot be reduced to those of its parts'.

Living systems are organised in such a way that they form multi-level structures, each consisting of subsystems which are wholes in regard to their parts and parts with respect to their larger wholes. Arthur Koestler (1978) coined the word 'holons' to refer to these subsystems, which are both wholes and parts. Holons have two key tendencies: 1) an integrative tendency to function as part of a larger whole and 2) an assertive tendency to preserve their individual autonomy.

Systems theory engages in a framework that is simultaneously integrated, interdependent and autonomous. Fritjof Capra (1982a) captures this essential characteristic well: 'In a biological or social system each holon must assert its individuality in order to maintain the system's stratified order but, but it must also submit to the demands of the whole in order to make the system viable' (Capra, 1982b, p. 27).

Systems theory was not an attempt to usurp the theoretical frameworks firmly established in the scientific community, but to propose an additional perspective, more sympathetic to the turbulent and dynamic nature of organic processes. Systems cannot be understood simply by analysis. The properties of the parts are not discrete and intrinsic; they can only be understood in the context of the larger whole. Three particular aspects of a complex system are useful to understand, that is, pattern, structure and process (Capra, 1996), as shown in Box 1.1.

Box 1.1   Three particular aspects of a complex system

Pattern – the configuration of relationships among the different components of the system, that determine their essential characteristics.
Structure – the physical embodiment of the pattern of organisation.
Process – the dynamic activity involved in the system and how the variables interact with each other.

Source: Capra, 1996.

It is important to recognise that human organisations are complex systems which defy simplistic analysis. Indeed one of the key dimensions of a systems perspective is that it embraces complexity, admitting to levels of unknowingness, provisionality and uncertainty that the determinist perspective seeks to avoid. We may get near to the truth of why things happen as they do in human affairs, but we must always allow for the fact that our understanding is never likely to be complete. The scientist Werner Heisenberg (1959/1999) asserted that, 'what we observe is not nature in itself, but nature exposed to our method of questioning' (Heisenberg, 1959/1999, p. 58).

A systems framework can help us to make our method of questioning more reflective of the complexity present within a human system. What it has never claimed to do is to offer blueprints of how organisations could be managed more efficiently. Systems theory is more a discipline of enquiry, than a plan for action.

Some significant pioneers of systems theory

The early work on developing systems theory during the 1940s and 1950s was undertaken by a number of academics.

Ludwig von Bertalanffy (1901–1972) was a biologist working in the United States, who also took an active interest in cybernetics, education, history, philosophy, psychiatry, psychology and sociology. His interest in the interdisciplinary relationships of different disciplines and fields of knowledge led him to propose a unifying concept – General Systems Theory. This was a framework for analysing, understanding and describing groups of objects that work together and produce a result.

Anatol Rapaport (1911–2007) was a Russian mathematician and psychologist, and one of the key contributors to the building of studies now known as General Systems Theory. He was particularly interested in the potential application of the theory to psychological conflict. He offered insights into the study of game theory, social networks and semantics.

Kenneth Boulding (1910–1993) was English by birth but moved to the United States where he married the distinguished sociologist and peace researcher Elise Boulding. His particular contributions were in the fields of political science, sociology, philosophy and social psychology. He coined the phrase 'psychic capital' to describe the accumulation of desirable mental states.

William Ross Ashby (1903–1972) was an English psychiatrist and pioneer of cybernetics. He proposed the Law of Requisite Variety, describing the necessary dynamic equilibrium of a system. He also developed the Good Regulator Theorem, which shows how autonomous systems need to develop an internal model of their environment in order to persist and achieve stability and dynamic equilibrium.

Gregory Bateson (1904–1980) was an English anthropologist who contributed to the development of the double bind theory. His interest in systems and cybernetics focused on an interdisciplinary study of the structure of regulatory systems and the role of feedback in adaptation. He was married to Margaret Mead (1901–1978) the American cultural anthropologist.

Charles West Churchman (1913–2004) was an American philosopher and systems scientist who undertook pioneering work in operations research, systems analysis and ethics. He articulated the relevance of General Systems Theory to complex human contexts such as conflict and management in organisations. He was a strong critic of positivist, reductionist and incrementalist approaches. He asserted that the extreme rationality and instrumental nature of these approaches left little room for ethical and moral considerations.

Lynn Margulis (1938–2011) was an American biologist who developed endosymbiotic theory – advancing concepts of the dynamics of cell networking and interdependence. Among her famous axioms is – 'Life did not take over the globe by combat, but by networking'.

Francisco Valera (1946–2001) was a Chilean biologist, philosopher and neuroscientist. He was interested in embodied cognition, suggesting that the human mind is largely determined by the form of the human body. All aspects of cognition – ideas, thoughts, concepts and categories are shaped by aspects of the body. These include the perceptual system, the intuitions that underlie the ability to move, activities and interactions with our environment and the naïve understanding of the world that is built into the body and brain. His later work built on ideas developed from research in linguistics, cognitive science, artificial intelligence, robotics and neurobiology.

Ilya Prigogine (1917–2003) was a Russian-born Belgian whose key work was on dissipative structures. These are characterised by the spontaneous appearance of symmetry breaking and the formation of complex and sometimes chaotic structures, where interacting particles exhibit long-range correlations. This theory was seen as a useful way to make a bridge between natural science and social science.

Stuart Kauffman (1939–) is an American medical doctor and theoretical biologist who studies complex systems and the origins of life on Earth. He has argued that the complexity of biological systems and organisms might result as much from self organisation as Darwinian natural selection.

Benoit Mandelbrot (1924–2010) was a French mathematician who was the originator of fractal geometry. He suggested that a geometric shape can be split into parts, each of which is (at least approximately) a reduced-size copy of the whole, a property referred to as self similarity.

Humberto Maturana (1928–) is a Chilean biologist and philosopher. In his studies of constructivist epistemology he defined, in conjunction with Francisco Valera, the concept of autopoiesis – the tendency in organisms for self organisation and self creation. He proposed that scientific knowledge is constructed by scientists and not discovered from the world, and that there is no single methodology to acquire or construct knowledge, a concept that stands in distinct opposition to positivism.

One of the striking features of these researchers is the polymathic nature of their interests, and the deep complexity of their enquiries. These are scholars who were frustrated that the somewhat rigid and deterministic scientific paradigm they were working in did not permit them the levels of conjecture and speculation that the more elusive and fluid phenomena of biology, physiology and psychology called for. It is interesting to note that their pioneering methodologies honour the principles of the theory they were developing – the networking they engaged in, academic cooperation rather than competitiveness, and the interdependence of their thinking and their ideas. Theirs is very much a constructivist, rather than a reductionist approach.

A significant feature of this developmental process were the Macy Conferences (sponsored by the Macy Foundation) held in New York City, regularly between 1946 and 1953. The purpose of these conferences was to lay the foundations for a general science of the workings of the human mind. And they produced important breakthroughs in systems theory, cybernetics, and what later became known as cognitive science. Distinguished psychologist Kurt Lewin (1890–1947) was a participant.

Systems theory has evolved to another level, generally referred to as complexity theory (Coveney & Highfield, 1996; Lewin, 1995) and chaos theory (Gleick, 1988). Far from a state of total confusion, chaos is a system in which it is not possible to identify many of the most significant variables. The theory provides insights into the dynamics of non-linear systems such as families and other human organisations.

The Gaia Hypothesis (Lovelock, 1979) is one of the most interesting and accessible recent developments of systems theory. This hypothesis suggests that the biosphere and the planet Earth together form an interconnected and interacting system that sustains all life. In other words, Earth is a single organism.

Of particular interest to the study of human organisations are the theories of self organisation and autopoiesis which became associated with General Systems Theory in the 1960s. These theories are concerned with the processes of self organisation which are particularly relevant in the fields of organisational leadership.

Applying a systems approach to management and leadership

Up until the 1990s, the literature of leadership and management seemed to contain few references to a systems approach, or to systems theory. In retrospect, it is interesting to see how many of the pioneers of management theory were expressing ideas that would now be regarded as congruent with what is described as 'systems thinking' (Argyris, 1957; Handy, 1976; Herzberg, 1959; Jaques, 1965; Maslow, 1970; Mayo, 1945; McGregor, 1960; Moss Kanter, 1977; Pascale, 1990; Peters & Waterman, 1982; Revens, 1979; Schein, 1980; Schön, 1983).

The works of these writers reveal a steady and progressive movement away from the scientific and bureaucratic perspectives that had dominated the literature in the first half of the 20th century (Taylor, 1947; Weber, 1947), towards a paradigm in which work and working were regarded as human experiences which had to be respected and understood if managers were to encourage their colleagues to work to the optimum of their potential.

Some of the elements of this emerging paradigm were brought together in 1990 in one of the first texts specifically to challenge the rational, mechanistic and reductionist frameworks that still tended to dominate organisational life. This was Peter Senge's *The Fifth Discipline*. His opening paragraph sets the agenda:

> From an early age we are taught to break apart problems, to fragment the world. This apparently makes complex tasks and subjects more manageable, but we pay a hidden, enormous price. We can no longer see the consequences of our actions; we lose our intrinsic sense of connection to a larger whole. When we then try to 'see the big picture', we try to reassemble the fragments in our minds, to list and organize the pieces. But as physicist David Bohm says, the task is futile – similar to trying

to reassemble the fragments of a broken mirror to see the true reflection. Thus, after a while we give up trying to see the whole altogether.

(Senge, 1990, p. 3)

This is a bit like the picture in books about perception in which you can either see an old woman or a young one, but not both at the same time. We can discover that the picture contains both, and we can learn to switch from one to the other, but how ever hard we try we cannot see both simultaneously. Each requires a different way of looking. Senge goes on to say:

The tools and ideas presented in this book are for destroying the illusion that the world is created of separate, unrelated forces. When we give up this illusion – we can then build 'learning organizations', organizations where people continually expand their capacity to create the results they truly desire, where new and expansive patterns of thinking are nurtured, where collective aspiration is set free, and where people are continually learning how to learn together.

(Senge, 1990, p. 3)

This somewhat grandiose and idealistic claim has something of the – 'in a single leap he was free' – mode about it. He seems to take no account that throughout human history human beings have been creating the results they truly desire and collective aspirations have been set free – how else would humanity have made the spectacular and amazing discoveries and developments we have witnessed in the last 200 years?

Senge falls into his own trap. He sees the paradigm conflict in dualistic terms, suggesting that if we are to acquire the benefits of the one he extols, then we must give up the one we have become familiar with. As Thomas Kuhn (1970) has demonstrated, paradigm shifts are rarely achieved quickly and never without struggle. Vested interest is one of the most powerful of human forces, which is one of the reasons why social and political change so often lags behind that of science and technology. A systems approach teaches us that both paradigms have their place in the wider scheme of things and that a new way of thinking does not require us to destroy the one that seems to have served us well so far.

The current documentation about systems leadership has something of the same naïve belief – that there can be no progress without the new ideas that are now being promoted. It is not that deterministic, positivist and reductionist thinking is wrong, but that in some situations the framework is inadequate and incomplete, and on its own not able to meet the demands made on it.

One of the significant flaws in Senge's fascinating and potentially useful framework is the idea that we can simply give up the illusion that he suggests has held back progress. That what we have been taught in our childhoods, at our schools and colleges and in our various workplaces, is not now the best framework for engaging with the world. It just happens to be the one that was seen to be fit for purpose for the majority of human history, and will continue to be so in those areas where it is most appropriate. Systems theory, with its emphasis on the whole, will not allow us simply to eradicate those variables we do not like. The challenge is to see them as part of the indivisible whole.

What Senge proposes is the adoption of 'the learning organisation' – the development of a particular type of culture in which the shift from a reductionist paradigm to an holistic one can be accomplished simply by adopting his five disciplines. The real difficulty is that the leadership of such learning organisations will be undertaken by those who themselves have been raised in the very paradigm he is now advocating we destroy. While it was this notion of 'the learning organisation' that was taken up by leadership specialists as a promising advance in organisational thinking, it was grasped by policy makers in both public and private sectors as yet another panacea for generating a more productive and cost-effective workforce.

What Senge's approach does is to prompt the question about whether text, however erudite or insightful, can actually enable significant and enduring change in the mental models we employ, let alone bring about a burgeoning growth of learning organisations throughout the land. Attempting to build leadership development through text is itself anti-systemic. The proponents of text-driven change are failing to use systems thinking themselves. By pursuing a largely analytical and theoretical approach to leadership epistemology, they are failing to take account of the most significant and dynamic variables within human systems – the individual and sometimes eccentric thoughts, feelings and experiences of those who lead and those who follow. The difficulty for theorists is that these variables defy simple definition, even safe identification. They are elusive and in a constant state of flux – forming, reforming and transforming from one moment to the next. Power/coercive hierarchies decided long ago to ignore these variables, with the consequent loss of human potential and capability that ensued. Leadership is not a corporate ritual, it is demonstrated through individual acts of engagement that have no consistent context, format or sequence. Each leadership act of engagement is different from all others; no two can ever be the same. Coming to terms with such beguiling complexity is a challenge that makes rocket science somewhat simple in comparison.

Herein lies one of the chief difficulties with Senge's exciting framework. What we are taught, and how we are taught in our childhoods, tend to become the habits of our lifetimes. What virtually all leaders have learnt, by sometimes bitter experience, is that it is not easy to dismantle the frameworks that we have constructed to understand the world. We are not likely to give up casually mental models and frameworks that have taken our lifetimes to construct. As andragogic theories tell us (Mezirow, 1983), transforming our inner worlds is never a simple or straightforward business, often requiring the most sensitive and painstaking support.

In *The Fifth Discipline*, Peter Senge (1990, p. 6) sets out what he describes as 'five new component technologies'. These components are:

1   Systems thinking
2   Personal mastery
3   Mental models
4   Building shared vision
5   Team learning

He suggested that these were gradually converging to innovate learning organisations.

> Though developed separately, each will, I believe, prove critical to the others' success, just as occurs with any ensemble. Each provides a vital dimension in building organizations that can truly 'learn', that can continually enhance their capacity to realize their highest aspirations.
>
> (ibid., p. 6)

The book has been one of the management best sellers, and its framework has formed the basis of many leadership development programmes, but the components are proving very slow to converge.

Examining the potential usefulness of a systems perspective in educational leadership, Fullan (2005) questions the reliance that seems to have been placed on 'systems thinking'. He is sceptical of the practicalities of this: 'I do not think we have made any progress at all in actually promoting systems thinking since Peter Senge (1990) first raised the matter' (Fullan, 2005, p. 41).

Fullan goes on to say that while Senge is on the right track at the philosophical level, what he has to say in relation to effective learning organisations is not very helpful at the practical level. He observes that in the decade since the publication of what was described as a 'groundbreaking book': 'I don't think we have made any significant gains on defining the problem, let alone doing anything about it' (ibid.).

It is in the wake of Senge's initiative that a systems perspective in the leadership and management of services to children, families and schools has appeared as the latest nostrum for service improvement. Fuelled largely by the prolific activities of the National College for School Leadership, the cluster of ideas, approaches, beliefs and assumptions that are contained under the systems banner have something of a messianic quality about them, that at last we have finally discovered how to make people more effective.

The current systems leadership approach: some inconsistencies

The comments and observations that follow, under fourteen different headings, highlight the inconsistencies in the systems leadership approach, or 'systems approach' that was advocated by the National College for School Leadership (NCSL) and systems theory, or General Systems Theory, from which the systems approach was said to be drawn. These inconsistencies were discerned from reading the following National College for School Leadership documents:

- 'Seven strong claims about successful school leadership'
- 'School leaders leading the system'
- 'Leading networks leading the system' and
- 'Community leadership in networks'

(NCSL website, 2009)

My approach to these documents was to explore to what extent the ideas expressed in them drew from the theoretical principles of systems theory, and from which particular systems theory literature they derived inspiration.

1. *A basic incompatibility* – It is difficult to reconcile the idea of the management of a service which has become increasingly centralised, hierarchically organised and tightly regulated with a systems view, where interdependence is one of the key characteristics. In a web – one of the frequently used images of a system – there are no asymmetries of authority, power, control and function. In this sense the approach suggests a hindering or distortion of the paradigm shift advocated in Senge's approach.

In the approach promoted in these documents an attempt is being made to incorporate a systems approach, in which power is equally shared, interdependence is cultivated and initiatives accepted from anywhere, into a service where power is exerted from the top of the hierarchy, people are dependent on the rank above them and initiatives are imposed from above.

2. *A political imperative* – The tone of the documents is categoric and emphatic, assuming a set of principles already explored, agreed upon and established. It is as if the framework needed no debate, exploration or experimentation; that it has intrinsic virtue and should be taken on trust. In systems theory the relationship of a system to its outside environment is crucial, and a system will struggle to sustain its own integrity and autonomy.

3. *An outcomes focus* – The somewhat simplified and often self evident interpretation of a systems approach seems to be more concerned with ensuring outcomes than with understanding and engaging with the complex processes at work in human organisations. The challenges of applying a tight science to essentially turbulent and often unpredictable phenomena of organisms is the very reason systems theory was developed in the first place. The nature of an organic system is that no one part is more necessary, important or valuable than any other.

4. *The service landscape* – The systems leadership approach seems to be more concerned with the boundary structure of the service landscape, where traditional boundaries and insularities need to be removed, than it is with exploring how the various players in the professional struggle can build on their mutual aspirations. The documents are full of implied assumptions

that school leaders have never looked over their school walls at the educational landscape beyond. During the 1980s the then Conservative Government invested heavily in ambitious regional development programmes where school leaders came together to do all the things that are raised as innovations in the NCSL documents.

5. ***Denigration of the past*** – It is sad that within the documents so little from the past is regarded of value. It is as if the slate has to be wiped clean and the new dispensation installed as an instant makeover. There is nothing new in the fact that much of educational success over the years has resulted from creative, and imaginative leadership (HMI, 1977).

6. ***Grand strategy*** – There is something of the grand strategy in this approach. The drive to increase uniformity and standardisation in children's experience of education and of the roles that teachers undertake is reducing opportunities for the sorts of radical innovations in learning and teaching that were once regarded as the defining characteristic of the nation's best schools. Early in his advocacy of a systems approach to leadership, Peter Senge (1990) asserts:

> It's just not possible any longer to 'figure it out' from the top and have everyone else follow the orders of the 'grand strategy'. The organizations that will truly excel in the future will be the organizations that discover how to tap people's commitment and capacity to learn at all levels in an organization.
>
> (Senge, 1990, p. 4)

In this passage he does capture the essence of the systems approach which no amount of central control and imposition will achieve, a point endorsed by McNiff and Whitehead (2006):

> Social change was never mandated, nor did it ever begin with prescriptive models. John Hume, former leader of the SDLP in Northern Ireland, claims that the peace process began in people's minds. This also applies to social change; it materializes because individuals decide to come together, with the intention to change themselves and influence others to also change themselves.
>
> (McNiff & Whitehead, 2006, p. 62)

7. ***Groupthink*** – While Senge (1990) singled out systems thinking as his fifth discipline, he was at pains to emphasise that it is to our *ways* of thinking that we must pay attention. The advocates of the NCSL systems approach seemed determined to tell us *what* to think. Their documentation had nothing of the mysterious complexities of the mind, the enormous diversity in the ways individuals use their thinking and construct meaning. It was silent about the deeper aspects of effective leadership such as ingenuity, imagination, nous

and creativity. The danger inherent in this was that groupthink replaces initiative, enterprise and imagination. Instead of advocating the use of systems theory to illuminate the complexities of the psychological and social complexities of the educational world, it was being used to generate and spread a form of groupthink, in which individual creativity and intellect is suspended and an 'on message' thinking culture realised.

8. *The systems tag* – As used in the NCSL documentation, the term 'systems' refers to the cluster of ideas about how the government currently believed that services to children, families and schools could best be conceptualised. Apart from a strong tendency to managerial clichés, it is difficult to find anything that suggests that this conceptualization differs from ones that have always been held by effective educational leaders in the past. The documentation examined would make a little more sense if instead of the prefix 'systems' to leadership, the phrase – 'our current way of doing things' was used. This at least would free it from a somewhat nebulous connection with General Systems Theory. This documentation rarely departs from the general meanings associated with system, referred to in 'The confusion of terms' section, and there is no acknowledgement in the totally inadequate reference sections of these publications that any of the significant literature of systems theory has been consulted.

9. *Competitive virus* – Systems theory works on a principle of interdependence. This implies generative collaboration in which function is not compromised by power hierarchies, mistrust and competition. It is difficult to see how a systems view can be promoted at the same time as hard-edged competition is advocated as a key driving force for change.

10. *Feedback* – In systems theory, feedback is the means by which the system receives information that will help it to maintain homeostasis. In contrast to this, feedback in the systems approach advocated in these documents, and in educational policy generally, is not devised primarily to inform and enable, but to threaten and punish. This is another example that systems theory is in no way compatible with official educational thinking.

11. *Predictability* – Central to the approach to leadership in these documents is the importance of central control. School-based leadership is adopted as the agency for delivering government policy, rather than as the vital agency for developing effective learning and teaching. The documents reveal a determination to predict the consequences of action, a concept alien to systems theory. In his study of the emancipatory character of action research, Ben Boog (2003) refers to the work of Flood (2001) on the relationship of action research to systems theory:

> Systems thinking views action as embedded in the unpredictable complex systems which are in a continual process of self-creation and re-creation. In action research, it challenges people to reflect on the place and function of what you do or do not do as part of a dynamic whole. This

reflection can provide more insight into the potentialities and possibilities to act otherwise, and in this way can enhance human emancipation.

(Boog, 2003, p. 432)

12. *Systems thinking* – Systems thinking seems to be the resource for system leadership. The documents make constant reference to systems thinkers and what they do, but nowhere is there any reference to when and where the patterns and processes of systems thinking were laid down. Systems thinking is set out as the essential requirement of the new leadership dispensation. A monolithic approach is advocated in which a preferred way of thinking – referred to as systems thinking, takes precedence over any other. This must be one of the first instances in the literature of leadership and management that leaders have been told what and how they should think.

13. *The novel and unexpected* – It was the phenomenon of randomness that preoccupied many of the early systems theorists. The positivist paradigm rendered random phenomena largely unexaminable, yet they are now grist to the psychologist's mill and to all of those who recognise the complexity of human co-existence. The proponents of the NCSL systems approach seemed as determined as the logical positivists to keep the unknown and unmeasurable out of the framework, thereby ignoring one of systems theory's key tenets.

14. *Standardisation* – A further determination is the need to sustain a standardisation imperative in any framework for the management of education services. The model of leadership that the NCSL promoted was one of agency for installing and sustaining political and professional orthodoxy, with all the necessary depletion of professional authority that such control requires. To further this drive towards management uniformity, a set of standards for systems leaders was developed (Collarbone & West-Burnham, 2008, p. 83). They set out in a trio of bullet point lists of the 'knowledge', 'qualities' and 'actions' leaders would need to demonstrate to earn the prefix – 'system'. Absent from the knowledge list is any reference to General Systems Theory or the wide ranging ideas, concepts and frameworks that have developed from it. All three lists reflect the elements that any self respecting educational leader would have incorporated in their professional make-up. What is not clear is the precise nature of the systems element in these requirements. For example, one of the knowledge requirements is that system leaders will know about the complexities of the system and the policy-making process. Is there a check list of what these complexities are? Have there ever been effective leaders who have thought that human systems were simple and straightforward? Does knowing that human systems are complex enable you to be a better leader, making it easier for you to deal with the most intractable struggles?

The comments above are raised in the spirit of debate, since the documentation seems to have arrived free from the theoretical discourse that such a significant shift in the nature of professionalism deserves and requires. Freed of the systems cloak in which they are shrouded, many of the ideas and developments expressed in the documents have much to recommend them.

New directions in leadership development

While this report has been very critical of NCSL initiatives in leadership development, it is important to highlight one success of the National College for School Leadership. From its inception it worked steadily to engage with the profession, particularly those in senior positions, in a dynamic process of leadership learning. A learning dimension in professional practice is now an implicit characteristic of those who offer themselves for the most senior positions in our centres, schools and colleges. While this process of networked learning (Jackson, 2002) owes much to the government's drive for a new educational orthodoxy, it has enabled academics and practitioners to engage in a range of interesting, useful and productive development activities.

One example of an NCSL document that is free of the semantic and cultural imperatives of this orthodoxy is 'Seven strong claims about successful school leadership' (Leithwood et al., 2006). The report, compiled by a team of five education professors, each with a specialist interest in school leadership, is a summary of the key findings of a review of the literature. This was meant to lead to a large-scale empirical study to test out seven strong claims:

1   School leadership is second only to classroom teaching as an influence on pupil learning.
2   Almost all successful leaders draw on the same repertoire of basic leadership practices.
3   The ways in which leaders apply these basic leadership practices – not the practices themselves – demonstrate responsiveness to, rather than dictation by, the contexts in which they work.
4   School leaders improve teaching and learning indirectly and most powerfully through their influence on staff motivation, commitment and working conditions.
5   School leadership has a greater influence on schools and students when it is widely distributed.
6   Some patterns of distribution are more effective than others.
7   A small handful of personal traits explains a high proportion of the variation in leadership effectiveness.

One of the interesting features of this report is that while it contains no specific reference to the system leadership initiative being advocated at the time, and no references to material from the systems field at all, it does have a distinctly systems feel about it. In commenting on the seventh strong claim, the writers observe:

> Although not setting out to be research on leader traits, recent studies of leaders' efforts to improve low-performing schools have begun to replicate evidence from private sector research. This evidence warrants the claim that, at least under challenging circumstances, the most successful

school leaders are open-minded and ready to learn from others. They are also flexible rather than dogmatic in their thinking within a system of core values, persistent (e.g. in pursuit of high expectations of staff motivation, commitment, learning and achievement for all), resilient and optimistic. Such traits help explain why successful leaders facing daunting conditions are often able to push forward when there is little reason to expect progress.

(Leithwood et al., 2006, p. 14)

This finding raises the question of whether the pursuit of a standardised and uniform approach to leadership is likely to yield the best results in leadership development. This very brief summary report reveals more of the essential elements of a systems perspective than any of the other documents studied, and identifies many fruitful avenues for exploration.

What seems to be absent from the wider discourse on leadership development is a radical edge. Standardisation seems to have turned the debate and its accompanying developments inwards, towards safe havens of practice. Vital to any effective development in challenging times are intellectual explorations that examine, without fear or favour, radical departures from tradition. As the human race moved towards the second decade of the 21st century, it was struggling to accommodate and respond to an increasing threat to its systemic integrity. It is crucial that those who lead in education challenge the shibboleths of a deeply entrenched system, and inject imaginative new ideas that question the most basic assumptions. We are challenged by a quest for new educational and leadership futures. As futures theorists tell us (Hicks, 2006, p. xiii), there are three different sorts of future – preferable, probable and possible. In other words we can work for the future we would like, accept the one that seems likely or consider other, as yet unknown, possibilities.

Drawing on the spirit of a systems approach, it is possible to identify a number of areas where leadership development initiatives could be both timely and effective. The seeds of these developments have already been sown. What they now require is some bold thinking and energetic initiatives, through the building of networks of like-minded thinkers. Six possible developments are outlined below. In the spirit of systems theory they are arranged as a web as shown in Figure 1.1. None is more important than the others and between each of them there are powerful patterns of interrelationship and possibility. The six possible developments are:

1   Systems consciousness
2   Collaboration
3   Emancipation
4   Theory and practice
5   Research
6   Organisation

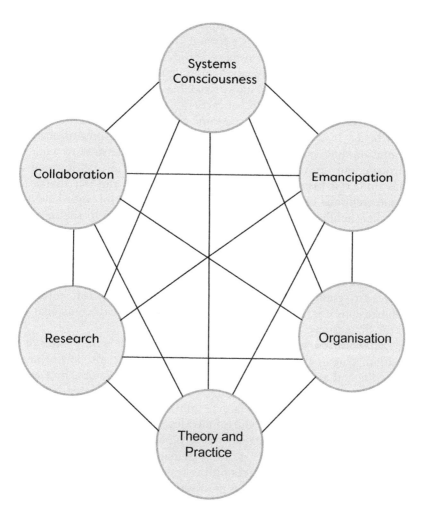

Figure 1.1 Leadership Development Web

1. ***Systems consciousness*** – Systems theory has a great deal of potential to inform and help in the processes of leadership learning and professional development. As was stated earlier, this potential lies more in the realm of insight and understanding than it does in the practicalities of leadership behaviour, strategy or vision. While it helps us to appreciate, for example, the central significance and importance of feedback, the theory cannot determine for us the form that feedback needs to take, nor the way it is offered.

The notion of variable complexity in living systems, so rigorously investigated by systems theorists, suggests that we recognise in the leadership environment such characteristics as fragility, inconsistency, messiness, complexity, elusiveness, ambiguity and unpredictability. Also that leadership will not be effective if it is applied as a formula in all situations. The message is clear – leaders need to be attentively and assiduously curious, constantly alert for subtleties and nuances, never afraid to adopt multi-perspective approaches, and prepared for the novel and unexpected. Leadership is a never-ending process of action, response and consequence.

Systems consciousness is not the same as systems thinking. It is more a way of being. It is concerned with recognizing the ever-present challenges of confusion, uncertainty and ambiguity, and being prepared to work with inadequate and insufficient data and information. The consciousness that comes from this assimilation builds a confidence in the fact that leadership interventions can rarely be planned to be successful, they have to be undertaken boldly, with sensitivity and care, responding to the significant variables as they emerge. Systems consciousness is strong on intuition and emotional fluency, traits not traditionally regarded as important dimensions of leadership.

Systems consciousness cannot be taught, but it can be developed, for we ourselves are systems. Its development will require engagement in the other five dimensions if it is to grow in awareness and become the force that energises the dimensions.

2. *Collaboration* – Intrinsic to the systems approach is the process of collaboration. One of the main differences between a systems view of organisational life and a deterministic one is the nature of hierarchy. In a systems analysis, the variables operate within a function hierarchy, each function dependent on all the others. In a deterministic perspective the hierarchy is one of power and control, in which individuals are separated by rank, status and authority and where dependency is vertical with each individual looking to those immediately above. Part of the excitement in recent years about the role and function of teams hinges on the realization that it is in teams that human potential often discovers its most supportive environment for growth, initiative, energy and application. Again this was seized upon as yet another panacea with organisations urged to reorganise along team lines before an understanding was acquired of the vital ingredients that need to be present if teamwork is to return the expectations invested in it.

Collaboration is certainly part of any radical agenda for leadership development, but our capacity to develop it is challenged by our formative and constant development in hierarchies where mistrust and competition are likely to be stronger variables than interdependence and mutual endeavour. As the proportion of staff within organisations who have managerial responsibilities expands (in the health service for example), an increasing number of staff will be trying to influence a declining number who are able to concentrate on their core professional work.

It is rapidly becoming a case of who will manage the managers. It might be wiser to conceptualise leadership as a process that springs from energetic and creative collaboration rather than that concerned with the separate work of individuals. Senge identified team learning as one of the five key disciplines of a learning organisation (Senge, 1990, p. 233), but there is little indication in any of the documents examined for this chapter that much thought has been given to a desirable shift from an individualistic to a collaborative approach. Such a shift needs to begin quite early in the schooling process if it is to develop the momentum and capability that will deliver rich rewards. Current orthodoxy is for an individualistic focus for classroom learning, with a performance and results culture inhibiting any hope of cooperation and collaboration in the learning process.

3. *Emancipation* – One of the most interesting and radical ideas to find expression in the action research literature in recent years is that of emancipation. This is not a new concept, but one well thought through and developed by Paulo Freire in the 1970s (Freire, 1970). The idea that human wellbeing and progress is deeply connected to freedom from oppression is not one that is welcomed in hierarchically arranged societies and institutions. In relation to management and leadership it was well formulated by Douglas McGregor in his groundbreaking study *The Human Side of Enterprise* (1960). He suggested that the way an organisation operates is related to the beliefs and assumptions of managers about the workers they manage. He initially outlined two contrasting perspectives, referred to as Theory X and Theory Y. The Theory X position suggests that people dislike work and try to avoid it. They have to be bribed, coerced and controlled and even threatened with punishment to perform adequately; most people wish to avoid responsibility and prefer being directed. The Theory Y position on the other hand suggests that people do like work and do not have to be forced or threatened. If allowed to pursue objectives to which they are committed most people will work hard and not only accept responsibility, but consciously seek it (Whitaker, 1984, p. 83).

Today McGregor's somewhat simplistic but persuasive formula is scoffed at by many knowing MBA graduates, but it stands up to rigorous examination. How powerfully, for example, the Theory X position reflects successive governments' attempts to tighten up and strengthen school management, apparently because politicians believe that professional staff cannot be trusted to devise appropriate curricula, plan a programme of lessons, create a scheme of work, develop their own approach to practice and then effectively evaluate the learning of their pupils. In addition punishments by naming and shaming are an integral and strongly defended part of this state-controlled dispensation.

The emancipatory position takes a Theory Y approach, believing that effective professional practice is best developed and improved when staff are helped to free themselves from restrictive work practices, inhibiting patterns of self disbelief and the threat of retribution for not performing to the required standard. Action research is one of the most powerful tools available to help organisations to confront what they find challenging, and to raise their awareness of those forces that inhibit creativity, stifle initiative and limit commitment. This is a dimension of learning that no ambitious organisation can afford to neglect.

Not only can professional learning be facilitated and supported by well-designed action learning projects, it can also be pursued more incidentally in daily work by cultivating a process dimension in which the nature of the working experience of members of staff is focused on and given attention. Central to the process of emancipation is the bringing to the surface of those thoughts, feelings and experiences which affect the way we act as professionals. It is the method for lowering the water table of the iceberg theory, and providing vital information to help the organisation to deal with those forces of interference that can prevent the generation of flow (Csikszentmihalyi, 1997) among each of its participants. Action research provides a powerful intellectual, methodological and ethical framework for leading change. Ben Boog (2003) notes the link between action research and a participatory world view, observing:

> The concepts of emancipation and empowerment are closely connected with the concept of participatory democracy. The values of equal rights, social justice and solidarity with the socially deprived can only be realized within a community that is organized along the principles of participatory democracy. Participatory here means communication and participation in decision-making. Participatory democracy is not only seen as a goal inherent to emancipation or empowerment, but must also be experienced in the practice of action research: in the relationship between researcher and researched subjects.
>
> (Boog, 2003, p. 428)

A further connection of importance is the growing understanding of action learning groups as powerful agencies for professional learning and for professional action. The systems processes at work in action learning groups are still not altogether clear, but there are strong indications that they have the potential to emancipate energy and creativity from working practices that are too unwieldy, and which do not allow the levels of introspection and disclosure that is necessary if emancipatory learning is to lead to action. The concept of *qualia* is significant here. Qualia is a term used in philosophy to describe the subjective quality of conscious experience, which is at the very heart of action research.

Understanding how differences in conscious experience can affect professional practice and organisational effectiveness, opening up the hidden areas within the system, can only help leaders to handle things more effectively. Perhaps action learning groups are one of the safest methodologies we have to explore those inner world dimensions that so affect an individual's capacity to work at their best. Emancipation is all to do with freeing things up and applies to all levels of human experience. It provides a way of understanding what holds us back from the full expression of our capability, and provides an exciting focus for learning and development. It is a key part of the systems consciousness outlined in the first area for development above.

4. *Theory and practice* – It has already been noted that systems theory has great potential to help us understand the complexities of professional life. Because human systems are characterised by diversity and difference in such aspects as location, context, history, aspiration and achievement, they need to have these variations taken seriously. Systems are not concerned with conformity; they thrive on particularities when these are allowed to function freely and without undue restraint. Systems theory, therefore, cannot provide a great deal of help with questions of what we do and how we do it.

One of the attractions of the systems world view is a concern for particularity. Systems theory encourages careful attention to contextual character and to the pattern of relationships that operate between the constituent elements. This is why the research dimension is so crucial. Research creates a rich environment in which theory and practice can combine in rich and powerful ways. A 'double hermeneutic process' (Boog, 2003) is created in which theory and practice are mutually sustained. The process thrives on iteration, with research into practice developing new theory, and new theory extending practice and so on. It is the capacity to theorise that is more important than particular theories themselves. This is no less true for leaders than it is for practitioners. Simply knowing a theory does not have great potential to change anything. Like praxis (Freire, 1970) where the constant iteration of reflection and action generates a momentum for growth, the combined interweaving of theory and practice can be synergetic – exciting to engage with and a powerful force for change.

The radical American educator Michael Apple (2006) stressed the importance of theory:

> the efficacy of our theories needs to be measured by our ability to work productively with theories that are almost always inadequate in some ways to push us 'further down the road' and enable us to see things that were hidden before. This suggests that theories must not be adopted as practical solutions to knotty problems, but as part of the processes involved in professional thinking, the means by which we sharpen the curiosity mentioned above, and the source of the experiments in possibility that are the stock in trade of any worthwhile leader.
>
> (Apple, 2006, p. 28)

Although Donald Schön's (1983) groundbreaking study of reflective practice has been around for nearly 30 years, there is still a great deal that has not been understood about this vital learning method. Used as one of the key methodologies in this web of potential developments, particularly in developing the relationship between practice and theory, reflective practice becomes both the means of enquiry and a focus of it. We need to know much more about how exploration of inner experience, for example, has the potential to unlock stifled dreams, passionately held professional ambitions and, perhaps even more importantly, those capabilities that are hidden under bushels.

5. *Research* – We are now at a stage in research history when qualitative research has achieved the respect of those who wish to study those phenomena that fall outside the framework of empirical enquiry. The various methodologies of this paradigm are now well tested, and their working principles laid down. We are now witnessing another significant shift in research practice in the emancipation of research from the tight confines of professional researchers. Practitioner research is rapidly becoming a significant feature of professionalism among those working in services to children, families and schools. While much of this research is undertaken by those professionals undertaking courses connected to qualifications, there is a need to extend possibilities and begin to embed research into the heart of professional practice. There is almost no professional activity that would not benefit from a research focus, and leadership has a great deal to gain from its methodical processes and its concern for social change.

Qualitative research has now provided us with a range of methods with which to explore the powerful but largely unexamined phenomena that generate the dynamic and often turbulent forces at work in human systems. It is important that we do not allow the current preoccupation with a hard-edged approach to research, concerned only with outcomes and results to inhibit our ambitions. While such research can be useful, it cannot provide the data that will help services to rise above the somewhat uniform and rigid requirements currently placed on them.

In such a determinist environment, there is less to attract leaders with ideas and imagination of their own. Increasingly they are becoming managers of policy and supervisors of prescribed practice. It is now necessary to create think-tanks to do the thinking that was once done by leaders. In the spirit of the Sigmoid Curve (Handy, 1994) it is necessary to plan for a more relaxed regime and to pioneer practices that can be adopted as opportunities arise. What we do know is that when practitioners themselves create and implement new and successful practice, the profession beats a path to their door.

Cultivating a research culture could be a most effective way of introducing a more promising change strategy than those traditionally adopted by many leaders. When practitioners become active partners in a clearly defined methodological process they can become emancipated from top-down requirements and their developing professional potential is given every opportunity to engage with all aspects of work. This research dimension links powerfully with each of the others in a truly systems spirit.

6. *Organisation* – So embedded in tradition are our organisational assumptions that any ideas for system change are regarded as unnecessary and undesirable. It is naïve to believe that the removal of hierarchical structures would bring anything but chaos and confusion to professional life. When the majority of workers are trapped in a power/coercive arrangement in their workplaces then they will develop a follower mindset and operate in ways that reinforce the Theory X assumptions probably still held by the majority of bosses. In educational institutions it is perhaps more important to pioneer alternative organisational forms, so that children and young people can have experience of responsibility and leadership from a much earlier age than is currently the case.

The most common organisational structure in centres and schools is that of the hierarchy with a senior management or leadership team. This means that the most senior members of staff have opportunities to develop the practice of collaboration outlined above, but this is not so possible for those lower down in the order. Two other structures have been suggested (Whitaker, 1997) – the project organisation and the loosely coupled organic network. Organic networks draw inspiration from systems theory and depart from tradition by:

> placing the head at the centre of a constantly changing pattern of small, task focused temporary teams. The pattern changes according to the organizational and developmental needs of the moment. This more flexible, organic arrangement, becomes possible when staff have become familiar with, and skilful in, management by project teams. The key feature is ad hocracy – teams are created, contingent on the current tasks and demands experienced within the school. A job of work becomes necessary, the task is defined, a team is set up, the job is done, the team disperses. Team membership is fluid and changes according to task and availability of staff. Teams are more in the nature of temporary partnerships than ongoing committees. Teams can be set up quickly, and get their work done in shorter time spans than normal. Staff develop enormous flexibility and constantly widen their experience through regular opportunities to work with specialist colleagues and take on important leadership roles.
>
> (Whitaker, 1997, p. 114)

Action learning groups have some of the characteristics of such an arrangement. This configuration offers exciting new professional challenges and opportunities for those at the top of the traditional hierarchy and considerably expands the professional development opportunities for members of staff at all levels. Such an arrangement could be pioneered as part of an action learning programme, provide an early opportunity for young staff to practice the leadership of a substantial piece of work, and also create the opportunity for learners to become involved. The introduction of collaborative leadership models into schools met with considerable success when it was undertaken in some Oxfordshire and Bristol schools by The Coverdale Organization (1989). What surprised the consultants from Coverdale was the sophistication of the year 5 children's ability to grasp a task/process action methodology and to implement it in their normal daily work. Perhaps a whole population of potentially effective innovators are lost because our habitual practice is to offer professionals leadership opportunities only when they are in mid-career.

Notes

1 Patrick Whitaker (1942–2010) was a primary head teacher, leadership consultant, local authority advisor and the author of several books on experiential learning, the nature of leadership and managing change in schools. He collaborated with Dr Margy Whalley over many years in the development and facilitation of leadership training for early years professionals.
2 The National College for School Leadership was established in 2000 and was replaced by the National College for Teaching and Leadership in 2013, which subsequently closed in 2014.

References

Apple, M. (2006) *Educating the "Right" Way: Markets, Standards, God and Inequality*. London: Taylor and Francis Group.

Argyris, C. (1957) *Personality and Organization*. New York: Harper & Row.

Ashby, R. (1956) *Introduction to Cybernetics*. New York: John Wiley & Sons.

Boog, B. (2003) The Emancipatory Character of Action Research, Its History and the Present State of the Art. *Journal of Community and Applied Psychology, 13*, 426–438.

Capra, F. (1982a) *The Turning Point*. London: Flamingo.

Capra, F. (1982b) *The Turning Point: Science, Society and the Rising Culture*. London: Fontana.

Capra, F. (1996) *The Web of Life: A New Synthesis of Mind and Matter*. London: HarperCollins.

Collarbone, P. & West-Burnham, J. (2008) *Understanding Systems Leadership*. New York: Continuum.

Coveney, P. & Highfield, R. (1996) *Frontiers of Complexity: The Search for Order in a Chaotic World*. London: Faber & Faber.

The Coverdale Organization (1989) *Management in Classrooms*. Internal Report.

Csikszentmihalyi, M. (1997) *Flow. The Psychology of Happiness*. London: Rider.

Flood, R.L. (2001). The relationship of 'systems thinking' to action research. In P. Reason & H. Bradbury (Eds.), *Handbook of Action Research, Participative Inquiry and Practice* (pp. 133–144). London: Sage.

Freire, P. (1970/1986) *Pedagogy of the Oppressed*. London: Penguin Books.

Fullan, M. (2005) *Leadership and Sustainability*. London: Corwin Press.

Gleick, J. (1988) *Chaos: Making a New Science*. London: Sphere Books.

Handy, C. (1976) *Understanding Organizations*. London: Penguin Books.

Handy, C. (1994) *The Empty Raincoat*. London: Hutchinson.

Heisenberg, W. (1959/1999) *Physics and Philosophy*. New York: Prometheus.

Herzberg, F. (1959) *The Motivation to Work*. New York: John Wiley & Sons.

Hicks, D. (2006) *Lessons for the Future: The Missing Dimension in Education*. Oxford: Trafford Publishing.

HMI (1977) HMI Series: Matters for Discussion No. 1. *Ten Good Schools: A Secondary School Enquiry*. London: HMSO.

Jackson, D. (2002) The Creation of Knowledge Networks. Paper Presented to the CERI/ OECD/QCA/ESRC Forum "Knowledge Management in Education and Learning", 18–19 March, Oxford.

Jaques, E. (1965). Death and the mid-life crisis. *The International Journal of Psychoanalysis*, 46(4), 502–514.

Koestler, A. (1978) *Janus*. London: Hutchinson.

Kuhn, T. (1970) *The Structure of Scientific Revolutions*, 2nd Edition. Chicago: University of Chicago.

Leithwood, K., Day, C., Sammons, P., Harris, A. & Hopkins, D. (2006) *Seven Strong Claims About Successful School Leadership*. London: DCSF and NCSL.

Lewin, R. (1995) *Complexity: Life on the Edge*. London: Phoenix.

Lovelock, J. (1979) *Gaia*. Oxford: Oxford University Press.

Maslow, A. (1970) *Motivation and Personality*. New York: Harper & Row.

Mayo, E. (1949) *The Social Problems of an Industrial Civilization*. London: Routledge.

Mezirow, J.A. (1983) critical theory of adult learning and education. In: M. Tight (ed.) *Education for Adults; Adult Learning and Education*. London: Croom Helm.

McGregor, D. (1960) *The Human Side of Enterprise*. New York: McGraw-Hill.

McNiff, J. & Whitehead, J. (2006) *All You Need to Know About Action Research*. London: Sage.

Moss Kanter, R. (1977) *Men and Women of the Corporation*. London: Basic Books.

National College for School Leadership (2004) *Community Leadership in Networks*. Nottingham, UK: NCSL. Downloaded from www.ncsl.org.uk (2009).

National College for School Leadership (2006) *School Leaders Leading the System*. Nottingham: NCSL. Downloaded from www.ncsl.org.uk

Pascale, R.T. (1990) *Managing on the Edge*. New York: Simon & Schuster.

Peters, T. & Waterman, R. (1982) *In Search of Excellence*. London: Harper & Row.

Revens, R. (1979) *Action Learning*. London: Blond and Briggs.

Schein, E. (1980) *Organizational Psychology*. New Jersey: Prentice-Hall.

Schön, D. (1983) *The Reflective Practitioner*. New York: Basic Books.

Senge, P.M. (1990) *The Fifth Discipline: The Art and Practice of the Learning Organization*. New York: Doubleday.

Taylor, F. (1947) *Scientific Management*. New York: Harper & Row.

(von) Bertalanffy, L. (1968) *General Systems Theory*. New York: Brazliller.

Weber, M. (1947) *The Theory and Practice of Social and Economic Organization*. New York: Free Press.

Whitaker, P. (1984) *The Primary Head*. London: Heinemann.

Whitaker, P. (1997) *Primary Schools and the Future*. Buckingham: Open University Press.

Chapter 2

Holding the baby
Leadership that inspires and contains ambition and anxiety

Karen John

Over 46 years of leading and managing within academic, mental health, social care and educational settings, my abiding aim, initially as a research psychologist, then as an Adlerian psychotherapist and supervisor, has never veered. I have sought to help individuals, families, staff teams, leaders, organisations and communities recognise and overcome the internal and external obstacles that interfere with their healthy and socially responsible functioning. In co-leading the Mentoring component of the Pilot and Roll Out of the England-wide National Professional Qualification for Integrated Centre Leadership (NPQICL), I mentored 23 Pilot participants over a one-year period, simultaneously recording and later analysing the issues and needs that emerged in the sessions (John, 2008b). Sixty-one per cent of those early years professionals confessed to feeling a *fraud* (or *impostor*, Clance & Imes, 1978) as a leader – feeling anxious and constricted for fear of exposure. Sixty-one per cent also felt unsupported by their line managers, experiencing confusion and lack of direction at local authority level (John, 2008b, p. 8). Since then, in mentoring, tutoring and supervising scores of early years leaders, I have found that few were confident in their leadership, and few felt supported, inspired or contained by their leaders. These are worrying findings given the evidence that systemic and democratic leaders need to believe in themselves and others, convey clarity of purpose and values, inspire others to be creative, take initiative and responsibility, and, crucially, contain their own and others' ambitions and anxieties. All of these while remaining open, curious and flexible in their leadership. I feel encouraged by what Adlerian psychiatrist and psychotherapist Rudolf Dreikurs (1971/1994) observed 45 years ago in his book, *Social Equality: The Challenge of Today*, "What we are currently experiencing are the birthpains [sic] of a new society: hardship, confusion and turmoil. But there is no ill caused by the democratic evolution that cannot be cured by more democracy" (p. x). This chapter focuses on 'holding the baby', namely what it takes to survive intact the challenges inherent in democratizing early years leadership and provision, keeping the baby safe and thriving. Specifically, I discuss:

- Challenges of leading integrated early years provision for children and families
- Leadership and management, *both* – with evidence from the neurosciences
- Parallels between leading and parenting
- Leadership that empathises, encourages, holds and contains – psychological understandings
- Supporting, containing and encouraging rigour through work-based supervision and
- Ecological systems that promote good authority and democracy

Challenges of leading integrated early years provision for children and families

In England, Early Excellence Centres (EECs) and Sure Start Children's Centres (SSCCs) were intended to be havens of support and hope for the future, where families on the margins of their communities were included in the planning and provision of services for their children, themselves and their communities (John, 2008b). The overarching purpose of EECs and SSCCs – and the surviving children and family centres and nursery provision – is that those they serve feel they belong, feel they are of equal value to others on this earth and feel themselves to be creative problem solvers with something valuable to contribute (ibid.). As can be seen in Box 2.1, there are a number of challenges in leading such aspirational provision.

Box 2.1   Challenges of leading aspirational provision

- Developing and providing high-quality integrated services that families and communities need and value
- Integrating different management structures, including unequal pay, poorly paid, unqualified staff from different disciplines and sectors, ensuring that staff members from various professional heritages are valued and respected
- Maintaining motivation, commitment and energy, even among low-paid staff
- Enhancing staff members' understanding and practice through supportive supervision and peer mentoring
- Preventing burnout through prioritizing the time and space for sharing and thinking about practice dilemmas and feelings in supervision and in staff meetings

- Sharing feelings and maintaining perspective in working with social disadvantage, challenging behaviours, complex family issues, and family and staff distress
- Fostering continuous professional development and increasing understanding and skills in order to improve provision and outcomes for children and families
- Encouraging innovation and new ways of working, e.g. flattening hierarchies, sharing leadership, theory and practice wisdom and encouraging reflective practice
- Inviting staff members to take initiative and responsibility and take the lead in researching their practice
- Coping with constant changes, demands and *disparagement* regarding the provision of support services for children and families – and the expectation of 'more for less'

Engaging members of the local community in developing and evaluating services requires commitment and tenacity, but doing so inspires commitment and greater realism about what is possible among those involved. The value for families of integrated services in a 'one-stop' setting is that they are able to access what they need with minimal effort, within a familiar context. For leaders and staff, integrating services and multi-disciplinary working affords opportunities to broaden perspectives and deepen and enrich practice approaches.

At the same time, in practice, it is far from easy to achieve equality of value and respect among staff members, especially when there are considerable differences in educational achievements, pay and conditions. Working with social disadvantage, challenging behaviours, complex family issues and distress can be contagious, especially when staff members are facing, or have faced, such challenges in their own lives.

Giving staff members opportunities to think about and share their feelings in staff meetings, regular individual and group supervision, and as part of professional development days, help to increase and maintain motivation, commitment and energy levels. Such opportunities also enhance staff members' understanding and skills and help to prevent burnout. Encouraging innovation and new ways of working, flattening hierarchies, sharing leadership, theory and practice wisdom, and inviting staff members to take initiative, responsibility and engage in researching aspects of practice increase staff members' confidence along with the quality of services for children and families.

With radical budget cuts in early years funding over the past eight years, by far the most undermining challenge for leaders has been coping with ever-changing goal posts and the expectation of 'more for less'. This challenge comes with the implicit, and sometimes explicit, suggestion that their accomplishments and efforts are inadequate, and that further cuts are directly related to the inadequacy of the leader, the staff and/or the setting.

Leadership and management, both – with evidence from the neurosciences

Valerie Hall (1996) helpfully observed that: "Leadership is philosophy in action with management an integral part. The women heads in the study were therefore simultaneously leaders and managers. Managing without leadership was unethical; leadership without management was irresponsible" (p. 11).

Like Hall, Margy Whalley and Patrick Whitaker (Whalley et al., 2005) suggested that there are more than semantic differences between *management* and *leadership*, with the management function being about *what* you do and the leadership function about *how* you do it. They were more explicit in specifying that the 'what' of management refers to all that is required for the achievement of the goals and aspirations of the organisation: documents of purposes, aims and targets, structures and systems, roles and responsibilities and operational procedures. In contrast, the 'how' of leadership refers to how staff members and others are encouraged to identify with and commit themselves to the organisation's aspirations and to work with enthusiasm, energy and effectiveness to achieve them.

Evidence from the neurosciences – Recent evidence from the neurosciences offers other ways to conceptualise and appreciate the differences between, and the importance of both, management and leadership functions. Older yet persistent findings regarding the lateralised specialisation of the *brain* confirm that the left hemisphere of the brain is adept at logical, sequential and analytical thinking, typically associated with management, while the right hemisphere is more intuitive, creative and socially attuned, typically associated with leadership. Moving beyond such dualism, newer evidence suggests that a healthy, *integrated mind* both influences, and depends upon, integrated, *whole-brain* functioning and interdependent and supportive interpersonal *relationships* (Badenoch, 2008; Cozolino, 2006; Franks, 2010; McGilchrist, 2009; Siegel, 1999, 2010; Siegel & Pearce-McCall, 2009).

Lateral brain functions – Psychiatrist Iain McGilchrist (2009) identified the different *foci* of each hemisphere of the brain, with the right attending to what is happening in the present moment, to the flow of connections, feelings and meaning in relation to others, nature and the environment. In contrast, but as McGilchrist argues, of equal importance, the focus of the left hemisphere is to provide stability by disassembling and analysing the information it receives from the right hemisphere – in order to create systems that can be relied upon. However, in so doing, the left hemisphere freezes what was flowing, rendering what was alive dead, disjointed instead of whole, favouring task over relationship or process. Observing that Western societies distort our shared, wider human experiences in valuing left brain functions – namely, notions of *independence* and *self-regulation* – McGilchrist's thesis is that the wellbeing of individuals and societies depends upon the healthy integration of the two hemispheres. That is, acknowledging and understanding the wisdom of the right hemisphere, and human evolution itself – that human survival and healthy development, including the development of an integrated and creative *mind* – arise through relationships with others, *interdependence* and *co-regulation*. The discovery of the *mirror neuron system* in primates (Di Pellegrino et al., 1992) and in humans (Rizzolatti & Craighero, 2004) have confirmed our inborn propensity to empathise with the feelings and actions of another.

Interpersonal Neurobiology – Daniel Siegel's Interpersonal Neurobiology (IPNB) (Siegel, 1999, 2006, 2010) has considered *mind, brain* and *relationships* as three interrelated, interacting and irreducible elements of human experience that create a conceptual framework for understanding how the human mind develops from the interactions of neurophysiologic processes and interpersonal relationships. In subsequent work, Siegel emphasised the importance of the *intrapersonal*, our relationship with our self, expanding the IPNB framework accordingly (Siegel, 2010).

Daniel Siegel and Debra Pearce-McCall (2009) provided an overview of IPNB, explicitly in the context of leadership, and as part of that overview, considered *consilient*, or parallel, empirical findings from a range of disciplines – the neurosciences, complexity theory, relationship and developmental studies, social relations, leadership and studies of consciousness and of psychological and neuroplastic change. In line with my abiding aim, Siegel and Pearce-McCall (2009, p. 2) pose IPNB-informed questions:

> What can we do, as individuals, in our relationships and in our organizations, to help create and maintain healthy minds, to facilitate health and well-being on small and large scales? How can we develop organizations that not only function well, but also are creative and flourishing?

They cited management and leadership consultant and academic Warren Bennis (2007), who identified leadership of our human institutions as one of four key threats to our planet, arguing that only 'exemplary leadership' can solve the other key threats, namely, 1) nuclear/biological catastrophe, 2) pandemic and 3) tribalism/assimilation – inviting their readers to consider how IPNB might contribute to the urgent need for exemplary leadership.

Siegel and Pearce-McCall (ibid.) stress that healthy minds and leadership are mediated by the integration, interdependence and connections among the components of the Interpersonal Neurobiology *well-being triangle*: our *neurobiology*, our *interpersonal worlds* and *our minds*. They helpfully define IPNB terms, which are summarised in Box 2.2.

**Box 2.2   Interpersonal Neurobiology –
definition of terms**

Triangle of wellbeing: Concordance in *attuned relationships, a
neurally integrated brain* and *a coherent mind,* which form three
points of the triangle used to examine movement towards healthy
functioning.

Integration: Linking together differentiated elements of a system into
a more complex whole; key to moving towards flexibility, harmony
and adaptability that accompany complexity and health in living
systems.

Relationships: Interpersonal connection, attention and interactions
and intrapersonal connection that involve sharing the flow of energy
and information.

Brain: The *mechanism* of the flow of energy and information as it extends
in the nervous system, distributed throughout the whole body.

Mind: "[M]ental activities that emerge from patterns in the flow of
energy and information within and between brains, with the key
feature of the human mind being a relational and embodied process
that requires the flow of energy and information" (Siegel & Pearce-
McCall, 2009, p. 4). The mind is further defined as having "a core
aspect of regulation" with nine functions: "body regulation, attuned
communication, fear modulation, response flexibility, insight,
empathy, morality and intuition. These are the established outcomes
and process of intrapersonal attunement and secure attachment"
(ibid., p. 5).

Intrapersonal, interpersonal and systemic leadership approach – In the
introduction of the National Professional Qualification for Integrated Centre
Leadership (NPQICL) course materials, Margy Whalley and her colleagues
(2005), like Siegel and Pearce-McCall (ibid.), argued for an intrapersonal,
interpersonal and systemic approach, and against a trait or tick-list approach,
to becoming and remaining effective as a leader:

> there is a vital fourth element, altogether more elusive and mysterious –
> that constellation of inner world components such as assumptions, percep-
> tions, beliefs, values, emotions, prejudices, thoughts, ideas and imaginings.
> It is these components that mark out one leader from another and that
> largely determine how each leader will behave in and experience any lead-
> ership transaction.
>
> (Whalley et al., 2005, Section 1, p. 6)

Like 'emotional intelligence', which gained popularity with the publication of Daniel Goleman's (1995) book, and analogous to Peter Fonagy's 'mentalization' (Fonagy, Twemlow & Sacco, 2005a), Siegel's (2010, p. 7) 'mindsight' refers to "our seventh sense, our ability to perceive the workings of our minds and the minds of others". Siegel (Siegel & Pearce-McCall, 2009; Siegel, 2010) contended that human enterprise and performance, including leadership, can be enhanced by incorporating neuroscience research findings about how our brains work.

Parallels between leading and parenting

A Google search of the expression 'children do not come with instructions' resulted in 27,800,000 results. Nonetheless, our experiences of being a child and being parented teach us a lot about how, or how not, to parent. Similarly, our experiences of being led from early childhood onwards inform our attitudes about leading and being led (Ferguson et al., 2006). A fundamental parallel between leading and parenting resides in the fact that we humans are born into a family hierarchy, dependent upon our parents, and/or other more experienced and powerful others, for our survival and wellbeing. Subsequently, every group or organisation we join will tend to have a hierarchical structure, led and managed by more powerful others, upon whom we are dependent for continued membership and a sense of wellbeing. From birth we find ourselves in groups comprised of older, more experienced others, who are – or whom we feel to be – more able and powerful than we are. Early on, when all is well, parents and older siblings are concerned for our welfare, look after our physical and emotional needs, guide our behaviour and development, cherish and respect us as unique individuals and encourage and support our learning and responsible participation in the give and take of family and community life (Dunn et al., 1999). Effective school and workplace leaders behave similarly.

We can see that neuroscience research over the past two decades offers models and metaphors for thinking about how early years settings and other services can be effectively developed, led and sustained. For example, effective early years provision depends upon encouraging and supporting individuals and interpersonal relationships, with leaders respecting and trusting each and every individual and team, engendering trust among staff members and earning staff members' respect and trust. Leaders' regular presence and meetings with individuals and teams are essential in affirming, aligning and realigning values and aspirations, and planning, setting and reviewing goals and expectations across the organisation. Integration of functions, keeping channels of communication open and encouraging co-operation are key means of inspiring and sustaining effective services, whilst inspiring leadership and creativity in others, as well as managing day-to-day operations, tasks and challenges across the organisation.

Long-standing and more recent findings from studies of leadership and of parenting show strong parallels between the two sets of roles and functions. Psychologist Kurt Lewin and his colleagues (1939) identified three different styles of leadership: 1) *authoritarian/autocratic*, 2) *participative/democratic* and 3) *laissez faire/free reign*. These parallel Adlerian formulations (Dinkmeyer & McKay, 1976/1989; Dreikurs, 1971/1994; Dreikurs & Soltz, 1964), and developmental psychologist Diana Baumrind's (1978, 1991) empirically based typology of parenting defines three distinct styles:

1 *Authoritative or participative/democratic* parents direct their children's activities in a "rational issue-oriented manner", encourage verbal give-and-take, discuss the reasoning behind their policies and solicit their children's perspective and exert firm control without attempting to over-restrict them (Diana Baumrind, 1978, p. 245).
2 *Authoritarian* or *autocratic* parents do not encourage verbal give-and-take, valuing obedience and punitive, forceful measures. They may be genuinely concerned or neglectful (ibid.).
3 *Permissive or laissez faire/free-reign* parents see themselves as an optional resource for their children, but not as active agents responsible for shaping or altering their children's on-going or future behaviour. Some may be very protective and loving, others self-involved and offering freedom in order to evade responsibility for their children's development (ibid.).

Research studies of the relative effectiveness of parenting and parent support programmes in the UK have shown that they were successful in bringing about shifts from authoritarian and permissive parenting to more authoritative, or democratic, parenting, e.g. increased understanding and sensitivity, along with more positive parent-child relationships and child behaviour (Anning & NESS, 2007; Chan & Koo, 2011; John, 2001). Large-scale studies of schools in Europe and North America have found that encouraging *mentalization*, that is, empathic, sensitive and more democratic leadership among teachers, with no alteration in curriculum, led to greatly improved attitudes, behaviour and achievement among pupils (Fonagy, Twemlow & Sacco, 2005a, 2005b).

Similarly, in the workplace, staff satisfaction, creativity and effectiveness have been found to depend upon authoritative/democratic leadership (Bennis, 1989, 1999; Eales-White, 1994; Hamlin & Sawyer, 2007; John, 2000). Human resources academicians Robert Hamlin and Jenny Sawyer's (2007) evidence-based UK study revealed that the most negative and ineffective form of leadership was the " 'traditional management paradigm' of command, control, compliance and coercion which still predominates in many if not most of public and private organizations" (p. 12). In contrast, the most effective leadership was associated with the " 'new management paradigm' of inclusion, participation, involvement, empowerment and openness" (ibid.).

Sociology professor João Formosinho and psychology professor Júlia Oliveira-Formosinho from the University of Minho in Braga, Portugal completed an external evaluation of the NPQICL, the aim of which was to gauge the *impact* of the programme on participants' leadership practice. This impact evaluation followed a small sample of NPQICL Pilot participants and a somewhat larger sample of participants in the NPQICL Roll Out. In the report of their initial qualitative research, Formosinho and Oliveira-Formosinho (2005) used two terms to describe what participants valued particularly about the NPQICL course as a whole. These terms were *epistemological homology* and *pedagogical isomorphism* (ibid., pp. 42–43), which reflected participants' feelings of being valued, respected and encouraged *in the same way* that they were being encouraged to encourage their staff teams, and that staff members ideally were encouraged to encourage children and parents – and parents ideally were encouraged to encourage their children (John, 2007).

Box 2.3 summarises – and provides a preview – of the key dispositions required of leaders and parents in democratic societies (Ferguson, 2011; John, 2008b, 2012a, 2014).

Box 2.3   Key dispositions required of leaders and parents in democratic societies

1   *Understanding* the purposes of their own and others' *feelings and behaviours*
2   *Applying democratic principles* of *authoritative* rather than *autocratic/authoritarian* or *permissive/laissez faire* structures
3   *Sharing power* and encouraging initiative, leadership and creativity in everyone
4   *Containing and surviving potentially toxic emotions and strategies* associated with constant change and uncertainty

---

These will be discussed in greater depth in subsequent sections of this chapter, but briefly, both leaders and parents need to: understand, and appreciate the purposes of, their own and others' feelings and behaviours; 2) *apply democratic principles* of *authoritative/democratic* rather than *autocratic/authoritarian* or *permissive/laissez-faire* structures, being leaders of leaders, inspiring, containing, encouraging and nurturing, rather than controlling, restraining, rewarding, threatening and blaming; 3) *share power* and encourage initiative, responsibility, leadership and creativity in everyone; and 4) *contain and survive potentially toxic emotions and strategies*, notably, anxiety, hostility, negative projections, envy and discouragement, which are associated with constant change, uncertainty, demands and pressure from above and below.

Leadership that empathises, encourages, holds and contains – psychological understandings

Parallels between neuroscience research and psychological understandings – There is consilience among neuroscience research and long-standing developmental and social psychology research and observations from psychodynamic and psychotherapeutic theory and practice that our healthy development, mental health and wellbeing depend upon the love, understanding and care of parents and caring relationships with others throughout our lives. For example, in contrast to Freud's (1901–1905/1953–1974) psychoanalytic and reductionist concepts of biological determinism and psychosexual development, as early as 1910, Alfred Adler's (1870–1937) Individual Psychology (1910/1914) stressed the reality that we humans are socially embedded, "the absolute truth of communal life" (Adler, 1929, in Ansbacher & Ansbacher, 1956/1964, p. 126). Adler further asserted the uniqueness and creativity of each individual and the *indivisibility* of the human mind and body, thoughts and emotions, as well as the individual and the social context; that being – and *feeling* – connected, respected and valued as equals by others are essential in promoting empathy, communication, contribution, co-operation and mental health. Adler (1931/1992, p. 70) wrote that empathy for another is "to see with their eyes and hear with their ears". He noted that from the beginning of life we are motivated by a felt need to belong and find a place in the social world and that we are purposeful and creative in our on-going efforts to do so. As discussed earlier, neuroscience research confirms that from birth the development of the brain and mind depends upon social interaction, emotional *attunement* and *co-regulation* – and that these needs and natural propensities are lifelong.

Freud and iceberg theory – While not the first to name or explore the workings of the unconscious mind or *the unconscious*, Sigmund Freud (1856–1939) placed unconscious processes at the centre of Psychoanalysis. In general terms, *the unconscious* refers to "a level of mind outside our awareness" and "a state characterized by a lack of awareness of ongoing internal processes" as well as,

> characterizing those internal processes that proceed in an implicit manner outside of consciousness . . . typically the cognitive, emotional and/or motivational processes. Physiological processes, to be sure, take place largely outside one's awareness but are rarely intended by users of the term.
>
> (Reber, 1985, p. 799)

Within Psychoanalysis, Freud focused on contents of the mind that were never conscious, for example, when we were infants and without language, but particularly, contents that were pushed out of awareness or *repressed*, because they were and remain threatening to us (Hall & Lindzey, 1985). He later specified a tripartite, dynamic model of the mind, consisting of the *id*, *ego* and *superego*.

Iceberg theory and group dynamics – The iceberg metaphor as it applies to groups is illustrated in Figure 2.1. Freud's focus on *the unconscious* was counter to the thinking of other 19th-century scientists and philosophers engaged in the then emerging science of psychology and interested in the conscious mind, the senses, thinking and imagining (ibid.). Now, prevailing schools of psychology, psychotherapy, counselling and the neurosciences agree that a good deal goes on outside of an individual's or a group's conscious awareness. Freud's contention that the mind is like an iceberg, with the small part we see being only its tip, or *iceberg theory*, alerts us to the unobserved mass of assumptions, expectations, fears and other feelings that lurks beneath the surface of interpersonal and organisational life. The iceberg metaphor suggests that it is not what can be seen above the surface of the water that will 'sink' relationships, a project or an organisation, but the much larger unseen mass below the surface (e.g. see Huffington et al., 2004; Obholzer & Roberts, 1994).

Understanding something about *group dynamics* – or the collective interactions and behaviour patterns that can be observed in groups, as well as the individual needs of group members – can help leaders limit the potential destructiveness of these largely unconscious processes in the workplace (John, 2000). The 'crowd' and 'herd instinct' theories of French social psychologist

Figure 2.1 Iceberg theory: unseen dynamics are what compromise group or team efforts

Gustave Le Bon (1841–1931) and English neurosurgeon Wilfred Trotter (1872–1939) influenced Adolf Hitler in the period leading up to World War II. Following that war, a number of psychiatrists and social scientists applied themselves to the study of social and group phenomena. Psychologist Kurt Lewin's (1948) Research Center for Group Dynamics at the Massachusetts Institute of Technology in the United States joined with the Tavistock Institute of Human Relations in London to launch the journal *Human Relations* and Tavistock Publications (Mosse, 1994, p. 3).

Group dynamics – Tavistock psychoanalyst Wilfred Bion (1961) developed an enduring theoretical framework for analysing the irrational aspects of small group behaviour. He distinguished two simultaneously operating tendencies in the life of small groups: the 'work-group' or 'task mentality' and the 'basic-assumption-group', the 'group maintenance' or 'process mentality'. In the *basic-assumption mode*, the group *avoids* the work task and attends to its preoccupation with meeting the 'collective unconscious' needs of group members in order to reduce anxiety and conflict.

According to Bion's theory, there are three basic assumptions that are common to all group members: *basic assumption dependency, basic assumption fight-flight* and *basic assumption pairing*. Despite the apparent irrationality of a group's observed preoccupations and behaviour, paradoxically each basic assumption mode is designed to ensure the group's survival. Depending upon the combination of group members' unconscious needs or the 'valence' of needs within the group, one or another of these basic assumption groups will predominate. However, in the life of a new group, *basic assumption dependency*, or the preoccupation with finding a leader who can meet group members' needs to feel safe, is most common. In *basic assumption fight-flight*, there is a search for a leader who can lead an attack on, or flight from, an imagined enemy; in *basic assumption pairing*, group members eagerly anticipate the coming together of two group members who can save them from the felt difficulties of present dynamics.

Bruce Tuckman's stages of group development – Bruce Tuckman (1965) identified a 'developmental' sequence – commonly referred to as 'Tuckman's Group Stages' – through which small groups pass: *forming, storming, norming* and *performing*, to which a fifth stage, *adjourning* or *mourning* was added later. In 'forming' members pretend to get along with others; in 'storming' the polite veneer is dropped, personal agendas are revealed and conflicts emerge; in 'norming' group members get used to each other and begin to develop trust; in 'performing' the group productively focuses its energy on the work task; and in 'adjourning' or 'mourning' the group dissolves. Tuckman observed that groups can get stuck and never progress to 'performing'.

Our fundamental psychological needs across the lifespan: the Crucial Cs – In an effort to integrate models of group and individual needs, I (John, 2000) linked Bion's (1961) group behaviour framework with the highly accessible Adlerian-based framework, the Crucial Cs (Bettner & Lew, 1990), which simply refer to four words that begin with the letter 'c', each of which stands for one of our *fundamental psychological needs* (Connell, 1990; Deci & Ryan, 1985; Ryan, 1995). These needs are: to *connect*, to feel *capable*, to feel we *count* and to have *courage*, as a quick way to identify individual team members' unmet needs. Indeed, the Crucial Cs were formulated by Adlerian psychologists Betty Lou Bettner and Amy Lew (Bettner & Lew, 1990; Lew & Bettner, 1996), as an easy way to remember our individual psychological needs, or *self-esteem* needs, through life.

Our fundamental social need to feel we belong or *connect* is extensively studied in research underpinned by attachment theory (Beckes & Coan, 2011; Bowlby, 1969/1982; Cassidy & Shaver's, 1999). When we feel disconnected from the group or team, we become overly dependent on others and seek undue attention from the leader and group or team members. Our need to feel *capable* or to improve is the subject of research on effectance or competence motivation – or its absence – among school-aged children. When we feel incapable, we tend to divert attention away from our feared inadequacy by getting into power struggles or fights with the leader or other members of the group or team. The need to feel we uniquely matter, have – and are seen to have – independent minds and desires of our own and are valued within the group, or to feel that we *count*, is related to research on the need for autonomy. When we feel we do not count, are undervalued, are insignificant, are not taken seriously or are overlooked by others, we feel hurt and apply ourselves to hurting back – and in our felt isolation, we engage in, or even enact, grandiose fantasies. The fourth Crucial C, *courage*, captures our need to feel that we can handle life and bounce back following disappointment, loss or failure – the core idea behind research on resilience. When one or more of our other Crucial Cs remain unmet, we become discouraged, can feel hopeless or helpless and invite others to give up on us – or with us (John, 2008b).

Another important aspect of the Crucial Cs (Box 2.4) is that they represent the developmental *differentiation* of our overarching and lifelong need to feel that we *belong*. That is, the need or inborn expectation to *connect* is evident at birth, the need to feel *capable* is discernible in the first six months of life, and the need to *count* asserts itself in the second year of life, when the *self* is powerfully, if ambivalently, felt, corresponding to 'the terrible twos'. The need to *count* is related to the on-going process of *individuation* (Jung, 1943/1953) or *separation and individuation* (Mahler, Pine & Bergman, 1975), the third phase of Margaret Mahler's 'phases of child development' and the third subphase of which Mahler and her colleagues termed *rapprochement* – or ambivalence about becoming independent or remaining dependent. Most students of human psychology and group dynamics would agree that this ambivalence persists through life as we struggle to be ourselves in our relationships and interactions with others.

Box 2.4 The Crucial Cs

If I have the Crucial Cs   If I don't have the Crucial Cs

CONNECT

I feel *secure*		I feel *insecure, isolated*
I can reach out,	I believe	I'm more susceptible to
make friends	**I belong**	peer pressure
I Cooperate		**I seek Attention**

I need *Communication Skills*

CAPABLE

I feel *competent*		I feel *inadequate*
I have self-control	I believe	I try to control others or
and self-discipline	**I can do it**	prove 'you can't make me'
		I become dependent
I am Self-Reliant		**I seek Power**

I need *Self-Discipline*

COUNT

I feel *valuable*		I feel *insignificant*
I can make a difference	I believe	I may try to hurt back
I Contribute	**I matter**	**I seek Revenge**

I need to *Assume Responsibility*

**IN ORDER TO LOOK FOR THE CRUCIAL Cs
THROUGH USEFUL MEANS, WE NEED:
COURAGE**

I feel *hopeful*		I feel *inferior*
I am willing to try	I believe	I may give up
I am Resilient	I can handle	**I use Avoidance**
	what comes	

I need *Good Judgement*

I AM ENCOURAGED   **I AM DISCOURAGED**

Misbehaviour is a symptom of someone who is discouraged about his or her ability to connect, feel capable and/or count through constructive means.

Source: B.L. Bettner & A. Lew: *Raising Kids Who Can*. Newton, MA: Connexions Press, 1990.

In the first year of life, most of us have plenty of *courage* – feel able to handle what life throws up. Indeed, as infants and toddlers, we need to be protected from a sense of our *omnipotence*. With maturing cognitive functioning, we become aware of our own 'smallness' and limitations, and at any stage of life, particularly when our sense of belonging, competence or significance is in jeopardy, we can become frightened and anxious about real and imagined threats – and lose our courage. The most effective leaders are those who appreciate and devote time to addressing group dynamics, individual needs and organisational and team development – and do what they can to support each person in the organisation to meet their needs to belong, to feel competent and significant – and to feel able to handle difficult situations. Box 2.4 illustrates how Betty Lew Bettner and Amy Lew's (1990) Crucial Cs framework incorporates Adlerian Rudolf Dreikurs's (1957/1968) Goals of Misbehaviour – attention, power, revenge and avoidance – or goal-driven, socially disruptive behaviours.

Family systems theory emerged in psychoanalytic psychiatry in the 1950s (Ackerman, 1954, 1958/1972; Bowen et al., 1957), not long after biologist Ludwig von Bertalanffy (1949/1952) began to publish articles related to his development of *general systems theory* (ibid., 1968). As Whitaker (this volume, p. xx) explains, a general systems perspective represented a shift from a linear causal model to models that required a *holistic* view of the *dynamics* involved, observing that organisms are complex, organised and interactive. A general systems perspective examines the way components of a system interact with one another to form a whole. Rather than focusing on each of the separate parts, the focus is on the connectedness, the interrelation and interdependence of all the parts, and how a change in one part affects other parts.

The application of a systems perspective has proved highly relevant and productive in the study and treatment of families and organisations, comprised as they are of individual members with a common history, emotional ties and strategies for meeting the needs of individual members and the group as a whole. Fundamental to family systems theory is that families organise themselves to manage daily challenges and tasks – adjusting to the developmental and other needs of family or group members. In order to understand the system, family and group therapists and researchers look at the family or group as a whole, with an eye to their tacit rules of interacting. A non-system approach attempts to understand the family or organisation by looking at individual members separately. A common analogy used by family systems and organisational theorists and practitioners is found in baking. That is, the cake that comes out of the oven is more than the eggs, butter, sugar and flour; it is how they combine to form something larger that is how we recognise the cake. Such is true with families and organisations; they are greater than their members; it is how they come together that defines them.

Psychosocial and ego development – Historians of psychological theory and treatment have cited Adler as the "first psychoanalyst to see humans as essentially social creatures" (Hall & Lindzey, 1985, p. 143). Other commentators have regarded Adler's Individual Psychology as the first social or community psychology (Ellenberger, 1970) and the first ego or self-psychology (Munroe, 1957) within which humans are viewed as actively creating and re-creating meaning, understanding and a sense of themselves and others throughout their lives (Loevinger, 1976). Many years after Adler first established Individual Psychology, neo-Freudians, Anna Freud, Heinz Hartmann, Robert White and especially Erik Erikson acknowledged not only internal and largely unconscious processes but also the importance of the social environment and those caring for infants and young children in the development and functioning of the ego or self, "which helped psychoanalysis to become more interpersonal and social" (Hall & Lindzey, 1985, p. 70).

Erik Erikson's psychosocial stages – Like Adler (1930), Erik Erikson (1902–1994) described a creative and vigorous ego that strives to adapt to its environment and to overcome challenges. Erikson (1959, 1968) evolved a flexible psychosocial stage theory, with *ego qualities* emerging and reflecting social and cultural features throughout life without being bound by time or culture. Erikson (ibid.) described eight distinct ego strengths associated with the positive resolution of each stage of psychosocial development. Table 2.1 lists Erikson's psychosocial stages, with the corresponding ego strength, along with its opposite, and underlying theme.

The term *ego strength* or 'ego stability' refers to a person's capacity to hold on to his/her sense of identity and reality, despite psychic distress or conflict between opposing internal forces and external demands (Sullivan, 1953). In order to shore up a threatened sense of self, the child or young person may *borrow* the primary carers' or other admired adults' strengths through *identification* (Ausubel, 1952). When understood by caring adults, this identification strategy can help the young person to discover and develop his/her own interests, abilities and courage, which in turn help in the development of sufficient ego strength to allow him or her to relinquish 'immature' defences, without falling apart, and gradually to develop more *mature* defences (Ausubel, 1952; Sullivan, 1953).

Carl Jung's individuation and transcendence – Like Freud, Carl Jung (1875–1961) conceived the nature of the *psyche* – his term for the mind – to

Table 2.1 Erikson's psychosocial stages, ego strengths and underlying themes

Psychosocial stage	Ego strength v. opposite	Underlying theme
basic trust – basic mistrust	hope vs. withdrawal	confidence/optimism v. doubt/faithlessness
autonomy – shame, doubt	will vs. compulsion	will/determination v. impotence/helplessness
initiative – guilt	purpose v. inhibition	realistic aims v. aimless
industry – inferiority	competence v. inertia	confidence v. uncertainty
identity – identity confusion	fidelity v. role repudiation	commitment/loyalty v. lack conviction – diffident/defiant
intimacy – isolation	love v. exclusivity	reciprocity v. enmeshment
generativity – stagnation	care v. rejectivity	care/nurture v. dismissive
integrity – despair	wisdom v. disdain	courage v. avoidance

develop as part of our human inheritance, and to be more unconscious than conscious. However, he differed from Freud in regarding us humans as holistic, purposive, creative and future-oriented throughout our lives (Hall & Lindzey. 1985). Within his psychodynamic school of Analytical Psychology, Jung uniquely focused on *the collective unconscious*, composed of *primordial images*, thought-forms or memory traces from our ancestral and even pre-human past. He held that these are not directly inherited, but give us a pre-disposition for certain ideas. At the same time, Jung held that our potential is fulfilled through personal experience, and that throughout life, the closely bound functions of *individuation* and *transcendence* are the superordinate processes through which we come to terms with unconscious material and by which we develop and achieve *wholeness* (Jung, 1943/1953). Individuation represents the more analytic set of processes – separating, differentiating and elaborating aspects of personality. Transcendence represents the more *synthetic* set of processes – synthesizing or integrating unconscious and conscious material, as well as within-system and cross-system integration that creates an effectively functioning whole. This involves coming to terms with the unconscious element of personality or the *shadow*, which includes the animal instincts and other unacceptable and unwanted aspects of the self (Jung, 1948/1959). According to Jung, the push towards wholeness is very strong, but repression and regressive personality forces may interfere with individuation and transcendence, and the ideal goal of complete differentiation, balance and unity is rarely if ever reached (Jung, 1948/1959).

Humanistic psychology – In the late 1940s and 1950s, two American psychologists, Carl Rogers (1902–1987) and Abraham Maslow (1908–1970), each studied with Adler, and like Adler and Jung, rejected Freud's psychoanalysis and instead embraced holism – or the indivisibility of mind and body, physical and mental wellbeing and individual and social circumstances. Today most psychologists and medical professionals accept holism and systemic thinking as givens. However, Rogers and Maslow led the humanistic movement in psychology, while at the same time developing their individual conceptual frameworks. Broadly, humanistic psychology asserts the dignity and worth of human beings, as well as their capacity for *self-realization* or *self-actualization*.

Carl Rogers and the actualizing tendency – Like Adler and Jung, Carl Rogers (1951, 1961) believed in an inherently creative human being who actively seeks to enhance his/her sense of self. Rogers conceived of the *actualizing tendency*, or the basic inclination of all individuals to fulfil their highest potential of 'human-being-ness'. Similar to Karen Horney (discussed below), Rogers held that actualization occurs when the 'ideal' self is congruent with the 'actual' self, and that *need-* and *drive-reduction* are part of the actualizing process. Rogers suggested that needs and drives are reduced in three ways: 1) seeking tensions that give pleasure, 2) being creative and 3) developing agency and mastery. Based upon his firm belief that clients have the capacity and strength to determine the course and direction of their therapy, Rogers developed the non-directive approach, which affords the client more control over the therapeutic process than generally given in other therapies. Also fundamental to Rogers's *client-* or *person-centred* therapy is the client-therapist relationship, that is, we therapists need to demonstrate: 1) *empathy* with the client's personal meanings and progress through therapy; 2) *non-possessive warmth* genuinely given to meet the client's needs – not the therapist's – which is enabling and not stifling; 3) *unconditional positive regard*, which is genuine without strings attached, demonstrating sincere trust and permitting the client to express that which is typically, or felt to be, unacceptable; and 4) *genuineness* or *congruence* in being deeply, sincerely and non-defensively ourselves in the role of therapist. It would seem that Rogers's experience of working with children, which led him to reject both psychoanalytic and behaviourist approaches, also led to concepts and therapeutic principles easily transferrable and helpful in developing more effective parenting and leadership strategies.

Abraham Maslow and the hierarchy of needs – Abraham Maslow's (1954/1970) 'hierarchy of needs', illustrated in Figure 2.2, offers a unique stage-like conceptualization, which indicates that in order to attend to 'higher needs', each of our basic needs must be met. The first of the 'basic needs' is the physiological requirement for food, shelter, etc.; the second is the need for safety; the third is the need for love, belonging and identification; and the

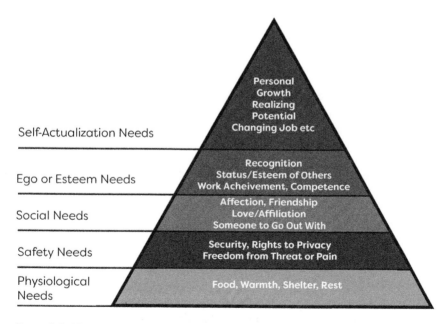

Figure 2.2 Maslow's hierarchy of needs
Source: adapted from Maslow, 1954/1970.

fourth is the need for respect and self-esteem. These basic needs are regarded as 'deficiency needs', but the crowning need is a different type, that is, the need for growth and self-actualization. Maslow argued that our lower needs are pre-potent when they are unsatisfied, but the higher ones predominate when the lower needs are satisfied. Stage theorists typically assert that individuals move through each stage of development in ascending order, and that the cognitive and emotional gains of each stage achieved always remain accessible to an individual. However, Maslow's hierarchy of needs offers a very useful framework within which to account for *regression* in adaptation and functioning, particularly when basic needs are not being met, are threatened or are felt to be threatened.

Loevinger's stages of ego development – Maslow's hierarchy of needs was included among the many stage and related theories of lifespan development that informed developmental psychologist Jane Loevinger's (1918–2008) integrated formulation of the stages of ego development. The main theories that Loevinger (1976) considered, and integrated into her nine-stage formulation were those of Freudian psychoanalyst Sándor Ferenczi, Carl Jung, Erik Erikson (with whom Loevinger worked early on in her career), psychoanalyst Margaret Mahler, developmental, constructivist psychologist Jean Piaget (1970), humanistic psychologist Carl Rogers on the process of psychotherapy, psychiatrist Harry Stack Sullivan on developmental epochs, philosopher and sociologist Theodor Adorno (Adorno et al., 1950), on authoritarian personality features and developmental psychologist Lawrence Kohlberg (1963) on moral development. Like Erikson, Loevinger resisted putting ages to the stages, which she argued would defeat the purpose of characterizing the *meaning making* and dilemmas at each stage. At the same time, she acknowledged that the earliest stages are rarely observed past childhood and that the later stages are impossible to reach in childhood. Whether or not one agrees with the notion of a lawful progression through distinct stages of human development – no skipping stages or *regressing*/going backwards – taken together, these formulations can increase understanding of an individual's ways of making meaning and their dilemmas and preoccupations. Loevinger's framework, which is summarised in Table 2.2, has been shown in a range of studies over many years to be a valid indicator of ego development and a useful means of understanding dilemmas and manner of relating to others across the lifespan (e.g. Syed & Seiffge-Krenke, 2013).

Karen Horney and Erich Fromm, other theories of interpersonal dynamics relevant to leadership – A number of psychiatrists and psychologists, notably German-born Karen Horney (1885–1952) and Erich Fromm (1900–1980), who began practising in the USA in the 1920s, developed their own understandings and approaches based upon interpersonal dynamics, which deviated considerably from their classic Freudian psychoanalytic training. Psychiatrist and psychoanalyst Karen Horney (1950/1970) drew on Jung, and especially Adler, believing in holism – the indivisibility of the physio-chemical,

Table 2.2 Loevinger's ego development theory*

Ego development stage (Erikson's stage)	Conscious preoccupation
(E1) Presocial and symbiotic (trust vs. mistrust)	Exclusive focus on gratification of immediate needs; strong attachment to mother, and differentiating her from the rest of the environment, but not her/himself from mother; preverbal, hence inaccessible to assessment via the sentence completion method.
(E2) Impulsive	Demanding; impulsive; conceptually confused; concerned with bodily feelings, especially sexual and aggressive; no sense of psychological causation; dependent; good and bad seen in terms of how it affects the self; dichotomous good/bad, nice/mean.
(E3) Self-protective (autonomy vs. shame)	Wary; complaining; exploitive; hedonistic; preoccupied with staying out of trouble, not getting caught; learning about rules and self-control; externalizing blame.
(E4) Conformist (industry vs. inferiority)	Conventional; moralistic; sentimental; rule-bound; stereotyped; need for belonging; superficial niceness; behaviour of self and others seen in terms of externals; feelings only understood at banal level; conceptually simple, 'black and white' thinking.
(E5) Self-aware conscientious-conformist	Increased, although still limited, self-awareness and appreciation of multiple possibilities in situations; self-critical; emerging rudimentary awareness of inner feelings of self and others; banal level reflections on life issues: God, death, relationships, health.
(E6) Conscientious (identity vs. role diffusion)	Self-evaluated standards; reflective; responsible; empathic; long-term goals and ideals; true conceptual complexity displayed and perceived; can see the broader perspective and can discern patterns; principled morality; rich and differentiated inner life; mutuality in relationships; self-critical; values achievement.
(E7) Individualistic (intimacy vs. isolation)	Heightened sense of individuality; concern about emotional dependence; tolerant of self and others; incipient awareness of inner conflicts and personal paradoxes, without a sense of resolution or integration; values relationships over achievement; vivid and unique way of expressing self.

(Continued)

Table 2.2 (Continued)

Ego development stage (Erikson's stage)	Conscious preoccupation
(E8) Autonomous (generativity vs. stagnation)	Capacity to face and cope with inner conflicts; high tolerance for ambiguity and can see conflict as an expression of the multifaceted nature of people and life in general; respectful of the autonomy of the self and others; relationships seen as interdependent rather than dependent/independent; concerned with self-actualization; recognises the systemic nature of relationships; cherishes individuality and uniqueness; vivid expression of feelings.
(E9) Integrated	Wise; broadly empathic; full sense of identity; able to reconcile inner conflicts, and integrate paradoxes. Similar to Maslow's description of the 'self-actualised' person, who is growth motivated, seeking to actualise potential capacities, to understand her/his intrinsic nature, and to achieve integration and synergy within the self.

* Source: adapted from Hy & Loevinger, 1996; Loevinger, 1976, pp. 24–25; Manvers & Durkin, 2001, p. 544.

emotional, cognitive and social aspects of being human, including the importance of the environment. Horney also embraced Adler's concepts of *safeguarding* the self, ego and self-esteem and attempting to overcome feelings of inferiority by striving for perfection, superiority and an ideal self, which she termed the 'search for glory' and saw as the effort to disown or *externalise* unacceptable parts of the self. Horney believed in basic human anxiety and hostility, first experienced when we are helpless infants, developing *techniques* (akin to Adler's *safeguarding* and psychodynamic *defences*), like perfectionism, self-hate and externalizing, for coping with those feelings. She distinguished between the 'idealised self' and 'actual self' – which a person often despises and rejects because of the failure to live up to the self-ideal. Horney (ibid.) also held that underlying a person's idealised and actual self is the 'real self', which like Jung's notion of differentiation, Roger's actualizing tendency and Maslow's self-actualization, emerges as a force towards *self-realization*, when a person sheds various dysfunctional techniques to deal with anxiety and conflicts.

Psychologist and psychoanalyst Erich Fromm, a colleague of Karen Horney's in Germany, attempted to combine the views of Sigmund Freud and Karl Marx (1818–1883). Fromm (1941) believed there is an inherent conflict between our animal limitations and our human possibilities, which he called the *existential dilemma* – the struggle to free ourselves and master the environment and our animal nature *and* the alienation from our roots in nature. He noted that the child who struggles to be free of its parents often feels lonely and helpless, and the society that struggles for freedom is likely to be endangered through isolation from other nations. Fromm observed that humans struggle continually for dignity and freedom, yet also yearn for connectedness, that human needs are of two types – those that reflect the existential dilemma and those that reflect our overall need to make sense of the world – and work towards a goal (Fromm, 1955).

Object relations theory and Melanie Klein (1882–1960) – Hungarian psychoanalyst Sandor Ferenczi (1873–1933) is credited with initiating *object relations theory*, which holds that the *psyche* develops primarily in relation to others during childhood. Relational analysts in the United States regard Ferenczi (1913/1916) as anticipating their emphasis on mutuality and intersubjectivity (Rachman, 2007). However, Freud first used the term *object* to describe things and people, in which the infant invests energy, known as *cathexis*, because those things or people fulfil the infant's *instinctual* needs (Stewart, 1992). Indeed, the term 'object' indicates a theory of instincts rather than a theory of interpersonal relationships (Hall & Lindzey, 1985).

Within *object relations theory*, an *object* is regarded variously as the recipient of an instinctual drive, usually a body part, like the breast or penis, but a *whole* object or person eventually becomes the focus of attraction (Klein, 1935/1986). So those who care for the infant also are referred to as 'objects', and early relationships in infancy are known as 'object relations' (Hall & Lindzey, 1985). In England, Melanie Klein is regarded as the founder of the *school of object relations* (Grosskurth, 1986), although Ronald Fairbairn (1889–1964) independently formulated his theory of object relations and popularised the term. Fairbairn's (1952/1981) theory holds that early experiences of objects become models for all experiences in later life. Also, in contrast to Freud's notion that the *libido*, or sex/life instinct/life force, was pleasure seeking, Fairbairn argued that the libido was *object seeking* and that the life force is *towards relationships with others*.

Object relations theory, particularly Klein's, remains the most influential theory within British psychoanalytic teaching and practice. During World War I Melanie Klein sought psychoanalysis with Ferenczi in Budapest, where she became a psychoanalyst herself – and where, in 1919, she began analysing children (Klein, 1926/1986). In 1921, Klein moved her practice from Budapest to Berlin, where psychiatrist and psychoanalyst Karl Abraham (1877–1925) later became her analyst and influenced her thinking with regard to early infant development. As with Fairburn's object relations theory, Klein was interested in a person's relationships with others, but Klein's focus was on the *intra-psychic* relationship between the self and the *mental representation* of others – formed in the earliest months of life – and how these representations affect lifelong mental functioning.

Klein argued for many years that her studies of infantile psychodynamics were elaborations of Freud's earlier theory and his evolved tripartite model of the mind (Mitchell, 1986). That is, she regarded her work as providing detailed insights and evidence of Freud's psychosexual development theory, as well as his later structural, dynamic system of the *id, ego* and *superego*. Freud's theory of psychosexual development specifies the *oral, anal* and *genital* phases. Within Freud's (1923/1953–1974) structural, dynamic model of the mind, the *id* is seen as the unconscious, primitive, need-driven and impulsive area of the mind, which provides energy for all three systems and operates by the *pleasure principle*. The *ego* is seen as the rational area, regarded by the individual as the self, capable of self-observation and efforts to conform to objective reality, but also developing defences to ward off fears and anxieties and protect self-esteem and operating by the *reality principle*. The *superego* represents moral standards, holding a *conscience* that punishes wrong behaviours and an *ego ideal* that rewards right behaviours; the *superego* is often seen as the *internalised parent(s)*.

Impressed with Klein's work, Freud's close colleague Ernest Jones invited Klein to come to England in the mid-1920s (Grosskurth, 1986). Around the same time, her close friend Alix Strachey (1892–1973) and her husband James Strachey (1887–1967), who together translated Freud's works, arranged for Klein to lecture at the Institute of Psychoanalysis in London (Mitchell, 1986). Klein lived in London from 1926 until her death in 1960 (ibid.). Through her observational and intensive analytic work with young children and adults, Klein evolved a much more elaborated model of mental development. Put simply, she proposed that the new-born possesses conflicting impulses of love and hate (ibid., p. 19) and described the ways in which these are experienced internally. Central to Kleinian object relations theory are the concepts of part objects in early infancy and whole objects in later infancy, both of which may be conceived of as either 'good', that is reassuring and satisfying, or 'bad', that is persecutory and frustrating.

The differences between Klein's and Freud's theories became fully apparent in 1934–1935 when Klein presented her most comprehensive theory of infantile development to date, 'The Psychogenesis of Manic-Depressive States', at the 1934 International Congress of Psychoanalysis in Lucerne (Mitchell, 1986), which was published the following year (Klein, 1935/1986). As Juliet Mitchell (1986) summarised, Klein "explored the borderland between the physiological and the psychological, with one emanating from the other under the provocation of the external world. In doing so she effected a shift in interest from the neuroses to the psychoses" (p. 31). "For Klein, what is unconscious is the biological and affectional condition of the human being . . . the life drive, the death drive and their affects" (ibid., p. 23). Also, based upon her work with children, Klein saw little distinction between *the unconscious, preconscious* and *conscious*. Klein's therapeutic and theoretical interest was more phenomenological and content-oriented than structural, focused on "finding the unconscious content of the phantasies and the work of the unconscious ego" (ibid., p. 24). In Klein's psychodynamic theory, past and present are one, since in early childhood and in unconscious phantasies time is spatial and not historical. "Infancy is a perpetual present" (ibid., p. 26), which is conveyed in part by Klein's use of the term *position* rather than *phase* or *stage*. Compared to Freud's notion that the child was the father to the man, in Klein we find, "the infant gave birth to the child and adult" (ibid., p. 27).

Klein's (1935/1986) account built upon her earlier observation that, during the first months of life the infant experiences sadistic impulses of annihilation towards the 'bad' part-object (breast). These sadistic impulses were seen to be projected/externalised, and then incorporated/introjected/internalised as paranoid fears of a persecutory/toxic part-object. This early phase was referred to as the *paranoid position*. Then near the end of the infant's first year and during the second year, when the ego becomes more organised and more in touch with reality, the young child identifies with the internalised and idealised image of the whole object/mother. The preservation, through incorporation/introjection of the good object/mother, is equated with the survival of the ego. However, together with the change from relating to the good/bad part-object (breast) to relating to the complete good/loved object (mother), the impulse to introject the good/loved object is curtailed by the young child's awareness of the potential contamination/annihilation of the loved object by the previously introjected bad/persecutory/toxic object, which threatens to destroy the good/loved object. Hence, within this impossible and anxiety-inducing situation of attempting to preserve the ego, as well as the relationship with the loved object, the young child experiences melancholia associated with 'loss of the loved object', also known as the *depressive position*.

From the *depressive position*, the good/loved object is idealised and seen as perfect, with the idea of perfection 'disproving' the fear of potential destruction or disintegration of the good/loved/object and ego – an early, unsuccessful attempt to mend the *split* between good and bad. Consequently, the *omnipotence* that characterises *mania* in the manic-depressive state is based upon the defence mechanism of *denial*, which is designed to protect the ego from internalised persecutors and the internalised good objects from destruction. The ego's

> attempt to detach itself from an object without at the same time completely renouncing it seems to be conditioned by the ego's own [gain in] strength. It succeeds in this compromise by denying the importance of its good objects and also the dangers with which it is menaced from its bad objects and the id. At the same time it endeavours ceaselessly to *master and control* all its objects, and the evidence of this effort is hyperactivity. . . . What to my view is quite specific to mania is the *utilization of the sense of omnipotence for* the purpose of *controlling and mastering objects*.
>
> (Klein, 1935/1986, pp. 132–133, her emphasis)

Klein distinguished between this manic attempt at reparation and true reparation, a primary goal in psychoanalysis. She considered the ability "to recognise our destructive impulses towards those we love, and to make reparation for the damage we have caused them, an essential part of mental health" (Segal, 1964, p. 89).

Klein's dramatic account of early object relations is the basis of the work of two of Klein's trainees Donald Winnicott and Wilfred Bion. Both these distinguished psychoanalysts built upon Klein's theories and offered valuable insights regarding how the psychodynamics that arise in early infancy remain a feature of childhood, adolescence, adulthood and group and organisational life – and how these can be mitigated.

Donald Winnicott (1896–1971) was a paediatrician and psychoanalyst, who was in analysis with James Strachey (1887–1967) for ten years and then with Joan Riviere (1883–1962), who became a key proponent of Klein's work. When he was already established in his career, he studied with Klein and found her observations and insights about infants and mothers more like his own than those of Freud (Winnicott, 1965, pp. 171–178). In the late 1950s, Winnicott (1958, 1965) introduced the notion of the 'good enough' mother, who from birth *holds* the infant in a safe place, helping the young child to survive imagined threats to his/her existence or *true self*. Through being held by the good enough mother, the infant/toddler perceives – and is helped to survive – imagined threats to his/her existence or *true self*. The *holding environment* serves as the 'transition space', which is achieved through the mother understanding, remaining calm and *surviving* the infant/toddler's rage and aggression. The developing infant/toddler then is able to move from 'unity' to having a personal existence – to think, trust, play. Winnicott observed that an effective holding environment grows and accommodates in order to meet the needs of the developing child, which is analogous to developmental psychologist Lev Vygotsky's (1896–1934) notion of the zone of proximal development (Vygotsky, 1978). In 1960, Winnicott (1965, pp. 140–152) introduced the concepts of the *true self* and the *false self*, equating the *true self* with 'being alive' and 'being', akin to Klein's notion of the *life force*. In contrast Winnicott held that the *false self* emerges in response to less than good enough mothering, when the young child conceals his or her real feelings and builds up a false set of relationships. At the same time, Winnicott (1964) observed that the *anti-social tendency* can be found in normal as well as neurotic or psychotic individuals and that anti-social behaviour is a cry for help and a need to be held.

Wilfred Bion (1897–1979) – Bion's Kleinian training was interrupted by World War II, which led him to study group dynamics. Indeed, Bion's (1962) work with shell-shocked groups of veterans was key to his concept of *containment* in groups, which he regarded as directly analogous to containment in the infant-mother relationship. Similar to Winnicott's notion of *holding*, but with the specification that within a mother's *reverie*, she *contains* and *detoxifies* split-off anxieties, or projections, and returns them to the infant, who introjects them in modified form. Bion observed that containment in therapy, in other supportive relationships and in groups or organisations makes possible *thinking*, which is a pre-requisite for positive action and functioning.

Similarly, a benign authority needs to demonstrate understanding of hostile projections, helping individuals to take them back, in detoxified form, as parts of themselves. He also observed that groups magnify anxieties and projections and that group experiences can induce psychotic phantasies and behaviour, all of which require containment. Consequently, the leader or *container* needs to survive negative projections and be able to manage his or her fears and anxieties – and not let these *leak* into the group or organisation.

Containment, thinking, feeling: Bion and the neurosciences – Figure 2.3 illustrates the relationship between thinking and feeling when we are contained emotionally, when we are frightened and when we are dissociated because of past, persistent or present trauma (van der Kolk, 2014). That is, the first circle shows that when we feel contained and safe, feeling informs thinking and thinking informs feeling, that is, there is integration between mind and body. The second circle shows that when we are frightened or do not feel heard, feeling swamps thinking – and we tend to feel *flooded* with emotion. The third circle shows that in response to actual or imagined past or present life-threatening fear, freezing and dissociation result in diminished thinking and feeling.

Summary of psychological understandings for leadership – In this survey of long-standing psychological theories, we see that healthy human development, mental health and wellbeing depend upon the love, understanding and care of parents and important others throughout our lives. As neuroscience research confirms, from birth, the development of the brain and mind depends upon social interaction, emotional *attunement* and *co-regulation*, and these needs and natural propensities persist (Siegel, 1999; van der Kolk, 2014). Alfred Adler (1931/1992) asserted that each individual is unique and creative, with life expressing itself in *striving* and *movement* – which others referred to variously as the *libido, life instinct* or *life force* – and that our meaning-making proclivity and biased apperceptions contribute to our uniqueness, about which there also is consilience across disciplines and theorists.

Furthermore, *holism*, or the indivisibility of the human mind and body, thinking and feeling and individual and social context is widely acknowledged, and also supported by neuroscience research. There is further consilience with regard to our shared fundamental psychological needs through life: that being – and *feeling* – connected, competent, respected and valued, and seen by others as self-directed equals – are essential in promoting empathy, communication, contribution, co-operation, mental health and resilience. Most theorists and researchers suggest that human development proceeds from actual and felt vulnerability and dependency to growth in body, mind and understanding, leading to gradual *separation* and *individuation* – but with healthy maturity being regarded as *self-integration* and recognition of our *interdependence*, rather than complete independence.

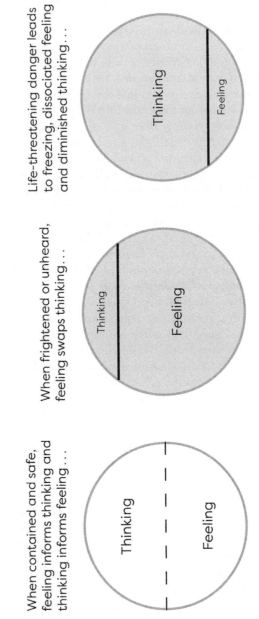

When contained and safe, feeling informs thinking and thinking informs feeling . . .

When frightened or unheard, feeling swaps thinking . . .

Life-threatening danger leads to freezing, dissociated feeling and diminished thinking . . .

Thinking

Feeling

Thinking

Feeling

Thinking

Feeling

Figure 2.3 The relationship between containment, thinking and feeling

Adlerian theory is particularly helpful in bringing together the varying accounts of how our very early experiences affect our later psychological functioning. Adler (ibid.) observed that when we are infants and young children, we are excellent observers but poor interpreters, that given the strength of our need to belong, we invariably make mistakes about ourselves and our value in relation to others and the world around us. These observations, and efforts to make meaning, contribute to our biases or *biased apperceptions*. What is more, from the beginning, we are aware of our vulnerability and dependency upon others, and from early on, both our human inheritance and our observations lead us to *strive* to overcome our perceived difficulties – and also to approximate, and accommodate to what we see others doing. Our earliest experiences typically include being a small person in a world of relative giants, and our observational skills can lead us to feel inadequate, less-than or inferior to others. From this position we tend to compensate by striving for superiority or perfection, which is illustrated in Figure 2.4.

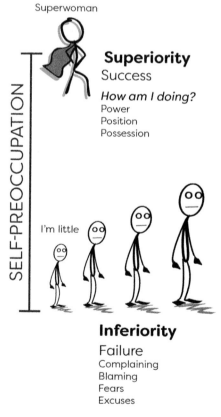

Figure 2.4 Striving to overcome feeling inferior

Within Adler's Individual Psychology, which accords with most of the other interpersonal theories surveyed, good mental health is associated with a positive sense of self, which leads to a positive interest in others and co-operation, and a desire to contribute to the good of the family, school, workplace and society as a whole, rather than a preoccupation with competitive striving to shore up an underlying sense of inadequacy. When we try to be better than other people, we demonstrate our concern with compensatory self-elevation and with our own prestige, rather than our concern for others. As we all know, when we feel good about ourselves we are more likely to help others, and when we help others, we tend to feel good about ourselves – and this has been confirmed in extensive and rigorous studies of happiness (Layard, 2005). It is when we feel unsure of ourselves that we seek superiority and become self-absorbed and preoccupied with 'how we are doing' (Adler, 1931/1992; Dweck, 2000; Sweeney, 1989). Discouragement, fierce competition, unrealistically high standards and over-ambition characterise many ineffective and unhappy human beings. High ambition is directly related to the depth of our feelings of inferiority. So Figure 2.4 also depicts our self-preoccupation in uselessly striving for perfection and superiority. One way to understand mental health problems is to see them as self-absorbed efforts to overcome feelings of inferiority and trying to do everything ourselves. This is akin to Klein's (1935/1985) notion of the infant's hyperactive and omnipotent efforts to master and control others as a manic response to depression associated with fear of their loss.

The difficulty with omnipotent striving for perfection is that we become caught in a manic-depressive see-saw, which can lead to withdrawal from others and life itself. While people need to be encouraged in *efforts* to 'get it right' and even to excel, expectations to *achieve* perfection inevitably lead to social and emotional difficulties (Adler, 1931/1992; Dweck, 2000, 2006). Mistakes are best regarded as aids to learning, not as failures. Research has confirmed that anticipating the danger of a mistake makes us more vulnerable to error; success is most likely when we concentrate on 'what we are doing' (Adler, 1931/1992; Dweck, 2000, 2006; Sweeney, 1989). Many homes, schools, workplaces and relationships are mistake-centred and fault-finding. Yet mistakes are unavoidable and generally less important than what we do after we have made one. This is what we mean when we talk about resilience. Moving towards and caring about others are more likely when we feel good about ourselves – that is, when we feel the Crucial Cs. We must carry on, maintaining our courage and facing life's challenges with hope and optimism. Figure 2.5 depicts the notion of moving towards others, cooperating in working together to improve things for everyone, compared with self-preoccupied striving for perfection and superiority. This requires 'the courage to be imperfect', a phrase coined by psychiatrist Rudolf Dreikurs (1970), Adler's most prominent proponent in the United States.

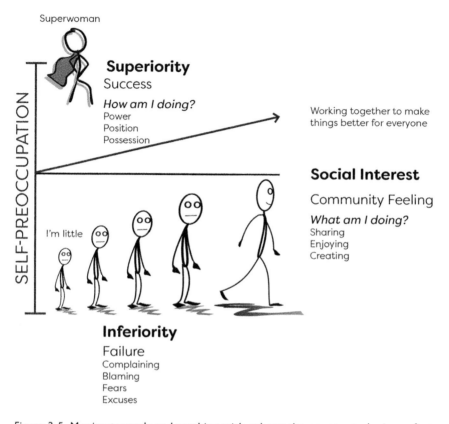

Superwoman

Superiority
Success

How am I doing?
Power
Position
Possession

Working together to make
things better for everyone

SELF-PREOCCUPATION

Social Interest

Community Feeling

What am I doing?
Sharing
Enjoying
Creating

I'm little

Inferiority

Failure
Complaining
Blaming
Fears
Excuses

Figure 2.5 Moving towards and working with others: the courage to be imperfect

Supporting, containing and encouraging rigour through work-based supervision

From a constructivist perspective, developmental and clinical psychologist Robert Kegan (1982) identified three overarching functions of good authority that promote healthy functioning and development and inspire and contain ambition, which can be seen to include parents, teachers and leaders, or supervisors in the workplace: 1) *continuity* or providing a stable and safe environment within which development is fostered, with minimal environmental changes; 2) *confirmation* or understanding, accepting and encouraging the person, where they are; and 3) *contradiction* – allowing the person to learn through increased awareness of physical and social realities and the needs and wishes of others. These three functions also can be seen as promoting our fundamental psychological needs (Deci & Ryan, 1985), which are summarised within the Crucial Cs framework (Bettner & Lew, 1990).

Sustaining ambitious services requires that leaders and staff take part in regular supportive supervision with someone they respect and trust enough to share their feelings, dilemmas, doubts and fears – confidentially, without fear of recriminations. Whether or not the supervisor has intimate knowledge of the supervisee's job, he/she needs to have enough understanding of the supervisee's context, circumstances and issues to offer empathy, a wider perspective, support and challenge.

If early years practitioners are to provide the kind of encouragement necessary for the support, development and challenge of children and families (Bahlmann & Dinter, 2001), they need to be encouraged, supported and challenged as well, ideally through clear leadership structures and formal supervision. Within the professions of counselling, psychotherapy, social work and social care, it has long been accepted that people who work under pressure, with complexity, discouragement and distress, are at risk of becoming overburdened, discouraged and distressed as well (John, 2008b, p. 56). Those practitioners traditionally have been required to take part in regular supervision, which helps them to look at their practice, how their work is affecting them and to maintain, or regain, a healthier perspective and more helpful distance from the needs of others. Long-established social care organisations that work with children and families have well-developed supervision policies and procedures that link with safeguarding and protecting the welfare of vulnerable children and adults, as well as with performance management and staff development.

Ideally, policies, procedures and leadership, along with inter- and intra-organisational recognition of the importance of safeguarding, provide the overall *container* and mechanisms for *holding* the strong emotions that are aroused by issues that arise in our efforts to protect children (John, 2008a, 2012b). However, promoting and safeguarding the wellbeing and healthy development of children, families, communities and staff teams – and working across professional boundaries within threatened and changing organisations – are all about managing complexity and contradiction. To do so we need to be able to recognise, contain and survive our own and others' pain, fears and anxieties. These aspects of emotional intelligence – *recognizing, containing* and *surviving* our own and others' strong emotions, rather than disowning, projecting or 'leaking' those feelings onto others – require support structures and safe spaces, such as individual and team supervision, that offer regular opportunities for reflecting and communicating openly, sharing perceptions, practice dilemmas and concerns with others, and together deciding on ways forward.

Emotional contagion and the rule of optimism – As suggested above, when we work with distress, discouragement or hopelessness we are at risk of feeling distressed, discouraged or hopeless as well. This is sometimes referred to as *emotional contagion*. That is, our innate ability to empathise with others' experiences makes us vulnerable to 'catching' their feelings, including their sense of urgency – that something must be done *right now*. As those who work with young children know, they often experience and express their needs with intensity and urgency, which are more or less understood and contained by those who care for them. In reviewing our work with children and families, we need to look at how the work is affecting us and how we might regain and maintain perspective. Often we need to slow things down and review circumstances and options, systematically and carefully – involving all those who are supporting the child(ren) and family involved. This does not mean that we deny or cut off from a child, parent or family's need or pain, or retreat into paperwork (Menzies-Lyth, 1991), but that we are able to achieve realistic hopefulness and identify more effective ways of thinking about and working with them.

A reluctance to register difficulties can arise from the optimistic view that parents are inherently loving and resourceful and that inadequate, even harmful, parenting is due to unfair circumstances in parents' lives, which prevent them from parenting as well as they might. Early years practitioners work hard to build positive, respectful and supportive relationships with parents, and they are often successful in helping parents to understand and meet their children's needs and to care for them more lovingly and effectively. It can be hard to admit that the needs of some parents are such that they are unable to consider the needs of, or look after, their children adequately, and we need to intervene.

The very prospect of children being taken into care can make it hard for us to take action. We may worry about what will happen to them, whether they will be looked after any better within the care system – or perhaps we have had experience of care proceedings going wrong. Ironically, it is at times when we most need to reflect carefully and attempt to anticipate the probable outcomes of any action we may take that things can spin out of our control. This has to do with the phenomenon of emotional contagion, as well as with professional differences in ways of perceiving and responding to safeguarding matters. Open communication and dialogue within individual and team supervision, along with integrated working and partnerships with trusted colleagues in other agencies are essential in ensuring the implementation of coordinated and well-considered safeguarding procedures.

What constitutes effective supervision? An effective supervision policy and structure within early years settings demonstrate a commitment to positive working relationships, foster open communication among managers and other staff and promote good practice. Supervision requires all staff to take time away from the day-to-day demands of their jobs and reflect on their work on a regular basis. Yet, early years practitioners can feel uncomfortable with the term 'supervision', which can seem to imply being *overseen*, and this can evoke fear of being under surveillance, at risk of being judged or deemed inadequate in some way. While 'performance management' is one of the three key functions of supervision – with the others being support and development – research suggests that good performance is more likely when a manager/supervisor is respectful, assumes a collegial stance and comes alongside the staff member, inviting them to review their work and discuss any pressing issues – and suggesting that together they might achieve a clearer and wider perspective (Hamlin & Sawyer, 2007), ultimately enabling 'super-VISION'.

Models of supervision for early years settings – Most staff supervision within early years settings is provided through the line management structure. As well as reflecting current financial constraints, there are dynamic issues that make line management supervision a logical approach. For example, within children's centres, the governing body or management council and the head are responsible for ensuring that the setting's aims and services conform to public policy and meet the needs of children, families and the community, ensuring that provision is effective, efficient and in line with quality standards, safeguarding and other health and safety regulations. This is accomplished most directly through line management accountability structures, ideally, within which mutual respect, trust and responsibility among members of management and staff are promoted and demonstrated on a day-to-day basis.

At the same time, it is important to acknowledge an on-going debate about whether a line manager with little or no experience of a staff member's specialist area of work, or of her or his professional heritage, can fulfil effectively the role of supervisor. This has been a crucial issue for children's centres, since the integration of services and inter-professional working became central features of how they organise and offer their services. The view that the line manager cannot provide adequate supervision tends to be felt most acutely when a staff member is the only one filling a unique role – for example, the only social worker, teacher, outreach worker, special needs worker, speech and language therapist and/or the staff member feels that the purpose of her or his role, profession or approach is not understood by her or his line manager or other members of the team. Such multi-disciplinary and inter-professional team dynamics need to be addressed within staff supervision and leadership mentoring.

Functions of supervision – Hawkins and Shohet (2006) pointed out that supervision within the helping professions has multiple functions. Kadushin (1976) described three main functions within social work supervision – *develop*, *support* and *manage*, and Proctor (1988) identified the processes within counselling supervision that directly parallel Kadushin's (1976) functions: *formative* (develop), *restorative* (support) and *normative* (manage). There is inevitable overlap among these functions, as depicted in the 'Map of supervision functions and tensions' (Figure 2.6). Even though each function concerns particular issues vital to the effective supervision of staff members, balance among the functions is vital.

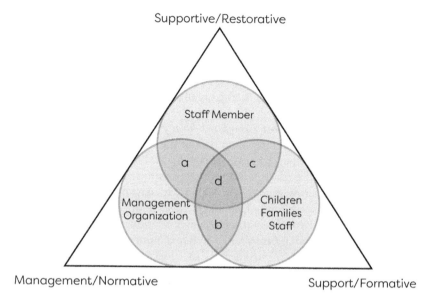

Figure 2.6 Map of supervision functions and tensions

Development or formative – While supervision is not training, this function concerns the development of skills and understanding through exploration and reflection, which can help to identify training needs. Of concern are: 1) the needs, behaviours and feelings of children and/or families, 2) the staff member's confidence, reactions and responses in their work with children and/or families, 3) the staff member's interactions with children, families and/or other team members, 4) the consequences of the staff member's actions and attitudes and 5) alternative ways of responding and interacting.

Management or normative – Supervision is also not the same as performance management, yet this supervisory function concerns issues of quality control and safeguarding of the children and families who use services, ensuring that aims, principles, policies and standards are upheld. Because of the complexity of leading and managing integrated services, the managerial or normative function of supervision also needs to hold a commitment to multi-disciplinary and inter-professional collaboration.

Supportive or restorative – Finally, supervision is not counselling. Rather this function focuses on how a staff member's work with children, families and other team members is affecting them. Inter-professional perspectives and values, despite a commitment to multi-disciplinary collaboration, will raise issues for staff members – such as feeling de-skilled – that need to be explored and understood. As noted above, those working on an intimate and empathic level with others are liable to over-identify with their pain, discouragement or distress, take on their feelings, give too much, cut off and/or suffer burnout. Appropriate support in supervision can help staff members achieve appropriate distance and perspective.

Tensions in the workplace – The letters a–d in the 'Map' in Figure 2.6 refer to tensions that arise inevitably in any organisation:

a   **Individual-management interface** (*loyalty to self vs. loyalty to work*) – Supervisees explore themselves as part of the organisation or team effort. This may include an exploration of personal values and beliefs in relation to those held by the team, setting or organisation and how any mismatch is managed. Supervisees may also examine management expectations and whether and how well they feel able to meet them, along with their own expectations of the team, setting and organisation.

b   **Management-client interface** (*over-involvement vs. over-retreat*) – Supervisees attempt to strike a balance between the twin dangers of 'over-involvement' with clients (or staff) and 'over-retreat' from their distress into administrative work (first identified by Menzies-Lyth, 1991), authoritarianism or over-professionalism.

c   **Individual-client interface** (*transference-counter-transference*) – Supervisees examine their reactions to and interactions with clients (or staff) and what they and others may be 'transferring' from their own life experiences and relationships into present day work encounters.

d   **Overall Picture** (*integration, balance and direction of work*) – Supervisees attempt to integrate the various aspects of themselves and their work, achieve as much balance as possible and find positive direction.

Over time, it may become apparent that certain functions and tensions are commanding much greater attention than the others. This provides clues to the nature of problems in the workplace, within the team, for individual team members or within supervision. Area '*d*' and the concept of *balance* are central to this model of work-based supervision.

Responsibilities of supervisors and supervisees – Supervisors need to establish a shared view of the value and importance of supervision and lead the process of establishing a supervision agreement and a positive supervisory relationship with each supervisee. Supervisors also have responsibility for ensuring regular supervision sessions take place, booking a mutually acceptable private space, keeping summary records of supervision sessions and being open to give and receive constructive feedback. Supervisees need to value the importance of supervision and contribute to an effective process by preparing for, attending, actively engaging in supervision, acting on decisions and being open to give and receive constructive feedback.

Supervisory skills – Training is essential in the introduction of supervision, ideally involving the entire staff team. Box 2.5 provides a summary of the skills supervisors need in order to assume their role effectively. These appear under the headings of understanding, skills in managing supervision sessions, skills in handling the practice of supervision, attitudes and on-going training.

Box 2.5   Supervisory skills inventory

Understanding

1   Understand the purpose of supervision
2   Clear about the boundaries of supervision
3   Understand the managerial, supportive and development elements of supervision and the interplay among them
4   Have adequate experience and knowledge of the area of work in which supervising

Skills in managing supervision sessions

1   Explain to supervisees the purpose of supervision
2   Negotiate a mutually agreed and clear contract
3   Maintain appropriate boundaries
4   Set a climate for supervision that is empathic, genuine and congruent
5   Maintain a balance between managerial, supportive and development functions
6   End a session appropriately and on time

Skills in handling the practice of supervision

1   Use good listening skills
2   Give feedback that is clear, balanced, specific and owned
3   Usefully focus on: the content that supervisees bring; the supervisees' own intervention skills with clients and relationships with colleagues and clients, including dynamic and safeguarding issues and the supervision relationship itself
4   Offer own experience appropriately
5   Develop a capacity for self-supervision in supervisees, i.e. help supervisees problem solve and find their own solutions, and refrain from telling and instructing

Attitudes

1   Commitment to the role of supervisor
2   Comfortable with the authority inherent in the role of supervisor
3   Encourage, motivate and carry appropriate optimism
4   Sensitive to supervisees' needs
5   Sensitive to individual differences: race, gender, age, religion, nationality, marital status, sexual orientation, disability, class, personality, education and training

Commitment to own on-going training

1   Receive own supervision
2   Commitment to updating own practice and supervisory skills and knowledge
3   Recognise own limits, identify strengths and weaknesses as a supervisor
4   Get regular feedback from supervisees, peers, own supervisor, manager, mentor

Supervision promotes wellbeing – Hopefully the foregoing description of the purposes, functions and dynamics of formal one-to-one supervision have made clear how regular supervision sessions can contain, support, encourage development and foster self-management among practitioners whose work requires them to contain, support, encourage development and foster self-management among children and families. Good working relationships are developed when formal and informal support combine to help staff feel they are important and valued members of the team.

Organisational equal opportunities policies generally aim to ensure that all staff maximise their ability to perform effectively in their current job, have their individual skills and abilities recognised and, as far as is practical, are encouraged and supported to grow and develop personally and professionally. Staff supervision is a key part of, and provides a formal means to promote, these egalitarian principles across a setting. That *all* staff and leaders are required to take part in and contribute to the effectiveness of their own and others' regular supervision – as both a right and a responsibility of their employment – provides an overall container for what is meant to be a positive process.

Ecological systems that promote good authority and democracy

In sharing the wisdom of Adler regarding the importance of good authority and democratic relationships and structures, I invariably find that leaders

and practitioners of educational, health, social care and community services for children, young people and families welcome and embrace Adlerian ideas and seem eager to put them into practice (John, 2011). They
recognise the need for a more equal society – and respectful relationships
between and across age groups, individual and socio-cultural communities
and private and public spheres (John, 2012a). At the same time, I regularly encounter doubt, confusion and discouragement about the reality,
or prospect, of flattened hierarchies, of being able to trust one's own or
others' *social interest*, when promoting social equality and democratic practices within the workplace, within classrooms, within families and in other
contexts.

As Adler (1910/1914, 1938) and Dreikurs (1971/1994) observed, democracy requires new ways of relating and leading, yet we struggle to identify and
develop *good authority* (John, 2012a; Pitt-Aikens & Ellis, 1989). More often
than not, those with leadership and management roles and responsibilities
deny, misuse or abuse the power they hold (ibid.). Lord Acton's warning, in
his 1887 letter to Bishop Mandell Creighton (1904), that: "Power tends to
corrupt and absolute power corrupts absolutely" (p. 373) provides a clue to
some of what gets in the way of democratic leadership.

Ferguson (2011) observed that while there are Adlerian books that describe
democratic parenting, "Fewer publications exist to show how administrators
of organisations can be democratic leaders" (p. 434). Even when leaders and
managers recognise and appreciate the importance of thinking systemically
about group needs and dynamics (John, 2000), as well as individual needs
for belonging, self-direction and significance (Teslak, 2010), they still express
their fears or frustrations about taking steps towards more transparent and
participative organisational structures. These fears inevitably arise from their
biases, notably from:

1   An underlying dim view of human nature, or 'Theory X' (McGregor,
    1960), used to justify authoritarian management;
2   Experience of the self-centred and uncooperative behaviour of "some
    people who ruin it for everyone"; and especially,
3   Uncertainty about how to be a democratic leader, that is, how to be *both*
    egalitarian *and* authoritative.

A few years ago, I (John, 2012a) carried out textual analyses of three books
on the topic of authority and democracy: 1) Alexis de Tocqueville's (1835–
1840/1998) *Democracy in America*; 2) Bertrand Russell's (1949/1960) *Authority and the Individual*; and 3) Rudolf Dreikurs's (1971/1994) *Social Equality:
The Challenge of Today*. Table 2.3 is a slightly modified version of the previous
one (ibid., p. 124), which summarised thematic concordance across texts with
regard to factors that undermine and factors that strengthen good authority
and democracy. These factors now appear under four overarching headings:
1) governmental stance, 2) societal expectations, 3) community attitudes and

Table 2.3 Factors that undermine and strengthen good authority and democracy

Factors that undermine good authority and democracy

Governmental stance	Societal expectations	Community attitudes	Individual feelings
Government lacks will to further democracy	**Society promotes disconnection**	**Community encourages shallow pursuits**	**Individuals feel anxious and meaningless**
social equality not guaranteed	individualism	pursuit of wealth/greed of possession	no higher purpose/ conformity of opinion
abuse of power oppressive bureaucracy	social isolation tyranny of majority	commercialism perfectionism	loss of meaning lack of confidence

Factors that strengthen good authority and democracy

Governmental stance	Societal expectations	Community attitudes	Individual feelings
Government takes social lead	**Society takes responsibility**	**Community holds social values**	**Individuals feel social belonging**
social values, equality of worth and dignity	community feeling and engagement	freedom of choice and scope for initiative	social belonging, pleasure and pride in belonging
social justice	civic morality	moral purpose	dignity and worth
material security social welfare and responsibility interrelatedness	mutual support and co-operation connection to cosmos	creativity, pleasure in contribution inner freedom	higher purpose in engagement being part of the human community

4) individual feelings, which helped me to take a systemic approach in the case study to be discussed.

Thinking systemically, what undermines authority and democracy at the governmental level is that *government lacks the will to further democracy*, social equality is not guaranteed and there is the likelihood of abuse of power and oppressive bureaucracy. *Society promotes disconnection*, individualism, social isolation and the tyranny of a 'majority'. The *community encourages shallow pursuits*, including wealth and greed of possession, commercialism and perfectionism.

Individuals feel anxious and a sense of meaninglessness; there is no higher purpose, conformity of opinion, a loss of meaning and a lack confidence.

Conversely, what promotes authority and democracy at governmental level is that *government takes a social lead*, including articulation of social values regarding the worth and dignity of all, social justice, material security, social welfare and social responsibility, and the interrelatedness of all. *Society takes responsibility*, including promotion of community feeling and engagement, civic morality, mutual support and co-operation and a connection to the cosmos. The *community holds social values*, including freedom of choice and scope for initiative, moral purpose, creativity and pleasure in contribution and inner freedom. These conditions help *individuals to feel social belonging*, including pleasure and pride in belonging, dignity and worth, a higher purpose in engagement and the sense of being part of the human community.

Case study: when good authority is undermined – In England, integrated, local services for young children and their families, known as *Sure Start Children's Centres* (SSCCs), evolved rapidly from 1998 through 2010, with the New Labour Government making available unprecedented funding to local communities in an effort to improve the life chances of poor and socially disadvantaged children and families. In 1998, 250 *Sure Start Local Programmes* (SSLPs) were established, some alongside *Early Excellence Centres* (EECs), the first settings to provide integrated nursery education, child care, adult support and training and other community resources. The number of SSLPs rose to 524 in 2000–2001. Then, between 2004 and 2006, as part of Phase 1, most of the existing 100 or so EECs and other well-developed integrated settings were designated as the first 800 SSCCs in the poorest neighbourhoods across England. From 2006 to 2008, Phase 2 designations brought the overall number to 2,500 SSCCs, including somewhat less disadvantaged communities; and from 2008 to 2010, designations of Phase 3 SSCCs brought the total number to 3,500.

Like the majority of Phase 1 SSCCs, in the late 1990s, Millbank (name changed to ensure anonymity) brought together a traditional nursery school and a social services day care centre for "children in need", working in partnership with social workers, health visitors, community paediatricians, and speech and language therapists. Nursery staff members were predominantly teachers, while day care staff members were nursery nurses or family support workers, with levels of education, qualifications and terms and conditions below those of teachers. Previous heads and deputies had been defeated in their efforts to lead the integration of Millbank and resigned. Despite past leadership difficulties, high levels of need in the local community, expansion of Millbank's catchment area and increased funding in 2006–2008 led to rapid growth and recruitment of more qualified and experienced leaders and staff members.

A highly experienced, confident and inspiring Head of Centre and two talented deputies proved able to contain long-standing divisions and discouragement in the team. This was not easy, given that seven members within the staff team of 60 were 'registered disabled' – with four being newly recruited staff members suffering from depression. Not surprisingly, there were frequent, and often prolonged, absences from work. Adding to the Senior Leadership burden was that team leaders with young families had negotiated part-time working patterns.

I had facilitated a Millbank Team Day in the early 2000s not long after their 'integration', and I supported the Acting Head for a brief period soon afterwards. I did not become involved with Millbank again until late 2008 when someone I supported in another setting, a relatively new, visionary and conscientious leader, Jan, was appointed as a deputy at Millbank. Within nine months, the Head retired, Jan was encouraged to apply and was appointed Head Teacher.

Jan enjoyed real success as a democratic leader – consultative, innovative and 'friendly-but-firm'. At the same time, the challenges were many, with major building work and frequent staff absences, which led to overwork, stress and resentment among other staff team members. There also was lack of effective leadership in the classrooms for the youngest children, due to team leaders working part-time, and to lower educational attainment and lower pay than in the 'nursery' classrooms. Constant bureaucratic changes in national and local authority (LA) expectations and targets were additional pressures. Jan managed all of these challenges very competently, but inadequate leadership at LA level, especially inadequate and inconsistent support from LA human resources (HR), contributed to Jan's growing feelings of discouragement.

The crunch came after several months of following the complex HR procedures necessary to terminate the employment of a depressed staff member, on grounds of excessive absences and poor performance. At the 'final' disciplinary hearing, when Jan expected the termination to proceed, the HR officer instead urged Jan to find the staff member 'alternative' work within the setting. It was that incompetence and lack of understanding of the structure and needs of a SSCC that prompted Jan to resign. The large majority of staff at Millbank was truly sorry to lose Jan, but losing head teachers was very familiar to them. Fortunately, with my and long overdue LA support, the two deputies together were able to claim their 'good authority' and take the staff team and setting forward confidently, effectively and democratically. However, neither wished to apply for the permanent Head of Centre post.

In analysing this case study of when good authority was compromised by factors that undermined leadership, I applied Bronfenbrenner's (1979) ecological systems theory, in which he delineated nested environmental systems that influence individual development and behaviour, as well as the interconnections among more immediate, less proximal and wider contexts. Adapting Bronfenbrenner's model, in the manner first illustrated by Garbarino (1982), I transferred the headings from Table 2.3 to Figure 2.7, which presents four concentric circles, with the: 1) Individual at the centre, 2) Community

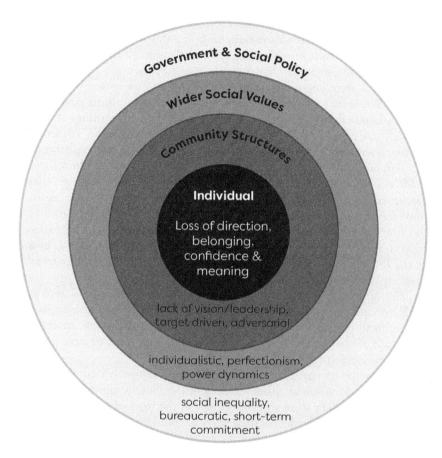

Figure 2.7 When good authority is compromised

structures enveloping the Individual, 3) Societal values enveloping the Individual and the Community, and 4) Government and social policy enveloping all.

As can be seen in Figure 2.7, beginning with the outer-most circle, the Government's social policies at the time of the case study through the time of writing promote social inequality and bureaucratic short-term approaches in addressing social issues. UK governmental policies and wider society both value individualism and the myth of perfectionism, favouring the radical capitalism and power dynamics of the US. In contrast a smaller gap between rich and poor has been found to be associated with much higher physical, social and emotional wellbeing among the populations of many other wealthy European countries, or social democracies (Wilkinson & Pickett, 2009).

Following the 2008–2009 economic crisis and persistent recession, there have been massive reductions in government spending on social care, including *Sure Start Children's Centre* budgets being slashed by more than a third in the two years following the last general election (Butler, 2013). Budget cuts and 'management of change' – the latest euphemism for making staff redundant – were beginning to be felt. There are now extensive closures of children's centres and nurseries across England. A common governmental stance when making cuts had been to point out the shortcomings of services, with all the perniciousness that attends blaming the victim. For example, centres have been told: "You have failed to work with the right families", "Unemployment in your area has not been reduced", "Children have not made enough progress". These alleged failures ignore the facts, e.g., that the catchment area was changed only recently, that reduction of local unemployment is outside the scope or remit of the service or that English is not the first language of most of the children. Instead of admitting to having little commitment to supporting vulnerable children and families (Feinstein et al., 2007), or the grandiosity of their expectations of services, particularly given successive cuts of social care services over many years, government policies and actions undermine the confidence of leaders and staff alike. Unfortunately, the local community, as led by local authorities, tends to be hierarchical, bureaucratic, target-driven and often adversarial, demonstrating a lack of vision or values, apart from those prescribed or determined by central government.

The absence of egalitarian values, short- or long-term commitment to social justice, or vision at either national or local levels, together with lack of appreciation of the nature and complexity of the work of early years settings, mean that the senior leaders of these services shoulder all the responsibility for these vital elements in demonstrating social interest and encouraging democratic ways of working. The leaders of the setting featured in the case study recognised the importance of treating staff members respectfully, helping them to feel a sense of belonging, worth and value, offering them scope for self-direction and encouraging them to assume responsibility for themselves and others – in the same ways they encouraged staff to interact with parents and children, and parents to interact with children (John, 2007).

Yet, to some extent the feelings and behaviour of staff members got in the way of maintaining a viable service for the children and families using the Centre. In my experience, this is not uncommon among staff working with discouraged communities for relatively low pay (John, 2008a, 2008b). Discouragement is contagious, and many staff members are drawn to social care positions hoping to work through their own discouragement (ibid.). Just as helping young children to manage intense feelings requires reassuring adults who remain confident, calm and contain their distress, anxious and fragile staff members require confident, calm and containing leadership (ibid.).

The case study demonstrated how a leader's confidence and good authority were undermined and proved difficult to sustain in the absence of governmental, societal or local commitment to egalitarian values and action. This may seem to be a pessimistic ending of this chapter, but it is precisely because modern life and 'holding the baby' can feel so precarious that we need 'leadership that inspires and contains ambition and anxiety'.

References

Ackerman, N.W. (1954). Interpersonal disturbances in the family: Some unsolved problems in psychotherapy. *Psychiatry*, 17, 359–368.

Ackerman, N.W. (1958/1972). *The Psychodynamics of Family Life – Diagnosis and Treatment of Family Relationships*. New York: Basic Books.

Adler, A. (1910/1914). Trotz und Gehorsam [Defiance and Obedience]. Reprinted in Heilen und Bilden [Healing and Forming] (pp. 84–93). Munich: Reinhardt.

Adler, A. (1930). *The Education of Children*. New York: Greenburg.

Adler, A. (1931/1992). *What Life Could Mean to You: On the Psychology of Personal Development*. Oxford: Oneworld Publications.

Adler, A. (1938). *Social Interest: A Challenge to Mankind*. London: Faber & Faber.

Adorno, T.W., Frenkel-Brunswik, E., Levinson, D.J. & Sanford, R.N. (1950). *The Authoritarian Personality*. New York: Harper & Row.

Anning, A. & National Evaluation of Sure Start (NESS) Team (2007). *Understanding Variations in Effectiveness Amongst Sure Start Local Programmes: Lessons for Sure Start Children's Centres*. Reference: NESS/2007/FR/024. Nottingham: DfES.

Ansbacher, H.L. & Ansbacher, R.R. (1956/1964). *The Individual Psychology of Alfred Adler: A Systematic Presentation of His Writings*. New York: Harper Torchbooks.

Ausubel, D.P. (1952). *Ego Development and Personality Disorders*. New York: Grune & Stratton.

Badenoch, B. (2008). *Being a Brain-Wise Therapist, A Practical Guide to Interpersonal Neurobiology*. New York: W.W. Norton.

Bahlmann, R. & Dinter, L.D. (2001). Encouraging self-encouragement: An effect study of the encouraging-training Schoenaeker-concept©. *Journal of Individual Psychology*, 57 (3), 273–288.

Baumrind, D. (1978). Parental disciplinary patterns and social competence in children. *Youth and Society*, 9, 238–276.

Baumrind, D. (1991). The influence of parenting style on adolescent competence and substance use. *Journal of Early Adolescence*, 11, 56–95.

Beckes, L. & Coan, J.A. (2011). Social baseline theory: The role of social proximity in emotion and economy of action. *Social & Personality Psychology Compass*, 5 (12), 976–988.

Bennis, W. (1989). *Why Leaders Can't Lead: The Unconscious Conspiracy Continues*. San Francisco, CA: Jossey-Bass.

Bennis, W. (1999). The end of leadership: Exemplary leadership is impossible without full inclusion, initiatives and co-operation of followers. *Organizational Dynamics*, 28 (10), 71–80.

Bennis, W. (2007). The challenges of leadership in the modern world. *American Psychologist*, 62 (1), 2–5.

Bettner, B.L. & Lew, A. (1990). *Raising Kids Who Can*. Newton Ctr, MA: Connexions Press.

Bion, W.R. (1961). *Experiences in Groups*. London: Tavistock.

Bion, W.R. (1962). A theory of thinking. In E. Bott Spillius (ed.) *Melanie Klein Today: Developments in Theory*, Bion, W.R. (1962). *Learning from Experience*. London: Heinemann.

Bowen, M., Dysinger, R.H., Brodey, W.M. & Basamania, B. (1957). Study and treatment of five hospitalized family groups with a psychotic member. Paper Delivered at American Orthopsychiatry Association Meeting, Chicago, 8 March 1957.

Bowlby, J. (1969/1982). *Attachment and Loss*, Vol. 1. New York: Basic Books.

Bronfenbrenner, U. (1979). *The Ecology of Human Development*. Cambridge, MA: Harvard University Press.

Butler, P. (2013). Hundreds of Sure Start Centres Have Closed Since Election, Says Labour. *The Guardian*, 28 January 2013.

Cassidy, J. & Shaver, P.R. (eds.) (1999). *Handbook of Attachment Theory*. London: Guilford Press.

Chan, T.W. & Koo, A. (2011). Parenting Style and Youth Outcomes in the UK. *European Sociological Review*, 27 (3), 385–399.

Clance, P.R. & Imes, S. (1978). The impostor phenomenon in high achieving women: Dynamics and therapeutic intervention. *Psychotherapy Theory, Research and Practice*, 15 (3), 241–247.

Connell, J.P. (1990). Context, self and action: A motivational analysis of self-system processes across the life-span. In D. Cicchetti & M. Beeghly (eds.) *The Self in Transition*, pp. 61–97. Chicago: Chicago University Press.

Cozolino, L.J. (2006). *The Neuroscience of Human Relationships: Attachment and the Developing Social Brain*. New York: W.W. Norton.

Creighton, L. (1904). *Life and Letters of Mandell Creighton*. London: Longmans, Green & Co.

Deci, E.L. & Ryan, R.M. (1985). *Intrinsic Motivation & Self-Determination in Human Behaviour*. New York: Plenum Press.

(de) Tocqueville, A. (1835–1840/1998). *Democracy in America* (translated by H. Reeve, revised by F. Bowen, abridged with an introduction by P. Renshaw). Ware, Herts: Wordsworth Classics of World Literature.

Di Pellegrino, G., Fadiga, L., Fogassi, L., Gallese, V. & Rizzolatti, G. (1992). Understanding motor events: A neurophysiological study. *Experimental Brain Research*, 91, 176–180.

Dinkmeyer, D. & McKay, G.D. (1976/1989). *The Parenting Handbook – Systematic Training for Effective Parenting (STEP)* (3rd ed.). Circle Pines, MN: American Guidance Service.

Dreikurs, R.R. (1957/1968). *Psychology in the Classroom – A Manual for Teachers* (2nd ed.). London: Harper & Row.

Dreikurs, R.R. (1970). The courage to be imperfect. In R. Dreikurs (ed.) *Articles for Supplementary Reading for Parents*. Chicago: Adler Institute.

Dreikurs, R.R. (1971/1994). *Social Equality: The Challenge of Today*. Chicago: Adler School of Professional Psychology.

Dreikurs, R.R. & Soltz, V. (1964). *Children: The Challenge*. New York: Hawthorne.

Dunn, J., Deater-Deckland, K., Pickering, K., Golding, J. & ALSPAC Team (1999). Siblings, parents & partners: Family relationships within a longitudinal community study. *Journal of Child Psychology & Psychiatry*, 40 (7), 1025–1037.

Dweck, C. (2000). *Self-Theories & Goals: Their Role in Motivation, Personality & Development*. Hove, East Sussex: Psychology Press.

Dweck, C. (2006). *Mindset: The New Psychology of Success*. New York: Random House.

Eales-White, R. (1994). *Creating Growth from Change: How You React, Develop, and Grow*. London and New York: McGraw-Hill.

Ellenberger, H. (1970). *The Discovery of the Unconscious: The History and Evolution of Dynamic Psychiatry*. New York: Basic Books.

Erikson, E.H. (1959). Identity and the life cycle. In *Psychological Issues. Monograph 1*. New York: International University Press.

Erikson, E.H. (1968). *Identity, Youth and Crisis*. New York: W.W. Norton.

Fairbairn, W.R.D. (1952/1981). *Psychoanalytic Studies of the Personality*. London: Routledge.

Feinstein, L., Hearn, B., Renton, Z., Abrahams, C. & MacLeod, M. (2007). *Reducing Inequalities: Realizing the Talents of All*. London: National Children's Bureau.

Ferenczi, S. (1913/1916). Stages of development of the sense of reality. In *Sex in Psychoanalysis*. Boston: Gorham Press.

Ferguson, E.D. (2011). What Adlerians consider important for communication and decision-making in the workplace: Mutual respect and democratic leaderships style. *Journal of Individual Psychology*, 67, 432–437.

Ferguson, E.D., Hagaman, J., Grice, J.W. & Peng, K. (2006). From leadership to parenthood: The applicability of leadership styles to parenting styles. *Group Dynamics: Theory, Research, and Practice*, 10 (1), 43–56.

Fonagy, P., Twemlow, S.W. & Sacco, F.C. (2005a). A developmental approach to mentalizing communities: I. A model for social change. *Bulletin of the Menninger Clinic*, 69 (4), 265–304.

Fonagy, P., Twemlow, S.W. & Sacco, F.C. (2005b). A developmental approach to mentalizing communities: II. The Peaceful Schools experiment. *Bulletin of the Menninger Clinic*, 69 (4), 265–281.

Formosinho, J. & Oliveira-Formosinho, J. (2005). *National Professional Qualification in Integrated Centre Leadership (NPQICL) Pilot Programme, An Evaluative Research Study*. Corby, UK: Pen Green Research.

Franks, D.D. (2010). *Neurosociology: The Nexus Between Neuroscience and Social Psychology*. London: Springer.

Freud, S. (1901–1905/1953–1974). VII. The case of hysteria, Three essays on hysteria and other works. In J. Strachey (ed.) *The Standard Edition of the Complete Works of Sigmund Freud* (24 Volumes). London: Hogarth Press & Institute of Psycho-Analysis.

Freud, S. (1923/1953–1974). XIX. The ego and the id. In J. Strachey (ed.) *The Standard Edition of the Complete Works of Sigmund Freud* (24 Volumes). London: Hogarth Press & Institute of Psycho-Analysis.

Fromm, E. (1941). *Escape from Freedom*. New York: Rinehart.

Fromm, E. (1955). *The Sane Society*. New York: Rinehart.

Garbarino, J. (1982). Sociocultural Risk: Dangers to Competence. In: C. Kopp & J. Krakow (eds.). *Child Development in Social Context. (pp. 630–685). Reading*, MA: Addison-Wesley.

Goleman, D. (1995). *Emotional Intelligence*. New York, NY, England: Bantam Books.

Grosskurth, P. (1986). *Melanie Klein: Her World and Her Work*. New York: Knopf.

Hall, C.S. & Lindzey, G. (1985). *Introduction to Theories of Personality*. New York: John Wiley & Sons.

Hall, V. (1996). *Dancing on the Ceiling: A Study of Women Managers in Education*. London: Paul Chapman.

Hamlin, R.G. & Sawyer, J. (2007). Developing Effective Leadership Behaviours: The Value of Evidence-Based Management. *Business Leadership Review*, IV (IV), 1–16.

Hawkins, P. & Shohet, R. (2006). *Supervision in the Helping Professions* (3rd ed.). Maidenhead: Open University Press.

Horney, K. (1950/1970). *Neurosis and Human Growth*. New York: W.W. Norton.

Huffington, C., Armstrong, D., Halton, W., Hoyle, L. & Pooley, J. (2004). *Working Below the Surface: The Emotional Life of Contemporary Organizations*. London: Karnac.

Hy, L.X. & Loevinger, J. (1996). *Measuring Ego Development* (2nd ed.). Mahwah, NJ: Lawrence Erlbaum Associates, Inc.

John, K. (2000). Basic needs, conflict and dynamics in groups. *Journal of Individual Psychology*, 56, 419–434.

John, K. (2001). Measuring children's social functioning. *Child Psychology and Psychiatry Review*, 6 (4), 181–188.

John, K. (2007). Encouraging the discouraged to encourage the discouraged to encourage the discouraged. . . . In *UK Adlerian Year Book*, pp. 25–53. London: The Adlerian Society UK and Institute of Individual Psychology (ASIIP).

John, K. (2008a). *Leadership Mentoring and Staff Supervision in Children's Centres*. Corby, UK: Pen Green Research.

John, K. (2008b). Sustaining the leaders of children's centres: The role of leadership mentoring. *European Early Childhood Education Research Journal, Special Issue: Leadership & Management*, 16 (1), 53–66.

John, K. (2011). Theoretical underpinnings of the NPQICL: Inspiration and grounding. In L. Trodd & L. Chivers (eds.) *Interprofessional Working in Practice: Learning & Working Together for Children & Families*, pp. 145–153. Milton Keynes: Open University Press.

John, K. (2012a). Authority and democracy 100 years on. In *UK Adlerian Year Book*, pp. 107–129. London: Adlerian Society (UK) and Institute of Individual Psychology.

John, K. (2012b). Supervision, Parts 1–4. *Nursery World*, 28 May, 25 June, 23 July, 20 August 2012.

John, K. (2014). A case study of efforts to lead democratically when good authority is undermined. In *UK Adlerian Year Book*, pp. 82–94. London: Adlerian Society and Institute of Individual Psychology.

Jung, C.J. (1943/1953). On the psychology of the unconscious. VII. Two essays on analytical psychology. In *Collected Works of C.J. Jung*. Princeton, NJ: University Press.

Jung, C.J. (1948/1959). The shadow. IX.ii. Aion. In *Collected Works of C.J. Jung*. Princeton, NJ: University Press.

Kadushin, A. (1976). *Supervision in Social Work*. New York: Columbia University Press.

Kegan, R. (1982). *The Evolving Self: Problem and Process in Human Development*. Cambridge, MA: Harvard University Press.

Klein, M. (1926/1986). The psychological principles of infant analysis. In J. Mitchell (ed.) *The Selected Melanie Klein*, pp. 58–68. London: Penguin Books.

Klein, M. (1935/1986). Contribution to the psychogenesis of manic-depressive states. In J. Mitchell (ed.) *The Selected Melanie Klein*, pp. 116–145. London: Penguin Books.

Kohlberg, L. (1963). The development of children's orientations towards a moral order. *Vita Human*, 6, 11–33.

Layard, R. (2005). *Happiness*. London: Penguin Books.

Lew, A. & Bettner, B.L. (1996). *A Parent's Guide to Understanding and Motivating Children*. Newton Centre, MA: Connexions Press.

Lewin, K. (1948). *Resolving Social Conflicts: Selected Papers on Group Dynamics*. New York: Harper & Row.

Lewin, K., Llippit, R. & White, R.K. (1939). Patterns of aggressive behavior in experimentally created social climates. *Journal of Social Psychology*, 10, 271–301.

Loevinger, J. (1976). *Ego Development*. San Francisco, CA: Jossey-Bass.

Mahler, M.S., Pine, F. & Bergman, A. (1975). *The Psychological Birth of the Human Infant.* New York: Basic Books.

Manvers, J. & Durkin, K. (2001). A critical review of the validity of ego development theory and its measurement. *Journal of Personality Assessment, 77,* 541–567.

Maslow, A.H. (1954/1970). *Motivation and Personality.* New York: Harper & Row.

McGilchrist, I. (2009). *The Master and His Emissary: The Divided Brain and the Making of the Western World.* Padstow, Cornwall: TJ International.

McGregor, D. (1960). *The Human Side of Enterprise.* New York: McGraw-Hill.

Menzies-Lyth, I. (1991). Changing organizations and individuals: Psychoanalytic insights for improving organizational health. In M. Kets de Vries (ed.) *Organizations on the Couch,* pp. 361–378. San Francisco, CA: Jossey-Bass.

Mitchell, J. (ed.) (1986). *The Selected Melanie Klein.* London: Penguin Books.

Mosse, J. (1994). Introduction: The institutional roots of consulting to institutions. In A. Obholzer & V.Z. Roberts (eds.) *The Unconscious at Work,* pp. 1–8. London: Routledge.

Munroe, R.L. (1957). *Schools of Psychoanalytic Thought.* London: Hutchinson.

Obholzer, A. & Roberts, V.Z. (1994). *The Unconscious at Work: Individual and Organizational Stress in Human Services.* London: Routledge.

Piaget, J. (1970). *Biology and Knowledge* (2nd ed.). Edinburgh: Edinburgh University Press.

Pitt-Aikens, T. & Ellis, A.T. (1989). *Loss of Good Authority – The Cause of Delinquency.* London: Penguin Books.

Proctor, B. (1988). Supervision: A co-operative exercise in accountability. In M. Marken & M. Payne (eds.) *Enabling and Ensuring.* Leicester: Leicester National Youth Bureau and Council of Education and Training in Youth and Community Work.

Rachman, A.W. (2007). Sandor Ferenczi's contributions to the evolution of psychoanalysis. *Psychoanalytic Psychology, 24* (1), 74–96.

Reber, A.S. (1985). *Dictionary of Psychology.* Aylesbury, Bucks: Penguin Books.

Rizzolatti, G. & Craighero, L. (2004). The mirror neuron system. *Annual Review of Neuroscience, 27* (1), 169–192.

Rogers, C.R. (1951). *Client-Centred Therapy: Its Current Practice, Implications and Theory.* New York: Constable.

Rogers, C.R. (1961). *On Becoming a Person: A Therapist's View of Psychotherapy.* London: Allen & Unwin.

Russell, B. (1949/1960). *Authority and the Individual.* Boston: Beacon.

Ryan, R.M. (1995). Psychological needs and the facilitation of integrative processes. *Journal of Personality, 63,* 397–427.

Segal, H. (1964). *Introduction to the Work of Melanie Klein.* London: Heinemann.

Siegel, D.J. (1999). *The Developing Mind: How Relationships and the Brain Interact to Shape Who We Are.* New York: Guilford Press.

Siegel, D.J. (2006). An interpersonal neurobiology approach to psychotherapy: Awareness, mirror neurons, and neural plasticity in the development of well-being. *Psychiatric Annals, 36* (4), 248–256.

Siegel, D.J. (2010). *Mindsight: The New Science of Personal Transformation.* New York: Bantam Books.

Siegel, D. & Pearce-McCall, D. (2009). Mindsight at work: An interpersonal neurobiology lens on leadership. *NeuroLeadership Journal,* (2), 1–12. www.NeuroLeadership.org

Stewart, W. (1992). *An A-Z of Counselling Theory and Practice.* London: Chapman & Hall.

Sullivan, H.S. (1953). *The Interpersonal Theory of Psychiatry.* New York: W.W. Norton.

Sweeney, T.J. (1989). *Adlerian Counseling – A Practical Approach for a New Decade*. Muncie, IN: Accelerated Development.

Syed, M. & Seiffge-Krenke, I. (2013). Personality development from adolescence to emerging adulthood: Linking trajectories of ego development to the family context and identity formation. *Journal of Personality and Social Psychology*, 104 (2), 371–384.

Teslak, A.G. (2010). "Buying in" and "checking out": Motivation in the workplace. *Journal of Individual Psychology*, 66, 116–129.

Tuckman, B.W. (1965). Developmental sequence in small groups. *Psychological Bulletin*, 61 (6), 384–399.

van der Kolk, B. (2014). *The Body Keeps the Score*. London: Allen Lane.

(von) Bertalanffy, L. (1949/1952). *Problems of Life: An Evaluation of Modern Biological and Scientific Thought*. New York: Harper & Row.

(von) Bertalanffy, L. (1968). *General Systems Theory*. New York: Brazliller.

Vygotsky, L.S. (1978). *Mind in Society: The Development of Higher Psychological Processes*. Cambridge, MA: Harvard University Press.

Whalley, M., Whitaker, P., Fletcher, C., Thorpe, S., John, K. & Leisten, R. (2005). *NPQICL Programme Course Leaders' Guide*. Nottingham: NCSL.

Wilkinson, R. & Pickett, K. (2009). *The Spirit Level: Why Equality Is Better for Everyone*. London: Penguin Books.

Winnicott, D.W. (1958). *Through Paediatrics to Psychoanalysis: Collected Papers*. London: Tavistock.

Winnicott, D.W. (1964). *The Child, the Family, and the Outside World*. London: Addison-Wesley.

Winnicott, D.W. (1965). *The Maturational Process and the Facilitating Environment*. London & New York: Karnac.

Chapter 3

Leadership as activism

Margy Whalley

I have been a leader of an integrated centre for children and families in Corby for 35 years and have experienced every one of Labour's new early years initiatives from 1997 to 2010 and the subsequent cuts and radical policy shifts under both the coalition government (2010–2015) and the Conservative government from 2015. I also have 30 years experience of designing and developing leadership professional development opportunities for leaders in ECEC settings in this country and overseas.

It seems to be the right time to be asking fundamental questions about leadership in the early years phase. My two main concerns in this chapter are firstly to consider leadership within Early Childhood Education and Care settings (ECEC) as emancipatory practice. In the 21st century it seems to me that leaders have to conceptualise and construct their practice as part of the struggle for social justice and social change, and this profoundly impacts on the way that services are co-designed and co-developed *with* the community. Secondly I want to reflect on how we train and develop future leaders, leaders who have a commitment to transforming the life chances of children and their families through harnessing the energy for change and social solidarity in communities.

Establishing the concept of integrated centres for children and families 1983–1994

> For anyone who is serious about social progress, this historical background is absolutely essential, because it helps to overcome the sustained and professional pessimism that is encouraged by the establishment in order to discourage anyone from carrying on with their campaigns for justice . . . hope is the fuel of social progress and we can acquire that hope most easily if we remember that throughout the whole of history it has always been the same.
>
> Tony Benn, 2003, p. 52

Pen Green in Corby, Northamptonshire finally opened as an experimental project in 1983 after eight turbulent years of discussion and negotiation between well-intentioned officers in the local authority, keen to innovate and establish the first multi-functional multi-disciplinary service for children and families in Northamptonshire, and local families in Corby who were deeply troubled with the idea that a 'problem family centre' was to be built in their community. Funding for this innovative 'pilot project' on Pen Green Lane was to be by Joint Financing through the Joint Consultative Committees on the County Council and the Area Health Authority. A radical decision was made, with far-reaching consequences, that the centre should be open 48 weeks a year and all staff, teachers, social workers and childcare workers were to be on the same conditions of service (Whalley, 1994).

The conceptualisation and early development of the centre clearly build on what had gone before. For example the work of the McMillan sisters Margaret and Rachel, who had developed ECEC provision at the beginning of the 20th century which integrated early education with healthcare services and adult learning opportunities in Deptford and in Bradford. This approach to integrating education, care, health and adult education was part of a transnational movement. Similar centres, such as the Lady Gowrie Centres (gowrieqld.com.au), were set up by the Australian Commonwealth Government in the 1940s in most Australian states and were strongly influenced by the work of the McMillan sisters and the work of Susan Isaacs (1930).

Our initial multi-disciplinary team of six staff built substantively on the work of pioneering centres such as the Dorothy Gardner and the Thomas Coram centres in London described in the literature as 'hybrid under 5 centres'. Local authority officers in Northamptonshire also visited the Hillfields Centre in Coventry which was offering a wider provision than either traditional nursery education or social services day care with very high levels of community engagement. Because the Pen Green centre occupied the empty shell of the oldest secondary school building (1930s) in the town, right next to the steelworks, the main employer in the town and imminently due for closure, local politicians and county counsellors were involved from the start. A local community social worker undertook a comprehensive data review and encouraged local families, in the spirit of the times, to set up a community action group whose members immediately requested representation on staff appointment panels and positions on the advisory board of the new centre. The political and structural relationship between the newly formed staff team and the local community was determined by the need for staff to be immediately accountable to a strong, vocal and somewhat militant local action group. This led to a partnership that was equal but different between workers in, and users of, the services, which has defined the way that services have developed over the last 35 years.

> Parents who are not defined as 'inept' and who are not competing for a scarce source are less likely to be passively grateful and deferential and to want to determine the nature of the service provided for their children.
>
> (Haddock, 1981, p. 7)

From community development to co-construction

Pen Green in 1983 was as much a 'community development project' as it was an 'early intervention project'. We owe a huge debt to the pioneers who developed community-based adult education initiatives in settlement projects at the beginning of the 20th century and radical community development initiatives in education and community health and social work approaches from the 1960s–1980s. Their innovative work informed our practice and helped us to develop a highly integrated service for children and families which went way beyond the 1980s approaches accurately described by Gillian Pugh (1988) who at the time directed the early childhood unit at the National Children's Bureau. Her synthesis of what local authorities were offering in terms of integrated services was as follows:

- **Co-ordinated services** – with multiple agencies engaged in focused activities
- **Co-located services** – where education social care and health moved into one building without necessarily any real shift in professional practice and
- **Collaborative services** – where staff were moving towards a shared philosophy without any formal shift in leadership or management structures

In 1994 when the first edition of *Learning to be Strong: Setting Up a Neighbourhood Service for Under-Fives and Their Families* (Whalley, 1994) was written, Pen Green staff were already articulating their philosophy as one in which participation was essential:

> We have come to understand the difference between inviting people to share in a finished piece of work (however beautifully tailored to their needs it might appear), and setting priorities and establishing principles together with the people who are going to use the services. Parental and family involvement was not tagged on as an afterthought nor as something that was secondary to the primary task of providing a quality nursery for children. We learnt that if we wanted real participation then we needed to share decision making from the word go.
>
> (Moss, 1992, pp. 43–44)

Pen Green was precisely the kind of multi-functional early years' provision that Peter Moss described at the time as having developed 'from a perspective which regards early childhood services a need a right of all communities and families, and as an expression of social solidarity with children and parents' (Opcit, 1992). In 1994 we had already had to fight a lengthy battle with the local authority when large swathes of our site were under threat of closure. The Pen Green 'Save our Site' group ran a major campaign including marches on county hall where parents, children and staff conducted civil action in partnership, the first of several major campaigns.

> I have to add *that hell-raising is a critical part of co-production and of the labour that it entails it must value.* Those with wealth, power authority and credentials hold those assets as stewards for those who came before and in trust for those yet unborn. They must be held accountable – and sometimes *that requires the creation of new vehicles that give rise to scrutiny, to questioning, to criticism, and to social protest.*
>
> (Cahn, 2008, p. 4)

Parents and staff at Pen Green were often criticised for getting *too* politically involved and for these incursions on the county council chambers. We were however well aware that counsellors were making decisions about the lives and futures of the children in a community they had never visited and it was important for families to make themselves heard (see Box 3.1).

Box 3.1   At Pen Green 'how' is sometimes more significant than 'what'

By encouraging families to participate in the re-shaping of the shared context in which they live out their individual lives

By supporting parents and children to become effective public service users

By building the capacity of children, families and communities to secure outcomes for themselves

By harnessing the community's energy for change and parents' deep commitment to ensuring that their children have a better deal

---

The degree of success of the political action that has been generated within the community is, as Warden states, 'one criterion for successful community education' (Warden, 1979). Corby parents who had been involved in this kind of community action became much more actively involved in their community. There had been very little parental involvement in local schools before 1985 but ex-nursery parents now became involved in all three of the governing bodies of local primary schools (see Box 3.2).

Box 3.2   Community participation driving service delivery

1981–1982
Campaign against the local Borough Council to re-roof local housing stock

---

1982–1983
LAG – Local Advisory Group against the Pen Green Centre
1983–1985
Parents conceptualising services
Parents appointing staff
Parents as volunteers
Parents sharing power
1985–1987
Parents as service providers
Parents engaged in their own learning
1987–1990
Parents as group leaders
Parents as community activists
1990–1997
Parents as co-educators involved in their children's learning
Parents as paid workers
1997–2007
Parents as trouble shooters
Parents as policy makers
Parents as co-researchers and evaluators
Parents as governors
2007–2012
Parents developing innovative projects – Total Place Corby
Parents developing websites, Facebook, Twitter
Parents running local, regional and national campaigns
2013
Parents and children as committed, critical and vigilant public service
    users
2016
Parents develop their own civic charitable bodies (CIO)
2017
Legal Advice Centre for SEND

At this point we were making judgements as leaders about the effectiveness of the integration of services for children and families in a number of different ways. From day one we had kept a comprehensive database on parental engagement and participation across a range of activities and interventions as well as comprehensive data sets on children's learning and development. We discovered, however, that the most powerful way to judge the degree of effectiveness of the integrated offer was from the perspective of the users of the service. Case studies became a very important part of our evaluative methodology. From the perspective of a child using the service it would be a truly integrated service if there was a warm and reciprocal relationship between parents and carers and a deep respect on the part of the staff for the learning that was going on in the home. Children's learning at home would be reflected in the day-to-day planning and practice in the nursery settings.

The ECEC team's responsibility was to build on the important relationships that children already had with their parents and extended family. In practice this would mean that Baby Nest staff would home visit and learn the rocking patterns of the infant or toddler, the lullaby that the parent sings to the child so that it is sung to the same tune in the nursery setting. ECEC staff would recognise the parents' role as their child's first educator and would be curious about the many ways that parents supported and extended their child's learning and provided experiences to excite and stimulate them. Staff would share the learning that was going on in the nursery setting through video vignettes and professional dialogues. From the start we demonstrated our conviction that the home learning environment was equally important to whatever we could provide in the ECEC setting. Through sharing child development concepts we developed a shared language that the parents and staff could use to powerfully describe the children's learning and development.

Parents, carers and grandparents as activists, mediating and brokering on behalf of their children

> What everyone needs in the ['new'] millennium is access to the Internet and a Grandmother.
>
> Blaffer Hrdy, 2009

'Activism' in early childhood education and care services like those at Pen Green can be described as a commitment on the part of ECEC leaders and staff to transform the life chances of children and their families, harnessing the energy for change within their local communities. Staff teams must know what they are offering is more than early education to make children 'school ready' or childcare for working parents. A 'pedagogy of activism' is where reflective teacher educators construct their practice as part of the struggle for social justice and social change. Powerful pedagogical engagement happens when staff in integrated centres are trained in many disciplines; early educators, teacher educators, social workers, adult educators, health workers understand that the primary objective of their role is actually to encourage participation. In this chapter and the chapters that follow the leaders and their strong leaderful staff teams are all activists.

My experience of working across three continents in Brazil (South America), Papa New Guinea (Oceania) and the UK (Europe), has taught me that there is often untapped energy in communities where parent/carer/grand-parent commitment often goes unrecognised. All the parents I have ever worked with have wanted more for the children than they had themselves. Parents and carers are also hugely aspirational; although perhaps not aspirational in the conventional sense of wanting a linear trajectory for the child from school to university, and a successful job with a probable move away from family and community but aspirational in that they hold high hopes that their children will be both happy *and* fulfilled. In the 21st century parents and grandparents want to be heard in the education system and they want to participate. They want their contribution to the education and the care of their children at home to be recognised and they want to work with and be listened to by those providing the education and care of their children in early childhood settings. Participation has to be the key to successful practice in integrated centres. The golden thread in improving outcomes for children is the parents' deep involvement in their own children's learning. We have to reframe our role as teachers and early childhood educators as *co-educators* working alongside parents (Easen et al., 1992; Athey, 1990).

Parent's knowledge of their individual child is absolutely critical and the knowledge that we have as professional educators is also important. However it is the combination of both sets of knowledge which we acquire through a knowledge-sharing approach that can fundamentally change outcomes for children (Arnold, 1997; Whalley & The Pen Green Team, 2001). Some parents may struggle to be advocates for their children because of their own social and economic challenges and their damaging experiences of family life or the education system. Developing your skills as an advocate on behalf of your child is relatively easy if you have experienced success in the education system but not nearly as easy if the education system you have been part of is flawed, and you have struggled through it for year upon year.

Increasingly social anthropologists and evolutionists such as Sarah Blaffer Hrdy (2009), development psychologists like Alison Gopnik (2017) and psychiatrists such as Sebastian Kraemer are recognising the critical role that early childhood educators in integrated ECEC settings have as 'allo-parents'. Allo-parents are those in the community who work with and support parents in the care and education of their children. We have a powerful responsibility in ECEC to work alongside parents and to make sure that they have all the information they need to support their children's learning and development. Pen Green staff embraced the responsibility to support parents and children on *their* terms in their own local community, long before these theories had been articulated, by using common sense and through deep engagement with local people. There is a certain irony as we painfully watch the dismantling of the welfare state and specifically mourn the loss of so many of Labour's Children's Centres that politicians and policy makers only come to realise the significance of powerful and innovative services when they let them slip through their fingers through yet another rationalisation of budgets.

Developments in integrated services between 1996 and 2006

By 1994 Pen Green was in a strong position to engage in national policy development, and with a strong committed and deeply reflexive staff group, confident and capable governors and strong support and challenge structures in place we could look out beyond our own county. Early years education and care in England was never in its convoluted history so centre stage as it was between 1996 and 2006. Throughout the early 1990s the Labour opposition party worked steadily to raise awareness of the importance of this 'new' integrated approach to education and childcare (Labour Early Years Task Force – Statement of Intent, unpublished 1995).

An early years enquiry team was set up by Labour with representatives from the voluntary public and private sector and expert leaders (including staff at Pen Green), from the traditionally divided fields of nursery education and day care/childcare. Coherence, access and accessibility were key issues for this working group but their overriding concern was with the development of quality services out of the 'great under 5s muddle' of the 1960s to the 1990s.

> This approach will replace the fragmentation and inequalities that currently exists between services. Instead of childcare for 'working parents', 'day care for children in need' and 'nursery education for 3 and 4 year olds' would be integrated, coherent and comprehensive early years services.
> (Labour Early Years Task Force – Statement of Intent, unpublished 1995)

There was a deep understanding and recognition by many of the early years policy makers, practitioners and academics who were invited to make representations to the enquiry team that developing such an integrated, coherent and comprehensive early years' service would take time.

> The principles are ambitious, the issues are complex and there is much ground to be made up after years of government neglect.
> (Labour Early Years Task Force – Statement of Intent, unpublished 1995)

This policy strand of multi-agency integrated working was bought to fruition by those same ministers, then in government, through the Early Excellence Centres Programme established in 1997/1998. A series of publications heralded what was described as a 'new [old] approach' to joint working in the early years and despite its unfortunate title the Early Excellence Centre Programme successfully encouraged effective partnership working across health, social care and education. Early Excellence Centres offered early education and childcare on one site, often with extended services before and after school. As the programme rolled out across the country many of the most effective Maintained Nursery Schools became Early Excellence Centres and subsequently engaged with the Neighbourhood Nursery Initiative and Sure Start. For some it meant a significant change in practice and new ways of working, for others it was an opportunity to secure wonderful new buildings without much evidence of any increased integration.

Subsequently around 1998 the Treasury and Home Office, working together with colleagues from the Department of Health and the Department of Education and Employment established a cross departmental review of provision with young children and began to address some critical questions in relation to preventative intervention and the importance of young children's service provision to prevent later social exclusion (July 14th 1998 Gordon Brown Spending Review). The outcome of a series of seminars and discussions and through the involvement of all government departments working together was the Sure Start programme (DfEE, 1999). For the first time government made a real commitment to:

- An emphasis on prevention
- A long term commitment (ten years)
- A method of working which was cross departmental and open to outside influences and evidence
- A method of working locally which built on community strengths and responded to local preferences
- A comprehensive evaluation of the programme from the start

(Glass, 1999)

The Sure Start programme's target areas were to be the 20% poorest districts across the country. It was set up to break the cycle of disadvantage. The government initially invested 200 million pounds on 250 programmes and this was described as a 'small step' for treasury and a giant leap for the early years community. It was certainly experienced as such in communities like Corby where Pen Green became one of the first trail blazer Sure Start programmes. A core offer of services which were provided by every Sure Start local programme included outreach and home visiting, support for parents and families, support for good quality play learning in childcare experiences, community healthcare and support for children and families with special needs. Subsequently the Sure Start programme was broadened out to include approximately 520 districts at a cost of over 500 million pounds.

The next intervention from the Labour government was the Neighbourhood Nurseries Programme which was launched primarily to support women who wanted to return to employment or training and subsequently, in 2003, the government launched the Children's Centre programme. The Children's Centre programme was potentially the most all-embracing programme and came nearest to Margaret McMillan's concept of a fully integrated inclusive service for children and their families providing high-quality flexible childcare 48 weeks of the year, early years education provision, adult learning and family support, parental outreach, child and family health services, support for children and parents with special needs and effective links with job centre plus and local training providers. The Children's Centres were supposed to act as 'service hubs' within their community; offering a base for childminder networks with links to local Neighbourhood Nurseries, out of school clubs and extended schools. Children's Centres also had a significant role to play in training the childcare workforce and the development of a childcare workforce career ladder. At Pen Green our local career ladder had been a work in progress from 1983 since we served a town with extremely low numbers of adults with further or higher education and we had to build local capacity and develop our own multidisciplinary workforce. For our staff group it was liberating to claim our place in the field as providers of very high-quality accredited adult professional development (see Figure 3.1). We worked with the local early years community as equal partners and developed courses that were highly relevant because they were driven by critical and current issues of practice. These courses were well received locally and increasingly take up became regional and national.

What became clear over the first six years of the Labour government was that quality early education and responsive childcare and family support were strands of an overall Labour policy to end child poverty by 2020. The policy focused on social/community regeneration and economic regeneration through getting women back into the workforce. What is less clear however is the degree to which these programmes, and others like them, were going to be effective in supporting the development of the most vulnerable children, promoting family life for all and developing the 'cultural capital' (OECD) that was needed to equalise children's life chances. "Poverty was to receive the greatest focus as the most immediate injustice and equality, social democracies flagship was forgotten or temporarily shelved." (Esping-Andersen, 1990).

Like most early years educators, Pen Green staff and parents applauded the concept of joined-up thinking and integration and were bowled over by the increased level of capital and revenue investment in early years; we had never envisioned this level of political support. However we were very aware that developing integrated services in the most challenged communities was a complex and challenging task. With support from DfE, and in partnership with the Innovation Unit we engaged with leaders of Maintained Nursery Schools and Children's Centres to identify what was happening across England (Whalley & Riddell, 2010).

Honouring the past is a critical principle of sustainability and in Children's Centres like the one we developed in Pen Green, we were very concerned with sustainability and sustainable development. We were 'building to last'. The powerful Corby Children's Centre network that has emerged is still thriving in 2018 despite a decade of drastic cuts to public sector funding. It has survived because it builds on a 100-year tradition of integrated services and locality working in this country. We wanted to ensure the 'new' children's

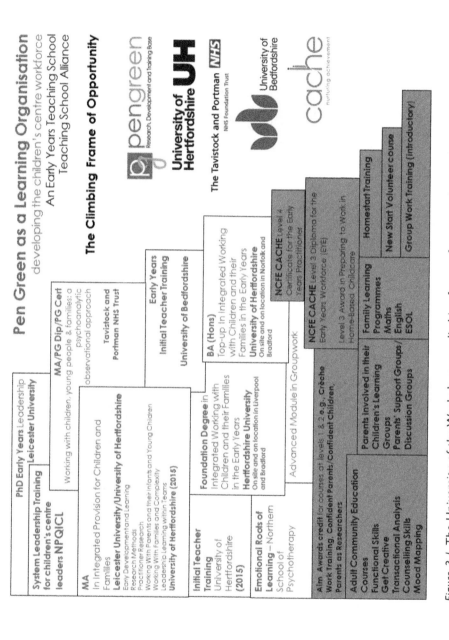

Figure 3.1 The University of the Workplace – a climbing frame of opportunity

centre services learnt the lessons of previous initiatives such as the combined integrated centres in the 1970/1980s (Ferri, 1981) and the Sure Start local programmes and Neighbourhood Nursery initiatives in the 1990s.

In 1983 the approach that we adopted at Pen Green as an integrated centre challenged existing traditionally delivered services. In 2006 Children's Centres still had to challenge traditional ways of working and they were meant to. Integrated services have to support the needs of both children and their parents. By 2006 an extensive range of courses were offered at Pen Green, adult community education with basic skills, family learning, access to GCSEs and A Levels, Foundation Degrees, BA Hons, Masters Degrees, alongside provision for high-quality early childhood education and care. Teachers, nursery nurses/childcare workers, adult educators, community social workers, health practitioners all had to work together to offer an extensive groupwork programme which in centres like our own, involved groups running in the morning, the afternoon, evenings and at weekends. These groups included fathers groups, single parent groups, survivors groups, parent and child groups and teenage parent groups, all of which needed to be regularly reviewed and evaluated. Staff in Children Centres had to be research active and capable of researching their own practice. Pen Green staff were research active from day one because in the 1980s researching, evaluating and demonstrating the efficacy of our work was the only way we could draw down funding locally, nationally and internationally. We constantly had to challenge our own practice and determine the relevance and accessibility of the services. Parents were highly involved in the research programme (Whalley & The Pen Green Team, 2017). Parents undertook interviews, documented their children's learning, kept diaries of their engagement with the centre and were involved in a mass observation project (McKinnon, 2014).

In the 1980s when Pen Green was set up, professionals often talked about 'hard to reach' families instead of services that were hard to access. It's still hard for many parents to access public services and Children's Centres. Indeed it may well become increasingly hard since local authorities have begun to decommission Children's Centres and many have become 'referrals only' generic 0–19 centres. Mairi, one of the parents that used the services at Pen Green, lived on a new aged traveller site. She evaluated our drop in services and undertook a study of the pedagogical influence of parents on the traveller site; she celebrated the way that parents were working with their children in her own community. Mairi had to draw our attention to the issues that made it difficult for other members of her community to use Pen Green services and we had to change our professional practice. Children's Centres are a powerful model of integrated services; they need to challenge traditional constructs of the child and the family. Staff in Children Centres need to be committed to a strength-based approach; valuing *all* parents as their child's best educators not just in their rhetoric but in reality.

Children's Centres need to be renamed as integrated centres for children and families. Their aim is to develop the capacity of children and parents to be competent users of services. Not just as 'clients' passively receiving generous dollops of the welfare state but equal and active partners in designing, developing and reviewing the effectiveness of what's on offer. In Children's Centres, as in all integrated services, we are often working with families who are struggling. It is vital in our research programmes and our practice that we help parents find their voice so that *they* can identify critical concerns. In this way we can build up multiple perspectives on issues of social injustice and inequality. Then we can develop more focused interventions within our open access community-based services. In the 21st century we have to provide services that are really responsive and accessible to all families within the community. At the same time we have to develop appropriate services for families where there are serious concerns around safeguarding issues; we have to make critical decisions all the time about the effective use of scarce resources and the decisions we make must be rooted in an evidence base.

In the Corby Children's Centre network, which is run through Pen Green, children may be referred by a number of different agencies and families will also self-refer. It is however vital that all families can access the services equally. Within Children Centres there should be no stigma attached to using the services. The loneliness and isolation that many parents can experience when they have their first child and often with subsequent children, means that they welcome the opportunity to attend groups like the Growing Together group that we run at Pen Green. In these groups parents meet weekly for support, staff document the children's development with video and dialogue with the parents. Psychotherapists, play workers, family support workers all help to run these groups which build on parents' deep interest in their children during infancy. Staff work hard to support parents appropriately and provide a containing and challenging environment for both adult and child. Children are at the heart of all of this work and it's vital that children's feelings are taken into account whilst offering services that support family life. Increasingly cuts to local authority budgets have meant that groups such as these are under threat and that staffing levels are significantly challenged.

Working in integrated Children's Centres is also about challenging our professional practice. We have to rebalance the power relationships between citizens and professionals and create flexible spaces where we can work in different ways with parents. We have to find a way to make services relevant and responsive for everyone so that all families want to use them. This involves staff in Children's Centres actively going out and working in the children's homes and in other settings within the community. It involves them meeting people where they are most comfortable and encouraging them to use specialist services if and when appropriate.

Pen Green's emerging leadership programme: the opportunities

The rapid expansion and development of integrated service for children and families through the Early Excellence Centre programme (1997), the Sure Start local programme (1999), the Neighbourhood Nurseries (2001) and Children's Centres (2003) created a huge demand for professional development for those early years practitioners appointed to lead the new services. The leaders in the new Children's Centres often had to recruit, employ or commission staff from other disciplines such as health, or social work or other education. In many cases these leaders would have previously been running relatively small establishments. Almost overnight they had to amalgamate disparate services with combative staff groups; for example a social services day nursery with an education-led nursery school. At the same time encouraging voluntary organisations and local health services to work collaboratively on the same campus. Centres expanded in both size and complexity, projects multiplied, budgets increased and in recent years severely decreased. National and local targets were identified but priorities shifted and changed all the time. Parental and community expectations were raised and at times disappointed.

Leaders within these settings and services came from a number of different disciplines; some were teacher trained and had first degrees but not all. Others had specialist training in adult education, social work or health visiting. Very few had been previously offered CPD or qualification courses in leadership and fewer still had effective mentoring, support or supervisory systems in place when they took up their posts.

The importance of leadership training had already been acknowledged throughout the primary phase (DfES; Excellence in Schools, 1997). In 1997 Margaret Hodge, then Minister for the Early Years and colleagues at the DfES recognised the need for leadership training and support for the newly established Early Excellence Centres. The decision was made to invest in a focused training and development programme for the leaders of these new services. Training courses were devised, developed and delivered at the Pen Green Research, Development and Training Base and subsequently a new purpose built Early Years Leadership Centre was constructed on the Pen Green campus so that a wider range of advanced level courses could be run for an increasing number of early years' practitioners from across the country.

Maintained Nursery School heads and early years practitioners in general were highly critical of the course content and the delivery of existing courses for primary heads (Winkley, 1998; Brighouse, 1998). However, they were concerned that the early years leadership training programme should have an equivalent status to training programmes provided for colleagues in senior management positions in schools (for example the National Professional Qualification for Head Teachers, NPQH, Head Lamp and the Leadership Programme for Serving Heads). Existing leadership courses lacked relevance to those leading multi-disciplinary multi-functional centres such as EECs or Sure Start local programmes, Neighbourhood Nurseries or Children's Centres which bridged private, voluntary and statutory services but equivalency was seen as essential if early years leaders were to be able to move between the early years phase and primary education (see Box 3.3).

Box 3.3   Development of a sustainable leadership programme for integrated Children's Centres

Programme of work 1999–2006

- Introductory days on Leadership for EEC's and Sure Start leaders
- Advanced modules in Leadership and Management
- Research bursaries for leaders
- International conferences and seminars
- International visits for NPQICL leaders from ECEC settings
- Development of the NPQICL course and materials; delivery of the pilot and roll-out with accreditation at Masters level
- Development of a full MA in Leadership and Management
- Support for the National roll-out programme of the NPQICL for two years through training, quality assurance and development of new materials
- Development of National Standards for Heads of Children's Centres

---

Integrated services and settings like Pen Green and other Children's Centres challenge our conceptualisation of leadership. The complex demands of running a Children's Centre means that the leader, or leaderful team, that drives the centre forward has to coordinate different models of early education, childcare, family support and adult community learning, into one institution. This requires a distinctive model of leadership professional development which celebrates complexity and actively promotes diversity. In Children's Centres leaders recognise that there is not one solution to any problem. Strong eco systems, in Andy Hargreaves's words, are 'bio diverse' (Hargreaves & Fink, 2006). Integrated services for children and their families and Children's Centres have to respond to their local community so they will all look different and this distinction is important. Hargreaves reminds us that standardisation is the enemy of sustainable development. It would not be appropriate for all Children's Centres to look alike or feel alike. They will all have had different starting points and be responding to different socio-cultural contexts.

It is absolutely the job of Children's Centre leaders to disequilibrate existing systems. If traditional approaches to working with children and families had been highly effective then we wouldn't have needed Children's Centres. Children's Centre leaders have to be community activists. In some cases they have to take on and challenge traditional bureaucratic systems and structures and they need support if they are to do this effectively.

Traditional leadership training requires the acquisition of a set of procedural behaviours which can be applied consistently in a range of situations. Early years' leadership work is significantly more complex than this and leads often to the need to focus on the inner experiences, values and understandings of the professionals involved (see Figure 3.2). ECEC Leadership work is inordinately unpredictable, dependant upon variables which cannot always be identified. The processes involved in helping leaders to develop effective practice require reflection, intellectual grappling and intuitive sharpness rather than learning prescribed strategies and tactics. It was clear to those of us at Pen Green who were developing the leadership professional development approach that leadership and management work in integrated centres and services is highly pressured and intensive. The varied and turbulent nature of community life can play havoc with carefully laid plans and leaders can find themselves engaged in a seemingly endless succession of ad hoc tasks and situations. What early years practitioner leaders needed was a professional development programme which dealt with both the strategic aspects of centre leadership management which also acknowledged the intensely extemporary nature of the work and provided guidance and help in handling these aspects with confidence. In other words any leadership course had to be designed to reflect the daily lives of leaders of Early Excellence Centres, Sure Start Local Programmes, Neighbourhood Nurseries and Children's Centres or their equivalent, and address the realities of their roles (Whalley et al., 2009).

The construction of the National Professional Qualification in Integrated Centre Leadership (NPQICL) was the task delegated to Pen Green and we immediately appointed a team which included senior staff and external consultants. Pen Green wrote the course materials and ran the pilot programme with 45 leaders and then took those participants on to complete an MA in Leadership. Subsequently the roll-out was managed through the National College for School Leadership. This meant that for the first time we had an innovative professional development opportunity for all ECEC leaders. Although the course was never a mandatory requirement for a leadership post in a Children's Centre, hundreds of leaders undertook the training. The objective of the new leadership training and development programme was to offer both professional development *and* ongoing professional support to leaders who had taken on these challenging new roles. At the same time a National Children Centre Network was developed to sustain leaders in their settings, a National Reference Group, made up of serving Heads from across the regions, was established to provide a bottom-up steer to the project.

Building Leadership Capability: sustain – our – ability
sustain – able – development

A developmental model of relationships between the impact of leadership professional development and outcomes for Children and Families

Building Resilient Children and Strengthening Families	Leaders who: •Are capable of building social and cultural capacity. Understand the need to encourage parents and children to be effective service users, have a highly developed understanding of 'progressive universalism' •Are offering additional support for those in lowest socio-economic groups •Offer focused support for the most vulnerable and those who find services hardest to access •Have an absolute commitment to developing parents' involvement in their children's education •Are able to develop a whole systems approach to support children and families within their centres in collaboration with the local community and strongly linked to other services
Organisational Development	Leaders who: •Are capable of building Children's Centres as learning communities •Have a strong focus on standards •Are concerned with sustainable development •Are able to develop skilled and well-qualified aspirational staff •Are systems leaders and can develop leadership capacity across the organisation, in the community and across agencies
Team Development	Leaders who: •Are capable of building a leadership team •Are able to utilize the strengths of staff with different professional heritages •Are able to build capacity through effective CPD linked to outcomes •Are able to build bridges with other agencies and develop a team around the child and family
Intra Personal & Inter Personal Development	Leaders who: •Are critically self aware and reflexive •Have a deep understanding of the 'primary task' of Children's Centres and the ability to communicate it to others •Are outcomes focused •Are connected to the wider early childhood field, deeper understanding of what different professional heritages can offer

Figure 3.2 Building leadership capability

Members of this reference group, initially chaired by the Founder/Director of Pen Green met regularly with the Department for Children and Families and the Minister and became strong champions for the field.

The development of this new leadership development programme was a paradigm shift in professional development for leaders in terms of:

- Conceptualisation and design
- Delivery team
- Recruitment
- Course content
- Learning environment: pedagogical spaces
- Andragogy (teaching and learning)
- Assessment (see Table 3.1)

Integrated centres for children and families also challenged traditional models of governance within public institutions. In a seminar presented at the Tavistock clinic, Tom Bentley (Fieschi and Bentley, 2006) described traditional models of governance as essentially monolithic, often alienating and sometimes persecutory. Children's Centres need to have models of governance that are porous, i.e. accessible, personal, engaging, adaptive and enabling. In Children's Centres parents and children don't use the services in one professionally prescribed way; they may start as a 'referred family' spending up to 37 hours a week in the community drop in. Subsequently parents may become volunteers, use the survivors group, go on to study, visit childcare settings in Europe, become parent managers, co-lead a national conference on parenting, sometimes become a paid worker. In Pen Green Children's Centre, around 54% of staff started off using the services as parents and went on to train in our own 'university of the workplace'. In a similar way children may start to use the centre from infancy; they may use the Baby Nest, take part in the nursery experience, go on to attend after school services and holiday play schemes. Alternatively they may just use a short part-time nursery session depending on the family's needs.

It seems to me there are four critical factors that have to be taken into account if integrated centres for children and families are to really work (see Figure 3.3). The first and perhaps most important factor is that staff in Children's Centres have to have a shared philosophy, a shared vision and shared values and a principled approach to practice. The second factor is the need for a multi-disciplinary multi-functional team with all or most disciplines represented or at the very least a team with strong connections to other agencies and highly effective data sharing. Thirdly, shared leadership and management is critical and a consistent way of working. It is extremely challenging for parents if practice differs significantly within the Children Centre. It is much more likely in an effective Children Centre that one will find a leaderful team of senior staff working alongside newly trained and newly qualified

Table 3.1 New paradigm of leadership professional development

Conceptualisation and design	Delivery team	Recruitment	Content	Learning environment: pedagogical spaces	Andragogy	Assessment
• Co-constructed at every stage • Derived from leaders' stories – critical incidents in practice • A multi-disciplinary approach • A multi-voiced approach • Leadership professional development as opposed to training for the acquisition of skills • Dual focus on leadership capability and academic capability	• Multi-disciplinary- social work, health, early years education, adult education, primary education, community work, research • Lead Practitioner and academics on the teaching team • Diversity of experience (phase and sector) • Balance of tutors and mentors • Access to an extended support team	• Application form and line manager support form • Telephone interviews • Face to face interviews • 'Graduateness' accepted as not all had first degrees • Regional mix • Multi-disciplinary mix • Diverse settings	• Leadership and management theories from across disciplines • Adult learning theories • Experiential and reflective learning theories • Theory generated by practitioners on the course and previous courses • New versions of professional knowledge • New theories drawn from practice	• Withdrawal areas and gardens • Large group area • Small group areas with protected 'pods' • Café and cybercafé • Open library • ICT and research support areas • Large surfaces on which to document learning • Photography and art work integrated into teaching and learning • Shared meals, excellent food, beautifully presented • Warm, friendly, supportive staff	• Constructivist approach to teaching and learning • Establishing the links between leadership and learning (andragogy, pedagogy and leadership) • Focus on task **and** process • Focus on practitioner research • Reflective journaling • Exploring the dynamic between theory and practice • Exploring the dynamic between reflection and action • Encouraging participants to critically appraise and challenge the tutors approach • Co-constructing at every level	• Self-assessment • Peer assessment **on** the course • Peer assessment **in** the workplace • Leadership capability assessment and academic capability assessment

The 'Primary Task' of integrated centres for children and families

Developing the children and family centres as a learning organisation

Involving parents in their children's learning

Encouraging parents to take up community education/adult learning opportunities

Children's Centres as the 'University of the Workplace' & 'Teaching Hospitals'

Ensuring all staff are well-informed rigorous thinkers with good supervision and support

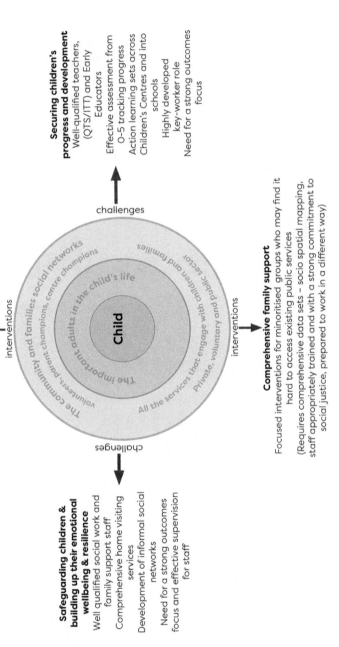

Securing children's progress and development

Well-qualified teachers, (QTS/ITT) and Early Educators

Effective assessment from 0–5 tracking progress

Action learning sets across Children's Centres and into schools

Highly developed key-worker role

Need for a strong outcomes focus

Safeguarding children & building up their emotional wellbeing & resilience

Well qualified social work and family support staff

Comprehensive home visiting services

Development of informal social networks

Need for a strong outcomes focus and effective supervision for staff

Comprehensive family support

Focused interventions for minoritised groups who may find it hard to access existing public services

(Requires comprehensive data sets – socio spatial mapping, staff appropriately trained and with a strong commitment to social justice, prepared to work in a different way)

Figure 3.3 The primary task of integrated centres for children and families

staff rather than one charismatic leader. Lastly, it is vital that services co-exist on one campus or are located within pram-pushing distance. For the parents and the children the services need to be highly visible and accessible. All four factors will need to be in place if a centre for children and families is to be a fully integrated and comprehensive service, responsive to all members of its local community.

Guardianship – working in multi-agency teams

In Children's Centres we are continually developing new versions of professional knowledge and this has been incredibly useful for our leadership professional development programmes. One of the most useful concepts that we developed at Pen Green has been the concept of 'guardianship' (see Figure 3.4). Depending on the historical starting point of the Children's Centre the weaving of professional roles may look very different but most professional disciplines will need to be present in most of the domains. For example a Sure Start programme that is working towards becoming a Children's Centre might well have had a family support team with outreach home visiting and a groupwork programme. They might have had a strong social worker either as centre head or as a member of the senior management team. Family support and home visiting services remain critical domains within any Children's Centre. A Children's Centre that started off as a maintained nursery school might well have had a very strong nursery education and care programme with an early childhood QTS teacher taking a strong leadership role possibly as head of centre or as the lead early years teacher. In any Children's Centre early years' education is a vital domain. In most Children's Centres there would still be some focused work with children from 0 to 3 years of age. In a Children's Centre that started its life as a Neighbourhood Nursery this might well be the strongest domain. The lead member of staff in this centre might have begun his or her career as a nursery nurse or an NVQ qualified childcare worker and may well have gone on to undertake additional professional development experience in a range of settings. This childcare specialist will need to network intensively with other professionals working in the same locality if they are to achieve a seamless response.

In the Pen Green Centre for Children and Families domains and strands of activity weave together to form a tartan which we consider to be pretty appropriate as the majority of our population in Corby in the first 10–15 years hailed from Scotland. Whatever the weave, the approach to working with children and families needs to be consistent and from all the evidence, the best way to work in effective Children's Centres is to adopt a community development approach. This is often described as *co-construction*.

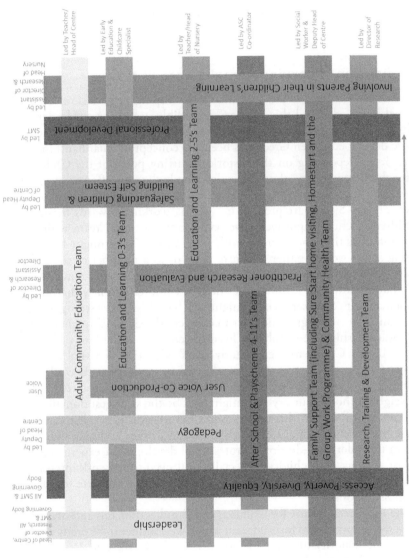

Figure 3.4 Guardianship at Pen Green

Co-production means delivering public services in an equal and reciprocal relationship between professionals, people using services, their families
and their neighbours. Where activities are co-produced in this way, both
services and neighbourhoods become far more effective agents of change.

(Boyle & Harris, 2009)

A fascinating new trend is the new tendency for local authorities to use this
term in their negotiations with the voluntary groups that they are increasingly
commissioning to develop and deliver public services. Paradoxically the co-construction event is often a paper exercise controlled through post-it notes and
large pieces of paper with very little focus on real negotiation or power sharing.

Staff in Children's Centres need to:

- Help individuals to be self-directing
- Encourage individuals to have more control over their own lives
- Be concerned with raising self-esteem and promoting learning as a life-
  long experience
- Work towards equality of opportunity
- Encourage boundary pushing and constructive discontent, i.e. not put-
  ting up with things the way that they are
- Encourage people to feel they have the power to change things

Working in this way everyone feels empowered to start or stop things, to
challenge others and meet challenges, to move out front or to fall back. This
community development approach is best described by Paolo Freire in his
writing on the importance of deep and sustained dialogue (Freire, 1970). In
Freire's words staff in Children's Centres have to have faith in other people's
strengths, they have to be prepared to relinquish as professionals their fear of
being set aside, they have to develop a shared vocabulary rather than assuming the vocabulary of an elite professional group, they have to give up the idea
that they have the exclusive hold on knowledge and truth.

Activism in the context of developing leadership throughout organisations and communities

Traditionally activism is about defining an enemy and taking it on through
protest and civil action. Activism in early childhood education is much more
about engaging with a specific problem through one's day-to-day work and
practice. When we dialogue with others and push ourselves to consistently
improve our own practice we become reflexive and can work at a deeper
level. In this sense it is reasonable to expect early childhood educators to act
with a critical stance and protest when there is injustice, alongside all their
other roles as pedagogical leaders. For example: developing relationships with
children and parents, working with other professionals and engaging in the

wider community. At times ECEC activism will require resistance to current trends and oppressive innovations; such as a preoccupation with teaching rather than a concern for learning. The alternative is compliance; where we accept a narrow curriculum and a didactic education model resulting in more and more children becoming alienated or excluded because of special needs and disabilities or mental health issues.

What we actually need in 2018, in the words of Michael Vandenbroeck et al. (2012), are reflexive professionals who are willing to:

- Value the 'other'
- Engage positively with difference
- Co-construct knowledge with children, parents
- Always act with a focus on change

Many ECEC leaders and educators will still be working in communities of oppression where families are living in conditions that are entirely unacceptable in the 21st century. Part of our engagement with these families is that we help them to realise that things don't have to be the way that they are. If early childhood education services work collaboratively with parents and the wider community and simply accept the ways things are, then there will be very little opportunity to transform children's life chances. Activism in the context of EEC settings consists of:

- Efforts to promote social, political, educational and economic reform
- Significant engagement and participation by public service users
- Consciousness raising
- Resistance leadership
- Capacity building within the community
- Collective action

One way or another I've been involved in all of these kinds of activism over the past 35 years. My form of protest has always been about taking responsibility for a 'specific something' and in that way I've had a strong sense of making a difference (see Box 3.4). As a newly qualified teacher in the UK 45 years ago I was reading Illich, Kohl, Freire and Goffman but I wasn't understanding the big issue that mattered most to me, injustice to children, which is systemic and closely linked to failures in government policy. Then I worked in Brazil, Papa New Guinea and Corby where *social injustice* was stark. My roots are in education, my passion has always been about teaching and my focus has always been the child who doesn't get heard. I've been concerned about children who are rich in possibilities but living in poverty and children with special rights whose entitlement is being denied. I've always been a strong trade union activist and even more so when working in ECEC, where many staff are earning less than the living wage with very little support for their practice.

My encounters with strong trade unionist ECEC educators in New Zealand have been hugely important and I have really appreciated their ironic ECEC anthem 'Don't Be Too Polite Girls' (http://unionsong.com/u263.html) and encouraged colleagues in this country to adopt it.

Box 3.4 Activism – lessons learnt from indigenous communities

- Take what people offer and build on it
- Pride matters; never humiliate, never blame
- Find new reciprocal ways of working
- Look to your elders for help
- Don't accept being minoritised
- Insist on complexity
- If you are seen as 'trouble' take it as a compliment
- Seize the day and leave no one behind

My personal theory is that when you are working in an environment where the social and economic conditions are very challenging and oppressive the integration of public services is essential. In these conditions we have to challenge existing systems and structures that don't work for poor people. Effective integration happens when people think systemically rather than in their professional silos. The integrated centres that have been most successful in the UK, the ones that have survived all the vagaries of political interference have been those centres that have been rooted in their community, responsive to their community and flexible, because communities obviously change over time. I think we have had an extended period with a very oppressive government which has left people working in the public and voluntary sector feeling very 'burnt out'. That's not helpful for effective integration. Although ECEC educators have become more politically aware, better at collaborating across the whole sector and stronger in a fight, it isn't healthy to be in a constant position of high alert when core funding is being challenged year on year.

When asked recently how Early Intervention could be improved, Dr Sebastian Kraemer reflected that most existing services still work separately and fail to communicate with each other. A salutary conclusion after all the years of prolific investment in ECEC. However he also commented:

> Children's Centres are the greatest social intervention since the foundation of the NHS. New Labour got a lot of things wrong, but they got that right. It is shameful that the coalition government is now making huge

cuts to those centres while declaring this it wants to protect them. We need better trained (and therefore better paid) staff in Children's Centres and nurseries.

(Kraemer, 2011)

Multi-disciplinary, multi-functional integrated services are inevitably complex. We are responding to a complex, changing and often chaotic world. The leaders of these settings have to learn to see being described as trouble as a compliment; they have to be thrifty in their use of public funds but should never be apologetic about the real cost of quality services which require well-trained staff. They have to seize the day and leave no one behind. Linda Lambert, writing about the education system makes this strong statement:

Everyone is born to lead in the same way that everyone is born to learn.

(Lambert, 2003)

Leaders of integrated centres for children and family can be seen as people in whom the dream of making a difference is being kept alive. Sustaining and supporting the achievements of centres for children and their families has been a privilege for all the staff and consultants employed by Pen Green over the last 35 years. The National Professional Qualification for Integrated Centre Leaders was a national response to the need to both support and challenge leaders of Children's Centres in their very demanding jobs. Over the next decade we will have to develop new ways of working. We need to celebrate the systemic approach that is described in the following chapters. Pen Green has already begun to engage with local authorities on system leadership professional development. We need confident, competent and reflective practitioners who are capable of developing leadership within their own Children's Centres *and* capable of working across localities. To support these leaders we need to create a national and international learning community; we are always stronger if we work together.

Imagine an early years centre in which all staff are beginning to be assertive; self critical and supportively critical of others, where the staff are deeply attached to each other, work cooperatively, respect each other's strengths, and celebrate each others' successes and failures. A centre in which the adults, parents and staff are rigorous thinkers, focussed and analytical, and yet aware of the rhythms of the organisation and their personal lives; where the work is rooted in the local community but also staff reach out, make their own views known and challenge local and central government over important issues. This would be a centre in which children's rich emotional lives were acknowledged and supported, where they were encouraged and cognitively challenged and their learning was promoted. In such a centre children could truly be the managers of their own possibilities.

(Whalley, Doctoral thesis 1999)

References

Arnold, C. (1997) Sharing ideas with parents about how children learn, in M. Whalley (ed.) *Working with Parents*, Hodder & Stoughton, London.

Athey, C. (1990) *Extending Thought in Young Children: A Parent – Teacher Partnership*, Paul Chapman, London.

Benn, T. (2003) *The Education of Children*. Greenburg, New York.

Blaffer Hrdy, S. (2009) *Mothers and Others; The Evolutionary Origins of Mutual Understanding*, The Belknap Press, Harvard University Press, Cambridge, MA, London, England.

Boyle, D. & Harris, M. (2009) *The Challenge of Co-Production*. Discussion Paper for NESTA, The Lab and the New Economics Foundation.

Brighouse, T. (1998) No time for bed, says Zebedee, TES September 225 1998:32

Cahn, E. (2008) *Co-Production: Manifesto for Growing the Core Economy*, New Economics Foundation, London.

DfEE (1999) *Sure Start Making a Difference for Children and Families*, DfEE Publication, Sudbury.

DFES, (1997) *Excellence in Schools: White Paper*, DfES Publications, London.

Easen, P., Kendall, P. & Shaw, J. (1992) Parents and educators: Dialogue and developing through partnership, *Children and Society*, 6 (4): 282–296.

Eisenstadt, N. (2011) *Providing a Sure Start: How Government Discovered Early Childhood*, Bristol University Press, Bristol.

Esping-Andersen, G. (1990) *The Three Worlds of Welfare Capitalism*, Polity Press, Cambridge.

Fieschi, C. & Bentley, T. (2006) *Governed States of Mind – Identity, Emotion & Everyday Democracy*. Seminar Presentation at Tavistock Clinic, London, 25th March 2006.

Ferri, E. (1981) *Combined Nursery Centres: A New Approach to Education and Daycare*, Macmillan, London.

Freire, P. (1970) *Pedagogy of the Oppressed*. Penguin Books, Harmondsworth. gowrieqld.com.au

Glass, N. (1999) Sure start: The development of an early intervention programme for young children in the United Kingdom, *Children and Society*, 13: 257–264.

Gopnik, A. (2017) *The Gardener and the Carpenter: What the New Science of Child Development Tells Us About the Relationship Between Parents and Children*, Vintage, New York.

Haddock, L. (1981) *Rydevale Community Nursery: A Case Study*. National Childcare Campaign Research Papers.

Hargreaves, A. & Fink, D. (2006) *Sustainable Leadership*, Jossey-Bass, San Francisco, CA.

Isaacs, S. (1930/1966) *Intellectual Growth in Young Children*, Routledge, London.

Kraemer, S. (2011) www.nurseryworld.co.uk/nursery-world/news/1105449/interview-dr-sebastian-kraemer

Lambert, L. (2003) Leadership redefined: An evocative context for teacher leadership, *School Leadership and Management*, 23 (4): 421–430.

McKinnon, E. (2014) *Using Evidence for Advocacy and Resistance in Early Years Services*, Routledge, London.

Moss, P. (1992) *Contemporary Issues in Daycare for Young Children*, pp. 43–44, HMSO, London.

OECD, *Pisa Survey* (www.oecd.org).

Pugh, G. (1998) *Services to Children Under 5: Developing a Coordinated Approach*. NCB, London.

Vandenbroeck, M., Roets, G. & Roose, R. (2012) Why the evidence-based paradigm in early childhood education and care is anything but evident, *European Early Childhood Education Research Journal*, 20 (4): 537–552.

Warden, J. (1979) *Process Perspectives: Community Education as Process*. Charlottesville Mid Atlantic Community Education Consortium.

Whalley, M. (1994) *Learning to be Strong: Setting Up a Neighbourhood Service for Under-Fives and Their Families*. Hodder & Stoughton, London.

Whalley, M. (1999) *Leadership in Early Years Settings*, Unpublished PhD thesis, University of Wolverhampton.

Whalley, M. et al. (2009) Developing and sustaining leadership learning communities: Implications of NPQICL rollout for public policy local praxis, *European Early Childhood Education Research Journal*, 16 (1): 5–38.

Whalley, M. and Riddell, B. (2010) *Critical Issues in 21st Century Children's Centres: Emergent Issues from a Series of Think Tanks*. Pen Green Publications, Corby, UK.

Whalley, M. & The Pen Green Team (2001) *Involving Parents in Their Children's Learning*. Paul Chapman Publishing, London.

Whalley, M. & The Pen Green Team (2017) Developing Evidence-based practice, in *Involving Parents in Their Children's Learning; A Knowledge-Sharing Approach*, pp. 16–40, Sage, London.

Winkley, D., with Pascal, C. (1998) Developing a radical agenda. In Pascal, C. & Ribbins, P. (eds) *Understanding Primary Headteachers*. Caswell, London.

Chapter 4

Who is taking responsibility? Becoming an authoritative leader

Elizabeth Klavins

Introduction

> The capacity to discover and participate in our unfolding future has more to do with our being – our total orientation of character and consciousness – than with what we do. Leadership is about creating, day by day, a domain in which we and those around us continually deepen our understanding of reality and are able to participate in shaping the future. This, then, is the deeper territory of leadership – collectively 'listening' to what is wanting to emerge in the world, and then having the courage to do what is required.
>
> Jaworski, 1996, p. 182

This chapter tells the story of my leadership journey over a twenty-five year period as Head Teacher of a maintained nursery school that developed into an integrated multi-functional children's centre. It offers an account of how and why I developed a passionate belief in systemic, democratic leadership and the challenges I encountered trying to implement theory into practice. I explain why I believe it is essential for leaders to become authoritative by taking responsibility for their designated role through purposefully inquiring into their leadership behaviours and actions. Such a process burrows down to the *deeper territory of leadership* (Jaworski, 1996, p. 182). This chapter also shows how knowledge gained through inquiry can be used to inform and, insofar as possible, shape the unfolding future. The messiness of democratic leadership caused by the interrelatedness and interconnectedness of all aspects that comprise an organisation is illustrated through the story of my engagement in action research as a leader-researcher undertaking a doctoral study. Experiencing leadership as a process of inquiry powerfully revealed the depth of understanding required for implementing systemic leadership theory in practice.

Awakening and conceptualising conscious leadership

Starting my career as an early years teacher in primary and nursery schools I experienced a sense of swimming against the tide. Trying to change simple things such as the time of school assemblies so that parents had time to communicate children's needs and children could be actively engaged at the start of the day rather than sedentarily listening became a major challenge. My personal beliefs and values regarding young children's education and development often felt thwarted, leaving me silenced and alone with my frustration. In 1991 I successfully applied for the Head Teacher position at Fairfield Nursery School situated in Accrington, a mill town in east Lancashire. Naively I believed that as a head teacher I would quickly develop a school where everything I held dear regarding children and families would be agreed and established. I soon discovered the challenges of developing a shared community vision and questioning beliefs about what constitutes effective practice. The phrase I came to detest was *well we have always done it like this*.

Government initiatives such as Neighbourhood Nurseries and Children's Centres saw many small nursery schools expand and change at a rapid pace between 2003 and 2006. My role as a nursery school head teacher initially involved working with a very small staff team of four, providing eighty part-time nursery places. I had a full-time teaching commitment and felt I knew staff, children and families well. The school, situated in a severely socio-economically deprived area of Accrington, served families who often struggled to meet their children's basic needs. I recognised that teaching could only provide effective learning outcomes if needs for security, shelter, warmth and food were met first. This led to opening an onsite a Neighbourhood Nursery in 2003, but local authority policy required us to set up a separate charitable early years provider. The pay and conditions for staff employed by the charity were less favourable than for the school staff due to the requirement to be totally self-sustaining, while providing services for the most deprived families. The development of Neighbourhood Nursery day-care provision for babies and children up to 5 years of age moved the building use from term time only, thirty-eight weeks per year, to being open for fifty-one weeks. The length of the day was also considerably extended from five hours to ten hours. The school became a designated children's centre in 2005, and this development entailed further strategic changes including: the development of the governing body; new staff appointments, notably the appointment of a Deputy Head of Centre, but also recruitment and development of an outreach family worker team; and a review of the pedagogical approach, in order to accommodate flexibility in patterns of provision and the development of the *Early Years Foundation Stage Framework* (EYFS), which became statutory from September 2008 (DFES, 2006). In 2008 the staff team had grown from four to forty-four and my role of Head Teacher had changed considerably.

Determined to improve outcomes for families, I worked passionately and tenaciously as Head Teacher of Fairfield Nursery School and integrated, multi-functional Children's Centre. After thirteen years, I reached a point when I felt I was working as hard as I possibly could. My work-life balance had completely disappeared, and yet I felt an absence of flourishing creativity in the workplace. Practice appeared repetitive rather than innovative. I found it impossible to take time for purposeful reflection on my leadership behaviour, and at that stage I probably would have regarded such a suggestion as self-indulgent when there was so much work to be done. Fortunately, an opportunity arose that transformed my professional life as a designated leader. Looking back on my life as a Head Teacher I visualise it as two distinct phases. Phase one involved working extremely hard whilst rolling deeper and deeper towards the centre of an ever-tightening coil. Phase two constituted a new beginning that involved awakening a new consciousness and unfurling the coil, as I began to inquire about the impact of my leadership behaviour and actions.

The new beginning started in 2004 when I accepted an invitation of academic study, i.e. participation in the Pilot of the National Professional Qualification in Integrated Centre Leadership (NPQICL). Initially I struggled with the andragogical principles of the study programme. The NPQICL programme's andragogical approach to learning was through sharing and reflecting upon the learners' stories. Sharing leadership experiences with other participants initially felt like I was wasting my time when there were so many work tasks back at the Centre that I could be doing. However, sharing stories with study colleagues provided a multi-faceted lens, offering different views and possible interpretations. Exploring theories relevant to my leadership experiences began to excite me as it helped me understand why trying to continually improve practice could be so challenging. This led to continuing engagement in academic study for my master's and doctorate, as part of a Doctoral Study Group at *Pen Green Research Base* in Corby, Northamptonshire. This encouraged me to research consciously my role as designated leader of such a rapidly changing organisation. It also led to the eventual realisation that working hard is not the same as taking responsibility. I came to recognise that working hard can easily result in over-functioning as a leader, which encourages dependency on the designated leader, who becomes the *implementer* (Lambert, 1998).

As a (NPQICL) pilot programme participant I was given the opportunity of what proved for me to be a transformational study visit to New Zealand. The visit provided an opportunity to stand back and take stock whilst also stimulating ideas and discussions with fellow participants. The Maori people of New Zealand have taken their Koru (spiral) symbolism from the unfurled new leaf of the native silver fern. The symbol depicts new beginnings. The spiralling pattern towards the inner coil of the fern refers to 'going back to the beginning'. It is a symbol of hope, perfection, rebirth, a new start, awakening, personal growth and purity. The Koru symbol depicts the start of my journey as a leader-researcher. Working to understand and learn from my leadership journey involved following an inward spiral of curiosity in order to uncoil it through processes of inquiry. The study visit awakened my recognition of a need to engage in a process of personal growth so that I could support the development of others. It gave me a desire to light fires of curiosity in others and develop a community of learners. I experienced a sense of new beginnings.

As the study visit progressed I visited several kindergartens and began to experience emotions that I now recognise were caused by disequilibrium as a result of my previous leadership trajectory. New Zealand kindergarten practice appeared to be so strong in placing the child at its centre. Talking to the teachers revealed strong, in-depth knowledge of theoretical concepts and how these related to their practice. I experienced a sense of awe and began to ask questions about the professional development opportunities for early years teachers. In answer, teachers talked about New Zealand's Ministry of Education's Educational Leadership Project. This was an independent Early Childhood Professional Development Project, and it fascinated me, opening up a whole new world of ideas. The centres involved decided upon a project including a bicultural focus connected to the use of Margaret Carr's (2001) 'Assessment for Learning: Early Childhood Exemplars'. The purpose being to develop aspects of: assessment, pedagogy and planning processes. Centres were selected for three-year research projects and were then known as Centres of Innovation. The Ministry's belief was that research should sit alongside policy. I observed the impact of involvement in research projects on Kindergarten teachers, described by one Papatoetoe Kindergarten participant in the following way:

> It takes teachers out of their comfort zones and challenges thinking. Continually shows and offers new possibilities. It makes one think outside the square. Shifts thinking and practice.
>
> (Personal Journal, March 2005)

One Centre of Innovation, Roskill South, was contracted to:

- Develop and document innovative learning and teaching through using Te Whariki
- Share information about innovative learning and teaching practices
- Work with researchers to find out what children and parents gain from research findings

The Centre used Learning Stories, an approach to assessment developed by Professor Carr (2001) at Waikato University following The Ministry for Education commissioned research 'Assessment for Learning: Early Childhood Exemplars'.

Learning Stories are based on the belief that developing good learning habits or dispositions is most important in Kindergarten, and that planning for learning is about knowing children extremely well. Individual children's stories were being told in the form of digitally illustrated narratives that were shared with parents and children. Children were involved in the illustrations and the writing of their stories at all stages. Every child I came across in this centre was keen to share his or her precious portfolio, and every child's stories were unique to the child. I found this practice to be effectively embedded in all the New Zealand Centres of Innovation. In visiting centres not involved in research projects, I noted that the use of Learning Stories, whilst implemented as good practice was not utilised as effectively. In fact the basic principles appeared to have been lost. Looking at many individual children's portfolios I found that the same Learning Stories appeared in every child's.

As a direct consequence of my learning in New Zealand I formed a proposition that those involved in leading the learning should be active participants in the process of its development.

Vision – a noble social intent

Learning from my observations I resolved to develop an organisation in which all practitioners would become leaders of practice. Marshall and Reason (1998) and Schön (1983) helped me to substantiate my underlying pedagogical observation that those involved in working directly with young children and families needed to engage with each other in exploring the relative effectiveness of their work. I envisaged that this could be achieved through engaging all practitioners in practice-based research as part of their everyday practice. My intent was to develop curious practitioners interested in deepening their understanding of their jobs in order to transform their practice. The term 'practice-based research' is used in this chapter to describe the engagement of early years practitioners in purposeful inquiry into an aspect of their work. I wanted practitioners to become empowered to lead practice developments through creating their own theories. My social intent was to move the hierarchical leadership model to a more organic, systemic leadership model, enabling everyone to be a leader of practice. I thought this would be a more sustainable and effective approach, consciously moving away from a *dependency-implementer* model (Lambert, 1998). This was the underlying proposition for my doctoral research *Repositioning Leadership in Early Years Contexts* (Klavins, 2015). The research was a qualitative, case-study project, which examined my leadership approach over a six-and-a-half-year period.

Untangling the messiness of democratic leadership

Through an iterative process of action research I discovered that amongst an all-female early years workforce, many held self-perceptions of being non-academic because they had struggled to gain qualifications or to feel recognised within institutionalised formal education. Practice and theory were regarded as two separate entities with very little engagement in relevant texts. As I began my own further studies I also realised that access to relevant literature was very limited in the geographical area where the centre was situated. I tried to instigate a centre book club with a view to eventually engaging practitioners in discussions about early years educational theory. The first and only book chosen by a staff member was Mark Haddon's *The Curious Incident of the Dog in the Night-Time*, and I felt pleased that whilst it was a fictional story it at least had some relevance to our work as it presented an autistic boy's story. The book club did not develop as I had anticipated, developing instead into a social group with a trip to pubs and a greyhound-racing track.

Self-perceptions held about learning capacities proved to be a psychological and emotional hurdle in striving to engage everyone in the process of developing practice-based research. In the first stage (Stage One) of my research I had selected and invited a small group of practitioners to form a Centre Inquiry Group that I would study as they engaged in practice-based research. They were all undertaking or planning to undertake a course of further study. The selection criteria for the 'Centre Inquiry Group' membership were based on the theoretical hypothesis that those engaged in further study courses were most likely to engage positively in a process of self-reflective and co-operative learning. Unfortunately my purposefully selecting a group who would engage in practice-based research made others feel de-valued, giving them a feeling of not being good enough. The Centre Inquiry Group chose to focus their practice-based research on the needs of children, parents and staff when children were starting nursery and separating from their parents. They worked to engage parents and all family workers in the research, requesting that they maintain journals documenting their experiences as children started nursery provision.

At this stage of my journey as a leader-researcher I had not realised the significance or likely impact of my study's social intent. I wanted something which seemed honourable, to flatten the hierarchical leadership model and empower others to take a lead on practice. I was to learn through inquiring about the impact of my leadership actions and behaviours that what I wanted for others was not necessarily what they wanted for themselves. Some practitioners were not yet ready to engage in practice-based research, nor to take on responsibility to engage in further learning. I now realise that some may never be ready. Practitioners began to get frustrated and cross with each other. Those who had engaged in the Centre Inquiry Group research experienced an urgent need to improve how we supported the transition process when children were starting nursery. They felt frustrated that other staff did not seem to recognise the need to change practice. Those who were being pushed to change practice by fellow team members became antagonistic towards them. The underlying feelings held by many were that they did not count anymore and had no voice. This became apparent from later Focus Group Discussions in Stage Two of my research, which was developed following discussions with Doctoral Study Group colleagues.

Through externally facilitated Focus Group Discussions practitioners were able to safely articulate their feelings describing themselves as non-academic and experiencing a sense that their work was not 'good enough'. This led to my recognition of the crucial need to recognise and understand the complexities of individual learners' identities, formed by a multitude of historical influences, and how these were expressed within organisational groups. Reports from the externally facilitated Discussion Groups were mostly very negative about the Centre's leadership approach, and it was very tempting to discard them as untrue. Practitioners' perceptions of how they were regarded by myself and other designated leaders appeared to be so at odds with my intended outcome.

It became evident that driving *my* vision forward unsettled many staff members and surfaced feelings of an absence of social justice and equality within the organisation. I learned that imposing an expectation of engagement in practice-based research upon practitioners in order to emancipate them from hierarchical practice directives was an attempt to impose a culture rather than co-operatively develop a culture. The vision of a workforce empowered by its engagement in practice-based research became problematic in its realisation. Practitioners had received unintended messages regarding what and whom I valued. They perceived me to value only those engaged in further academic study, and they viewed such study as something divorced from their working practice. Cultural values had been tacitly recast, and several members of the organisation felt excluded, with a loss of voice, connectivity and capability. Tensions between practitioners had begun to erupt, and for the first time after many years as a Head Teacher I experienced a sense of a disintegrating organisation. I viewed myself as a failure and considered resignation.

Working with the Pen Green Doctoral Study Group and an external provider of professional supervision I was encouraged and supported to actively seek feedback on the impact of my leadership actions and behaviour. Rather than reject the feedback from Focus Group Discussions I was supported to analyse, make links to relevant theories and gain an understanding of what lay behind the angst vocalised by practitioners. It became clear that the real research question was 'how a designated leader could '*create the conditions within which others will motivate themselves*' Deci and Ryan, (1985, p. 10). Creating an agreed learning culture could enable practitioners to flourish and become empowered but I could not empower them. Within such a culture it would be up to individuals to take responsibility for their own learning.

Engaging with relevant theory to develop further understanding

It was following Stage Two (Focus Group Discussions) of my leader-researcher journey that I returned to some earlier reading and began to fully connect with the significance of Torbert's (1972, 2004) theory. Torbert (2004) discussed the power that action inquiry holds in enabling anyone within an organisation to experience transformational learning, but stressed that first the person needs to be open to learning from the feedback received from others. He described this as making yourself vulnerable explaining that all too often, people behave paradoxically, defending themselves against the feedback, if they don't like it, rather than giving it proper consideration as being another person's perspective. Unless feedback can be considered and used as part of an experiential learning process, it will be at odds with a systemic leadership approach. I discovered that taking a position of leader-researcher engaging in the process of action research into leadership resulted in my feeling extremely vulnerable, with a desire to reject the feedback I had sought. I also realised that practitioners would vary in their readiness to be open to feedback from others if they participated in co-operative practice-based research.

Mezirow and Associates (2000, p. 19) described transformational learning as something that happens through the passage of time and through giving consideration to and 'reconstructing the dominant narratives'. My research required seeking out and considering from different perspectives others' narratives. It involved trying on practitioners' points of view in order to examine and interpret or transform how I perceived my own experience. Whilst I did not like the feedback from Focus Group Discussions I needed to accept the feelings expressed as the participants' emotional truths and attempt to look through their eyes.

Exploring relevant theories from Individual Psychology (Adler, 1927/1992), psychological needs and motivation (Deci & Ryan, 1985; Dweck, 1999) and group dynamics (John, 2000) helped provide possible explanations for the degenerative behaviours that I was witnessing. Recasting what appeared to be valued within the Centre had led to some practitioners feeling insecure, afraid of being unable to rise to the new challenge, feeling threatened by those who were engaged in further studies and feeling left out. Studying social philosophies of social democracy, equality and organisational values (Dreikurs, 1971; Giddens, 1988) helped me to recognise what was needed to move forward rather than abandon ship. I realised that seeing things from different angles or perspectives in order to gain new, creative ideas is crucial to the process of systemic leadership, which demands courageous leadership inquiry. This means peeling back the protective layers that we often unconsciously construct around ourselves. Engaging with relevant literature highlighted the importance of knowing how we know what we know, recognising that we know more than we can tell, that we hold memories as stories and that experiences shape our lives – and that all are crucial to understanding participants' behaviours within co-operative action research contexts.

Connecting with the theories and observations of Alfred Adler (1927/1992) about how improving awareness of oneself can lead to life-changing behaviours, it became apparent that I had to view my own leadership as a continuous process of learning from action-based research. Heron's (1996) co-operative action research philosophy suggested that, as a leader-researcher I was required to be a participatory subject of the research because my conscious and tacit behaviours impacted on the whole. I became strongly aligned to Judi Marshall's (2001) description of *Systemic Leadership* that involves purposefully seeking feedback about the impact of one's own behaviour accepting, analysing and making sense of it in order to inform future actions. I argue that failure to engage in such a process prevents the acknowledgement and exercise of *good authority* (John, 2012). Ultimately, failure to engage in such a process would have prevented me from taking responsibility and gaining a sense of authoritative leadership. As a result of taking responsibility for my leadership work, the constantly developing organisation became more creative and began to flourish by the time I retired in 2016. I desperately wish that I had been ready to engage in leadership as a process of inquiry when taking up my head teacher's post in 1991. Whilst the years leading up to 2004, when my leadership awakening began, had not involved purposeful inquiry I have still been able to draw on, reflect upon, analyse and learn from incidents that occurred during that time.

The impact

As a result of taking responsibility for my leadership, seeking and acting upon feedback from all practitioners, I worked to engage them on a voluntary, experimental level in practice-based research. They led this at a level for which they felt equipped. This formed Stage Three of my research, as I became an observational researcher. Practitioners worked in self-chosen groups, some at a very elementary research level focussing on an aspect of their work about which they were curious to know more.

One example of how this impacted on outcomes for children was how their art work moved from daily paintings completed over a short time period, taken home at the end of the day, to paintings revisited each day until the child felt it was complete. Practitioners became learners alongside the children and the results were stunning. Below is an example of how one little girl's talent was developed through a process of inquiry shared by the practitioner and the 4-year-old child (see Figure 4.1). The practitioner worked with the child whenever she wanted to return to her painting over the period of a week demonstrating great sensitivity in how she supported the child, for example to find answers on how to mix a lighter colour, where to start and what to do when her hand was shaking.

Learning from the experience of engaging in a continuous process of inquiry into my leadership behaviour expanded my knowledge and promoted a sense of responsible authority as a leader. This strengthened my resilience as a designated leader. It gave me an improved sense of self-efficacy – good authority – that led to a feeling of being at ease with the responsibility held. I felt able

Figure 4.1 Painting created by 4-year-old over five days, supported by staff member

to 'take responsibility'. Ultimately this helped to sustain my own and others' emotional well-being, leading an organisation within which all staff members were engaged in researching and improving their practice – and my remaining in headship until my retirement from full-time work in 2016.

The Centre now has an impressive professional library that is well used by practitioners. This was commented upon when discussing leadership in the Section 8 School Ofsted Inspection that took place in the term after my retirement. *'You even provide a research library to help with [practitioners'] studies'* (Ofsted 29th November, 2016). Ofsted also commented on how deeply reflective members of the organisation were. When retiring from my Head Teacher post, I was able to recognise and accept my own achievements. Staff were engaging and connecting with theory as part of their practice. This looked very different from eight years previously when my attempt to start a book club failed. Retirement celebrations were held in the wonderful, newly opened *Forest School* (Figure 4.2). Practitioners across the setting had researched, planned and developed the *Forest School* collaboratively over a three-year period without my involvement. This gave me confidence in the organisation's future sustainability.

Working currently as a part-time local authority school adviser involves working with head teachers who face organisational challenges as they strive to ensure the best possible outcomes for children and families. Many voice worries and concerns about being able to continue working in such challenging settings. Feelings of being overwhelmed and frustrated by practitioners who appear to lack creativity in their work are frequently expressed. I find myself gently encouraging head teachers to actively engage in a process of inquiry into their own leadership behaviour and actions. I suspect that this is sometimes met with a cynical thought of 'and where will I find time to do that?' and sometimes this has been voiced as 'but I am so busy'.

Having described why and how I was stimulated and encouraged to regard leadership as a continuous inquiry process, showcasing some of the outcomes for children and practitioners, I feel it is important to outline the methods used. What follows is not a manual of how to engage in the process of action research. It is offered simply as an example of how I engaged in such a process, a case study undertaken in a setting that is unique as every other setting.

Figure 4.2 Photo of Forest School walkway designed and created by staff members

A brief overview of research methods: how I actively discovered what was emerging in the organisation

The methodology was constantly revisited and explored, rather than determined at the outset. This reflected a response to findings from the first stages of the research, which indicated that a purposefully selected sample group had caused feelings of social inequality across the wider organisation. The methodology sat firmly within the paradigm of qualitative research described by Heron (1971) as a method of inquiry seeking to take account of human behaviour and to understand the reasons behind it. It explored the leadership of cultural change within the single and unique early years setting where I held the designated leadership title of Head Teacher.

I selected the medium of a reflective personal learning journal as an ongoing method for engaging in *first person action inquiry* (Torbert, 2004). This was supported by regular access to high-quality professional supervision. I undertook my inquiry as part of a practitioner-led action research Doctoral Study Group, which served as an on-going method of engaging in *second person action inquiry* (Torbert, 2004). This could also be described as an opportunity to seek out different perspectives in order to further my understanding.

Stage One

In the first planned fieldwork of the study I established a 'Centre Inquiry Group'. The Group consisted of six highly credible practitioners, or emergent leaders, from across the School and Centre teams.

The group was to provide a systematic way of exploring practitioners' emotions, feelings, cognitive challenges and skills, evoked by the introduction of practice-based research. I saw them in Reason's (1988) terms as *experiential researchers*, a group set up for the purpose of inquiry, who would be *action inquirers*, reflecting on their experiences in social action and *participatory*, sharing dialogue as a group. I intended that the group would provide an insight, as '*cultural experts in their setting*' (Stringer, 1999, p. 8), into the understanding of how and why things happened within the organisation as the concept of practice-based action research was introduced. The group was encouraged and supported to engage in practice-based research over a two-year period. I expected this method to generate data that would help me better understand the social and emotional phenomena of the organisation. The proposal was to research the journey travelled by this purposefully selected sample group of staff, the 'Centre Inquiry Group', as I worked to engage them in practice-based action research.

Following discussions at the initial meeting about the concepts of co-operative inquiry, journaling and reflection, I asked participants to keep a journal that would remain confidential to them. I suggested that the journals might help as an aide-memoire when discussing their thoughts and feelings about engaging in co-operative practice-based research.

Semi-structured audio-recorded interviews were conducted with the Sample Group following their work after a one-year period. Thematic analysis (Braun & Clarke, 2006) of semi-structured interviews with the Sample Group was undertaken. This involved looking for patterns or meanings within the responses.

Reviewing the overall approach and methods of analysis as part of the action research cycle in Stage One, I realised that I had employed a constructivist, theoretical approach. Using a purposefully selected research group, questions asked in the semi-structured interviews were based on my preconceptions. This resulted in limited, relatively shallow data. The use of a written note form of transcription from each of the semi-structured interviews was in itself an interpretative act (Braun & Clarke, 2006). Coding for the thematic analysis was based on the theories and questions held. Despite the limitations, positive developments in work with children and families resulted from the efforts of the Centre Inquiry Group. The Group decided to focus their practice-based research on children's separation from parents when starting nursery provision and how this could be better supported to minimise emotional trauma for children and parents.

Stage Two

Following a review of the original research method, in the true nature of cyclical action research, the methodology evolved. The second stage employed a 'random sampling' approach (Tracy, 2013). Every member of the organisation had an equal opportunity to participate. The proposal involved commissioning and processing two Focus Group discussion days, facilitated by a carefully selected External Facilitator, to which all staff members were invited. The Focus Group discussions were held one year apart. The aim of the second day was to explore some of the issues highlighted on the first day.

The focus group discussions were much more open-ended in their remit and staff were invited to form their own agenda. The purpose was to explore the tacit knowledge, experiences and feelings of working in the organisation. Staff were invited to participate on the basis that the final report would not disclose the identity or attribute comments to any named individual. Participants were informed that the final report would only be submitted to me after they had agreed on the final version.

The method of thematic analysis employed to analyse the Focus Group Discussion Reports was that which Braun and Clarke (2006) termed an 'inductive approach'. The open nature of the discussion groups meant that when analysing data from the discussion groups, themes emerging were not determined by my theoretical constructs as a researcher. I studied the reports several times and shared them for discussion with my Doctoral Study Group colleagues. I highlighted responses that I felt were pertinent to the research purpose and began to list recurrent or similar opinions as emerging themes. Published theories and research findings relevant to emerging themes were then studied in an attempt to understand potential explanations for underlying feelings expressed by the participants. The reports were then reviewed and scrutinised for further evidence, confirmation or contradictions. The depth and richness of the data from these analyses provided the main research findings. Resultant theories were then taken to participants for discussion during staff meetings.

Stage Three

After carefully considered discussions at a series of Centre practitioner staff meetings, professional supervision conversations and exploration with the Doctoral Study Group I realised that further attempts to engage staff in practice-based research needed to be non-threatening. A decision by the Senior Leadership Team was made to offer all Centre staff the opportunity to engage in co-operative practice-based research over a one-year period. For practitioners choosing to participate, two staff training days were allocated as staff-leave entitlement with the agreement that the equivalent twelve hours would be given to research activities. The time and place for the research work was to be decided co-operatively by those involved.

The research method consequently selected was 'Observation', described by Lofland and Lofland (1984) as systematic description of behaviour and incidents that occur in the researcher's social setting. I took the decision to be an observer as opposed to a participant. The intention was to stand back from the activities and actions taken by participants, observe and record observations in my (Personal Journal) field notes. I selected this method in order to avoid influencing participants and to allow myself as a researcher to capture the complexity of the situation. It was planned that after one year, participants would be invited to share their research work with each other in a market place evening. How they shared their findings would be up to them. Feedback on the process and experiences would be invited through anonymous post-it notes.

The Senior Leadership Team invited all staff to an evening where food was provided. All full-time staff attended. The importance of feelings expressed by staff during Focus Group Discussion days was acknowledged. An explanation of the aim of the research was articulated as a belief that practitioners working together to find out about an area of work that interested or fascinated them would enable them to be better informed and consequently inspired to lead changes in their practice. The opportunity was offered as being completely voluntary. It was explained that the work was an experiment to find out whether practitioners felt that engaging in practice-based research was an effective approach to self-evaluation and further improvement. It was stressed that there was no right or wrong approach to this work. At the end of the year they would be invited to give feedback and decide whether they wanted to use training days to engage in practice-based research in the future or return to traditional training opportunities.

Practitioners who opted to engage were asked to pin their written fascinations or areas of interest onto a research board placed in the staff room. A full month was allocated to this task, allowing time for thought and informal discussion. At a further evening meeting, proposed research titles were placed around the room and practitioners were asked to stand next to the title that interested them. They were then asked to think about how they would work as a group, and when and where they would meet. The questions shown below were made available to practitioners as guidance for optional consideration.

Project title: *What is your area of interest?*
Statement of purpose: *What do you want to find out?*
Actions: *What will you do?*
Theory: *What might/did you read?*
Ethical code: *How will you/did you protect and respect those involved?*
Findings: *What did you learn?*
Implications for practice: *What should we do as a result of your learning?*

Learning from leadership inquiry – becoming authoritative

Experiencing leadership as a process of inquiry led me to identify democratic processes that supported the development of systemic leadership. I learned through first-hand experience about the complexity and challenges of putting democratic principles into practice. I was able to make conscious decisions about my leadership behaviour and actions, informed by my learning. The challenge of individuals being at different stages in their professional and personal learning journeys – their unique luggage accumulated along the way – was realised. I was able to consider, better understand and respect practitioners' individual needs. Everyone has an inner world with perceptions, assumptions and beliefs that we may struggle to unveil and may sometimes never surface.

Becoming a leader-researcher in order to develop a co-operative research culture helped to surface some explicit and implicit assumptions held by individual members of the organisation, including my own. I found that it was only when the organisation's members were functioning in a manner that showed mutual respect, trust and consideration of each other that co-operative practice-based research could succeed as an agent of social change. Learning co-operatively involved recognising each other as equal participants (Dreikurs, 1971) whilst respecting differences. This involved actively seeking to know and understand the organisation rather than making assumptions about each other.

In Stage One of my doctoral study I had mistakenly assumed that all practitioners would be ready, willing and feel able to take more responsibility for developing their own practice. Suggestions of taking such responsibility were a frightening concept for some practitioners. The fear of not being 'good enough' and of getting things 'wrong' was voiced within the safety of the Focus Group Discussions. Whilst I could not change staff members' previous life experiences, as a designated leader I could consciously work to promote an organisational learning culture that would support practitioners to regard themselves as capable, courageous, collaborative learners able to shape future practice.

Taking the role of leader-researcher enabled me to learn from work experiences, exploring what was known and believed. It was important for me to gather data from leadership cues in order to gain some understanding of the organisation's emotional intelligence. The early stages of my research demonstrated that without such intelligence co-operative work between practitioners could not thrive. It would have been easier in many ways to dismiss my socially situated knowledge of tensions between staff as something best ignored, especially because it pertained to emotional intelligence rather than undisputed facts. Choosing to explore what lay beneath the surface of such tensions provided insights and understanding about the impact of my leadership behaviour. This enabled further actions to be more carefully considered, informed by the learning that had taken place. I gained an understanding that voices sought through my inquiry were inevitably the emotional constructs of the participants. I realised that I had unintentionally and unconsciously changed practitioners' views of what and whom I valued by selecting a small group of practitioners engaged in institutionally recognised further studies. Dreikurs (1971) recognised that emotions represent an expression of real beliefs. It took courage to hear and respond to practitioners' 'real beliefs', which were the unintended consequences of my own leadership behaviour. Feelings held by many appeared to be at complete odds with what I had intended. Through seeking information that was bubbling away beneath the surface I was able to respond in a responsible, well-informed manner and develop a positive learning community where all practitioners did indeed become engaged in co-operative practice-based research. Maintaining field notes in the form of a dated personal journal, revisiting these notes and identifying relevant theoretical frameworks helped me to understand and value practitioners' emotional constructs as a rich source of data, rather than rejecting them.

Regarding leadership as a process of inquiry required a willingness to release my sense of control and destination. Undertaking action research required valuing, inquiring about and learning from the process. This led to three distinct stages in my study. The methods used at each stage were in response to what was learned from the previous stage and became less controlled, more open and experimental in nature. Marshall and Reason (2007) suggested that through living life as an inquiry, nothing can be fixed, the route cannot be marked and the destination may be unknown. Such a cyclical process of action inquiry required me to be open, reflective, responsive and flexible. I initially found the route's uncertainty caused feelings of great apprehension but learning from the process this uncertainty became exciting.

Engaging in an action research cycle constantly raised new questions. Work shifted as learning occurred. As one problem appeared to surface it raised further questions or theories. Informed by learning from the study, the initial research question shifted from 'How can I motivate and support staff to lead practice developments through practice-based research within the Early Years setting?' to 'How can I create an organisational culture and conditions within which others are self-motivated to lead practice developments through practice-based research within the Early Years setting?' My willingness to be flexible and take the pathway directed by the research was essential as I engaged in processes of inquiry within a real-life organisation. Following the tensions that arose as a consequence of selecting Centre Inquiry Group members I needed to take restorative actions. Boulton (2006) *complexity theory* recognises that everyday events and interactions occur within the workplace, meaning that nothing is fixed. As a result, the envisaged destination may continually change. I had to adopt a willingness to be open and flexible and am able to recognise that this was a personal challenge because I like to feel a sense of control and certainty. This was obviously challenging when I also held a vision for a more egalitarian systemic leadership approach. I was able to seek support for changing my leadership behaviour through accessing high-quality professional supervision.

I discovered the imperative need to promote feelings of social equality so that individuals can feel confident in their social status, free of the fear of not belonging. Failure to do so brought tensions across the organisation that saw people start to pull in different directions. The sense of shared purpose began to disappear. I discovered the importance of using fully inclusive methods of inquiry when actively setting out to learn how practitioners could become co-operative leaders of their own practice. Coyne (1997) outlined the concept that any sample, intentionally selected is made in order to fulfil a direct purpose. Selection criteria by which choices are made are discriminatory, developed to meet the intended purpose. Glaser (1978) identified this as a common pattern of behaviour in research; with selection of a group believed to have the most potential in providing the information sought often leading to bias. Considered alongside Dreikurs's (1971) principle that humans can only participate and contribute if they feel that they belong, it is clear that purposeful selection results in feelings of being ostracised by those not selected. As some practitioners' sense of adequacy through the Inquiry Group work in Stage One of my study grew, other members of the organisation felt that their work was not valued and felt they were 'not good enough'.

In Stage Three of my research, inviting all practitioners to engage in practice-based research as an experimental, non-threatening approach proved much more positive. Lambert (1998) claimed that systemic leadership is about learning together, constructing meaning and knowledge collaboratively. She described this as a process of reflection within a group, encouraging the rethinking of practice. I found that co-operative inquiry groups enabled staff to learn together, holding such conversations and supporting each other in developing their knowledge. Having taken part in co-operative inquiry work, participants frequently commented on the benefits of hearing other people's viewpoints and ideas and began to regard themselves as learners. Creating opportunities for the entire staff team to explore their differences in values and needs through processes of co-operative inquiry helped us all to explore and re-establish the organisation's values. The requirement to consider the allocation of professional development periods when all practitioners could be available to work co-operatively over a long time period became a leadership priority. Paying attention to issues of power, equality, social justice, value frameworks and opportunities to take responsibility for supporting the development of democratic leadership behaviour needed to be constantly considered.

Establishing membership in the trusted Doctoral Study Group of like-minded people facilitated the articulation of my thoughts and feelings. Thought processes undertaken prior to meeting with the group in preparation for clearly articulating feelings became an essential tool in reflecting and learning from the muddle of everyday work experiences. Reconstructing narratives recorded in my personal journal led to *transformational learning* Mezirow and Associates (2000). For example, it helped me to understand the behaviour of several senior practitioners during an INSET day when an external trainer facilitated a session on outdoor play. They had come up with non-sensical excuses for why suggestions would not work in our outdoor space. This day took place at end of the first term following the rapid expansion into a children's centre. They had started the year working with new staff in an extended building, working to a new curriculum. It was a couple of years later when I revisited the incident with Doctoral Study Group colleagues and the staff involved that I understood the degenerative behaviour of those involved. They felt their voices had been lost; the strength of their professional relationships and their professional capability had been challenged.

My own experience of seeking then receiving feedback, which I was tempted to reject upon receipt from the Focus Group Discussion Facilitator, illustrated a requirement for appropriate support mechanisms. I experienced the value of high-quality professional supervision and membership in a trusted community-learning group, the Doctoral Study Group. These were essential mechanisms supporting as well as challenging me at all stages of my leadership inquiry. Being open to feedback required me to be at ease with different thoughts, ideas and perspectives, rather than regarding those termed by Zoller and Fairhurst (2007) 'dissenters' as the problem. Adlerian psychologists Boldt and Mosak (1998) argued that each memory acquired by a person to be stored as a story shapes the person's life. I began to genuinely understand the extent to which individual practitioners' stories shaped the way they received new information and experiences and construed meaning, that is, I was able to accept staff members' emotional constructs rather than reject them as untruths.

A question I discovered worth asking was: *What behaviours and consequential experiences are authorised unconsciously by the organisation?* Dreikurs (1971) suggested that feelings of inferiority deter social functioning yet it had become clear how easy it was to unconsciously give out unintended messages. Promotion of a 'growth mindset' identified by Dweck (1999, 2012) through paying attention to what was valued and celebrated in the organisation encouraged practitioners to regard themselves as learners. Positive learning dispositions such as perseverance and curiosity needed to be purposefully valued in the organisation above attainment of formal, institutionalised, academic learning qualifications. Findings from my research suggested that when practitioners engaged in self-selected co-operative inquiry group processes they began to regard themselves as learners.

The need to seek out the extent to which values were understood by designated middle leaders and the wider organisation's members also emerged from my study. Working co-operatively to develop knowledge transcended designated leader roles. In a complex organisation necessitating distributed leadership, engaging in a quest to understand leadership required inquiry into the effects of others' leadership behaviours in the organisation. Designated team leaders who held responsibility for others needed to understand their authority and be able to negotiate the differences and tensions that existed within their teams. It became clear that opportunities and processes were required through which all of us who held designated leadership titles could surface, discuss, explore and understand each other's values, behaviours and actions.

Inquiring into group functioning needed to become part of my leadership inquiry. Paying attention to group dynamics helped to protect individuals from pressures towards conformity, and was necessary for developing systemic work. Paradoxically I discovered a need to develop hierarchical organisational structures that provided containment for emotional turbulence and promoted professional relationships. The hierarchical structure's purpose was to bring individuals together as a systemic, whole organisation that was moving towards an agreed shared goal, whilst protecting individual rights and mediating different views. Such a view of a hierarchical organisational structure was very different from that of a top-down decision-making hierarchical leadership model.

Regulation was required to provide a sense of containment, justice and opportunities for individual initiatives, including mediation of individual rights, obligations and behaviour towards others. Mezirow and Associates (2000) recognised that failure to integrate new experiences results in feelings of chaos and anxiety. Looking for safety from such a state, John (2000) recognised the pattern of behaviour is to look for protection from the person seen as the most powerful individual, attributing great significance to designated leadership job titles. Leaders were encouraged to consider using their power over resources to regularly allocate time for practitioners from different teams to work and dialogue together. Practitioners were able to make links with each other through inquiries into fascinations and curiosities about their work. This served as a means of informing further practice improvements. Self-determined co-operative inquiry groups working on self-identified areas of interest were shown in my study to contribute effectively towards taking responsibility for sustainable improvements.

It was necessary to negotiate and establish agreed principles and behaviours by which practitioners could work in the form of a 'Community Learning Contract'. This served to prevent the monopolisation of stronger voices. I gained an understanding that in practice, the human qualities of individuals, who are the organisation, have the capacity to work towards a common goal; however, their lack of motivation or commitment to do so is what is likely to stop ideologies being realised (Adler, 1927/1992). Writing from a psychologist's perspective on group dynamics John (2000) highlighted the danger of the individual's need to connect easily leading to coercion. The way the group behaves and the beliefs it actively supports may not always reflect the individual's beliefs or behaviour. However, the individual may choose to support the group behaviour because of his or her need to feel a sense of belonging to this group. As a result, individuals within a group may feel an internal conflict or sense of tension. Through my research I discovered that when a person's needs to belong and gain a sense of self-esteem were not met, alienation occurred and disruptive behaviour was displayed.

The importance of developing systems for monitoring and evaluating that did not undermine feelings of trust became apparent. When leadership of practice was being developed at all levels of the organisation, devolution of authority required an increased need for accountability. The ultimate responsibility to meet externally regulated standards still sat with me as the appointed Head Teacher. A robust process for monitoring and evaluating work carried out by those taking on responsibilities was therefore required. Essentially, leadership when looked at in this context remained hierarchical in a structure of organisationally sanctioned roles. McGregor (1960) referred to the inconsistency in approach of delegation and trust, which often is undermined by policing staff behaviour. Consideration therefore had to be given to how such 'policing' was undertaken. Terminology again became important as support and monitoring meetings were established across the centre on a regular calendar. The agendas for the meetings were drawn up collaboratively with those involved.

Responding to practitioners' feelings that their work was 'not good enough', it was important to develop systems that promoted individuals' feelings of self-efficacy, self-confidence and courage. There needed to be a recognition and promotion of the view that excellence in practice was valued for its contribution in the here and now. Practice at any point had to be regarded as a stage in an evolutionary change process. Previous practice had not to be regarded as poor when learning for development took place. The use of language and attention to how thoughts and ideas about next steps were articulated required sensitive consideration. As previously mentioned, designated leaders needed to consider how they could nurture and support individuals' emotional learning dispositions. The courage to be imperfect, the development of a 'growth mind-set' supported by the works of Adler (1927/1992), Deci and Ryan (1985), Dreikurs (1971) and Dweck (1999) were requirements for practitioners' willingness to engage in co-operative practice-based research.

Consideration of how different levels of practitioner capability could be protected and supported became hugely important in promoting a fully inclusive learning culture. Giddens (1988) proposed that an inclusive society must provide for the needs of those who find themselves less able. My study illustrated how transformational learning can cause feelings of turbulence. Practitioners did not automatically regard themselves as having equal opportunities to take part in co-operative practice research because of their individual constructs of knowledge, skills and abilities. A non-threatening experiential approach enabled different levels of challenge to be appropriate to individuals. In practice this involved Inquiry Groups, working at a level of self-choice, developing research questions, method design, analysis of evidence and presentation of findings. Informed by the early stage of my unintentionally divisive research approach, I consciously decided to promote feelings of adequacy rather than inadequacy by praising practitioners' willingness to engage in the process of co-operative inquiry work, focussing on the outcomes when embarking on such a journey. This involved accepting the sometimes elementary nature of practice-based research work undertaken as a starting point, a brave first step on a new learning journey.

I identified the importance of developing a clearly articulated understanding across the organisation that 'academic learning' is a means of learning about the work being undertaken. Understanding how individuals perceived professional development was crucial. Some of the participants in my study initially identified engagement in inquiry or learning processes as an activity for those who were academic and wished to change their job roles rather than seeking feedback from their environment in order to improve their current work. I discovered that many practitioners initially appeared to regard learning as something extra to their job role, rather than it being intrinsic to their work. Whitaker (2009) recognised that the term 'academic' tended to make people think of cleverness or high intelligence rather than learning. This was of particular relevance to the early years practitioners who, as previously discussed, often regarded themselves as non-academic. As noted above, findings from my research suggested that when practitioners engaged in self-selected co-operative inquiry group processes, they began to regard themselves as learners. It was important that the emphasis was placed on 'practice learning' rather than 'academic learning' and that this was clearly articulated and shared at every opportunity across the organisation.

Practitioners' feedback from engaging in co-operative practice-based research indicated that they valued the opportunity to undertake their inquiry over a sustained one-year period. They reported that this promoted a deeper level of thinking and reflection. They also found that working over a sustained time period allowed relationships to flourish and for connections to be made with others in a meaningful way. Participants identified a further benefit of working with a group over time being the development of confidence within that group as they developed relationships. This informed how we began to plan the annual calendar for professional development work. I recognised the value and importance of creating opportunities for sustained periods of learning where staff from different teams could come together.

As previously mentioned, supervision played an important role in supporting the development of positive learning dispositions for practitioners and me. It supported and encouraged us all to learn from our experiences through exploring and learning from self-reflection. The role of professional supervision and allocation of resources to support it needed to be fully valued and given consideration. To help develop readiness for learning, Lambert (1998) recommended coaching individuals so that they are able to recognise the influence they can have upon their workplace, learn from their behaviour and have the courage to try new ideas, accept and take responsibility for their own actions. This was crucial to promoting feelings of social equality across the organisation.

I chose to inquire into my practice as a leader in order to bring theory, research and practice together. Sergiovanni (2001, p. 343) discusses the 'heart, head and hand' of leadership. Through engaging in processes of inquiry I was able to consciously pay attention to my heart, seeking to surface driving emotions, my head, engaging with theory in order to understand what I uncovered, and my hand, the actions I took. Such an approach allowed an opening up, and at the same time, taking control of my thinking. It facilitated paying attention to the process involved in reaching a goal, what this meant for my inner self as a leader, and what it meant for those for whom I held responsibility. It enabled me to feel at ease with myself as a Head Teacher, aware that I was consciously taking responsibility for my leadership role.

References

Adler, A. (1927/1992). *Understanding Human Nature*. Oxford: Oneworld Publications.

Boldt, R. & Mosak, H. (1998). Understanding the Storyteller's Story: Implications for Therapy. *Journal of Individual Psychology*, 5, 4.

Boulton, J. C. (2006). *Embracing Complexity: Strategic Perspectives for an Age of Turbulence*. Oxford: Oxford University Press.

Braun, V. & Clarke, V. (2006). Using Thematic Analysis in Psychology. *Qualitative Research in Psychology*, 3(2), 77–101.

Carr, M. (2001). *Assessment in Early Childhood Settings – Learning Stories*. London: Paul Chapman.

Coyne, I.T. (1997). *Sampling in Qualitative Research: Purposeful and Theoretical Sampling, Merging or Clear Boundaries?* London: Blackwell Science.

Deci, E.L. & Ryan, R.M. (1985). *Intrinsic Motivation and Self-Determination in Human Behaviour*. New York: Plenum Press.

DFES (2006). Statutory Framework for the Early Years Foundation Stage.

Dreikurs, R. (1971). *Social Equality: The Challenge of Today*. Chicago, IL: Henry Regnery.

Dweck, C.S. (1999). *Self-Theories: Their Role in Motivation, Personality and Development*. Philadelphia: Psychology Press.

Dweck, C.S. (2012). *Mindset: How You Can Fulfill Your Potential*. London: Constable.

Giddens, A. (1988). *The Third Way: The Renewal of Social Democracy*. Oxford: Blackwell Publishing.

Glaser, B. G. (1978). *Theoretical Sensitivity*. California: Sociology Press.

Heron, J. (1971). *Experience and Method: An Inquiry into the Concept of Experiential Research: Human Potential Research Project*. Guildford, UK: University of Surrey.

Heron, J. (1996) *Co-operative Inquiry: Research into the Human Condition*. London: Sage.

Jaworski, J. (1996). *Synchronicity The Inner Path of Leadership*. San Francisco, CA: Berrett-Koehler.

John, K. (2000). Basic Needs, Conflict and Dynamics in Groups. *Journal of Individual Psychology*, 56, 4.

John, K. (2012). Authority and Democracy 100 Years On. In: P. Prina, C. Shelley, A. Millar & J. Karen (Eds.), *2012 ASIIP Year Book: Celebrating 100 Years of Individual Psychology (1911–2011)* (pp. 107–131). London: Adlerian Spcoety (UK) & Institute for Individual Psychology (ASIIP).

Klavins, E. (2015). *Repositioning Leadership in Early Years Contexts*. Doctoral Thesis. Leicester: Leicester Theses, Department of Medical and Social Care Education.

Lambert, L. (1998). *Building Leadership Capacity in Schools*. Danville, Alexandria, VA: ASCD.

Lofland, J. & Lofland, L. (1984). *Analysing Social Settings: A Guide to Qualitative Observation and Analysis*. Belmont, CA: Wadsworth.

Marshall, J. (2001). Self-Reflective Inquiry Practices. In: P. Reason & H. Bradbury (Eds.), *Handbook of Action Research: Participative Inquiry and Practice* (pp. 433–439). London: Sage.

Marshall, J. & Reason, P. (1998). Collaborative and Self-Reflective Forms of Inquiry in Management Research. In: J. Burgoyne & M. Reynolds (Eds.), *Management Learning* (pp. 227–242). London: Sage.

Marshall, J. & Reason, P. (2007). Quality in Research as "Taking an Attitude of Inquiry". *Management Research News*, 30(5), 368–380 (University of Bath).

McGregor, D. (1960). *The Human Side of Enterprise*. New York: McGraw-Hill.

Mezirow, J. & Associates (2000). *Learning as Transformation*. SanFrancisco, CA: Jossey-Bass.

Reason, P. (Ed.) (1988). *Human Inquiry in Action: Developments in New Paradigm Research*. London: Sage.

Schön, D. (1983). *The Reflective Practitioner*. London: Ashgate.

Sergiovanni, T.J. (2001). *The Principalship: A Reflective Practice Perspective* (4th Ed.). Boston, MA: Allyn and Bacon.

Stringer, E. (1999). *Action Research* (2nd Ed.). Palo Alto, CA: Sage.

Torbert, B. & Associates (2004). *Action Inquiry*. San Francisco, CA: Berrett-Koehler.

Torbert, W.R. (1972). *Learning from Experience*. New York: Columbia University Press.

Tracy, S.J. (2013). *Qualitative Research Methods*. West Sussex: John Wiley & Sons.

Whitaker, P. (August 2009). Applying *Systems Theory to Leadership in Services for Children, Families and Schools – A Critical Review, with Suggestions for Future Developments*. Corby, UK: Pen Green Research (unpublished).

Zoller, H.M. & Fairhurst, G.T. (2007). Resistance Leadership: The Overlooked Potential in Critical Organisation and Leadership Studies. *Human Relations*, 60(9), 1331–1360.

Chapter 5

We all have the potential to lead because we all have responsibilities

Christine Parker[1]

My leadership narrative: living life as a learning leader

During my engagement in PhD study I had several roles as the author of the study. I was a lead researcher, I was an early years practitioner and I was the Headteacher of the primary school that was the research subject. I brought to these roles specific knowledge, understanding, experience, positions and passions which enriched the research study as well as creating research limitations. Specifically, I had lived and worked in Pakistan, I considered myself to be an expressive artist and I was an early years practitioner working within the primary school phase of formal education. I am writing this chapter about leadership and specifically primary school leadership in recognition of the struggles, celebrations, challenges and pain that practitioners experience. Having been a Headteacher for 16 years in both the early years and primary school sectors I conclude that there is not one model for organisational leadership.

The school learning community, the subject of my action research project, was a larger-than-average primary school with, at the time of writing, a capacity for 450 children. The school is an inner-city school in an area of high disadvantage. The school opened on the current site in 1897 and was originally a school for boys. Following Local Authority reorganisation in 1983 the school was given a new name and became an all through co-educational primary school for children aged 4-years to 11-years-old. The school is a culturally rich and diverse community. All the children attending were multilingual and over 90% were Muslim. Over 20 different languages were spoken and the children's countries of heritage were Pakistan, Afghanistan, India, Bangladesh, Portugal, Latvia, Lithuania, Czech Republic, Slovakia, Poland, East Timor and The Seychelles. The Pakistani heritage community was the majority minority community in the city. In 2014, the community celebrated the sixtieth anniversary of the arrival of the first Pakistani heritage immigrants. Although most of children attending the school are of Pakistani heritage the demographic was changing. In 2008, the percentage of Pakistani heritage pupils was at 93% and by 2014 was at 83%. This changing demographic can be explained by three contributing factors. Firstly, aspirational Pakistani heritage families have relocated to more affluent locations in the city. Secondly, a rise in immigration from other countries, including those Eastern European countries that have joined the European Economic Community. Finally, new immigrant families are housed in the school's locality, often in rented accommodation.

Through the PhD research process the term 'leadership narrative' evolved. It was important to present the stories of research as narratives and to recognise the emergent conceptualisation of school leadership. By combining the two words 'leadership' and 'narrative' two significant strands of theorising are honoured. A 'leadership narrative,' for the purposes of my PhD research project, was defined as the telling of either a leadership story or leadership journey. It is characterised by the exemplification of aspects of leadership including the identified research themes and the development of our thinking about taking a lead. In my research project a series of leadership narratives were created specifically with the purpose of making leadership visible. The research project line of inquiry was to ask whether collaborative action research is a sustainable approach to school development that promotes responsive leadership, accountability and aspirations in learning and successful outcomes at many levels.

In this chapter I shall reflect on my participation in several learning communities, how they operated, what difference they made and their relevance to early years and school leadership. I ask the question 'What resonates?'

One learning community I belonged to was a PhD Learning Group based at the Pen Green Research Centre, Corby. Members of this group are the authors of this book. The formation of the group was a motivation for me to access doctorate level study. Discourse and reflective research journaling were important research processes and embedded from the beginning. The PhD Action Learning Group was significant in sustaining everyone in their position as practitioner researchers (Schön, 1983). The group supported and challenged the process for each research project. This was a learning community, originally of six students and three tutors, created to engage in the processes of listening, reflecting, debating, challenging and learning. The group placed the leadership narratives within an innovative dynamic for doctoral study: a dynamic that added passion and rigour to the research process.

Living life as inquiry

I have been influenced in my leadership thinking by Judi Marshall who considers the proposition of 'living life as inquiry' (Marshall, 1999). Marshall advocates story telling as a key process for finding voice and acknowledging learning and research journeys as living life as inquiry. Throughout my career in early years education I have struggled with the connectivity between my personal and professional lives. I have felt resentment when the pressures of work have invaded my head space. What I have learnt during recent years is that I am one person who has a wide spectrum of pursuits in both my personal life and my professional life and that they overlap and that's fine. There is enough challenge and struggle for me to face and deal with as a human being without creating an unnecessary barrier. I have acknowledged how I am nourished by my interest and studies in the expressive arts. These are as much a part of my professional being as of my personal being. Therefore, for me to seek music and art as ways to express how I feel as a leader has a relevance as does seeking graphic representations to visualise my leadership learning. After all isn't this the purpose of the expressive arts? To provide stimuli for human responses, reconnaissance, release, relief and solace.

In my pursuit of living life as inquiry I take an holistic approach. This means that in my work life I acknowledge my concerns as a whole person. These include my political concerns for the world, my interest in aspects of the expressive arts, my belonging to a range of cultural groups such as that of my family, my colleagues and the PhD Learning Group I am a member of. I belong to the cultural group of people who have travelled, people who have learnt other languages, groups I belong to as an educator, a family member, a colleague, an artist, a dancer. For you there will be alternative cultural references.

Journaling continues to be a process I use to help me make sense of what I experience in the personal, the professional, the creative, the political, the emotional and social life that is me. The value and power of journaling and freefall writing, as creative methods of developing and strengthening leadership, have impacted on my understanding of leadership theory. Journaling and freefall writing (Marshall, 2007) are processes for deep reflection. My documentation is both chronological, thus keeping a record of actions and outcomes, and of a more theoretical nature, where thoughts are unravelled, analysed and set within the context of research literature. Sharp describes the value of reflection and developing the ability "to evaluate your own emotional literacy" (Sharp, 2001, p. 90).

In my role as an education practitioner, journaling has activated my reflections and learning. From the start of my formal career in 1980 I have documented my observations and evaluations of child learning and my learning as an adult practitioner. I was appointed as the deputy Headteacher of a nursery school in 1997 and it was from this time that I journaled with the purpose of unravelling leadership dilemma stories (NCSL, 2004). From the point of my first headship in 1999 this leadership journaling became increasingly a necessity for my professional and personal wellbeing.

There are times when I get stuck. I have no words to give, no means of expression to articulate my experiences. When I read about Marshall's process of 'freefall writing' I could see that this was a method I needed to explore, investigate and experiment with (Marshall, 2001). "Invoke the writer in you and your direct voice, whatever shape it takes" (p. 11). Writing for action research is about finding voice: finding your own voice as a researcher and locating and projecting the voices of your co-researchers and research participants. Marshall finds her voice through her reflection on the writings of Virginia Woolf. She calls this "Learning from Woolf: Working with Intent" (Marshall, 2007, p. 5). I am enamoured by and engaged in this crossing over of the arts and academic approach. It strengthens thoughts around life as a researcher/leader and how I am influenced by the creative arts. Freefall writing sits well within the idea of being a reflective practitioner (Schön, 1983). It provides a non-judgmental place that is safe. It enables the articulation of thoughts to test out before they are shared with others. It is the sharing with others that is so frightening. I define freefall writing to mean a technique to enable the writer to access and respond to thought processes in a way that is free and is not limited by formal writing conventions. Freefall writing has released me, enabled me and provided the confidence I needed as a researcher to write.

Having a blank sheet of paper and writing whatever came into my head without fear is a release and gives me the freedom to write. Although Marshall advocates writing by hand I have discovered that I can word process my thoughts. I didn't correct spelling and grammar errors unless I chose to share my freefall writing with others. The release allowed me to write in a range of genres, for example, storytelling, poetry and autobiography.

The impact of freefall writing

Freefall has liberated my approach to academic thought and writing. I have the right to write down what I am thinking in the first person. I have the right to feel justified in what I write. I do need to demonstrate that I am well informed by what others have said, what others have researched and how others lead their researcher and practitioner lives. Those references to others enhance and enrich what I think, reflect and do. I have absorbed much over the years, and developed my academic thinking. This academic thought is enriched by my life as a creative person, a human being, who has a range of political, artistic and cultural perspectives and viewpoints.

To illustrate the impact of freefall writing I have selected five extracts from my time as a researcher/leader. I have chosen the first extract because it demonstrates a direct link with Marshall's theory of freefall writing (Marshall, 2007). It was written two months following the European Early Childhood Education Research Association (EECERA) conference in Birmingham, 2010. This conference provided a platform for the PhD Action Learning Group to disseminate emergent findings.

Freefall writing extract one: 29.11.2010

My title shall come from the notes I made at Judi Marshall's keynote speech.

Everything in play at any one time

Why does this particular phrase appeal?

The notion of all aspects of self being present and being there as a resource to dip into is exciting. The use of the word 'play' appeals. Play as a construct that allows us to know something, an idea so well it goes beyond acquisition but onto an idea that can be used for creative purposes.

In my leadership role, I feel good about what I do when I sense that I am looking in from out and looking out from within. I can be fully engaged in a conversation, with a colleague, with a child, with a parent, with a professional who has come to work with us and be conscious of what I say, conscious of how I stand or sit and think ahead about what is important to value and to reject. In that role, as lead leader and lead learner, the more I am conscious of what I say and do, the more I learn from others and the encounter tends to be nourishing rather than toxic. This is not to say there is no challenge and it is easy. If this was so it is unlikely that the dialogue will change anything, the expected outcome of a learning encounter.

Extract two, has been selected because it exemplifies the notion of seeking metaphors and analogies across disciplines. I searched for musical terminology to reflect school leadership. This resonates with Wyse's discourse on the primary curriculum (Wyse, 2014) and Boog's musical metaphor of the 'Intermezzo' to clarify the time required for the initial stages of research (Boog, 2014).

Freefall writing extract two: 02.12.2010

I want to play with the notion of our leadership journeys, the Learning Stories being accompanied by music and images.

Playing with words, the language of music and art:

> Movement, Tempo, Composition, Colour, Theme and Variations, Rhythm, Density, Fluidity, Texture, Staccato, Legato, Two dimensional, Three dimensional, Binary Form, Ternary Form, Rondo Form, Sonata Form, Lyrics, Dance

The third extract relates to the notion of leadership following a path that is slow and therefore sustainable. 'Immer langsam' translates from the German as 'Always slow.' It was the advice of a German-speaking cowherd when my partner and I were tackling the steep slopes of the Dolomite mountains in Northern Italy in 1984.

Freefall writing extract three: 14.05.2011

Immer Langsam
    Notions of slow leadership resonate with me and then I thought of the German speaking cowherd we met in the Dolomites. "Immer langsam, immer langsam." This to me is the recurring theme of my leadership journey. You cannot accelerate human learning and development. Why is accelerating so desirable? Deep learning takes time and needs to be revisited in different ways. And that's the exciting element of the learning process. Wallowing is good. It's good for my soul.

Extract four demonstrates my continuing concern for the children in our learning community and the impact of the political world.

Freefall writing extract four: 06.08.2011

As a majority Muslim learning community, we have to acknowledge that the children are growing up in a hostile world. They have to be articulate individuals, who can be very clear about their position in this country and this world. They need to be able to articulate the contribution they are making to the communities beyond their own. It is interesting to note that Chris defines community (Watkins, 2005) and in that definition rejects notions of the community around the school that are warm and cosy.

The final extract shows my personal concern for my own learning and my aim to make leadership visible.

Freefall writing extract five: 06.08.2011

I am learning about leadership, I am learning about making notions of leadership visible. I am developing methodology to make that learning about leadership visible. At this point I am not sure what that looks like, not specifically. My theory is that by making that leadership visible, this will mean we will develop a shared understanding of what we mean by leadership and this deepening in our understanding will lead to a leadership that listens, provokes, challenges, celebrates, supports what is right and at the heart is the deepening of the children's understanding, widening of their knowledge and the creation of an organisational culture that is positive about agency, belonging, collaboration and diversity.

Visualising learning

I seek and find comfort in art and therefore it is not surprising that I search for images to represent my thought processes. I respond to what I see around me. Throughout my PhD research quest I struggled to make the research process visual. In this endeavour it has been important to recognise the influence of the predominant culture represented in the school learning community. From my perspective engagement with the Pakistani heritage community and culture has personal as well as professional resonance. Figures 5.1–5.6 are

Figure 5.1 The learning spiral

Figure 5.2 The bumps: representing either the action learning groups, or research themes or aspects of leadership

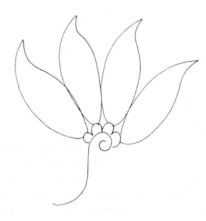

Figure 5.3 The 'paisleys': representing learning

Figure 5.4 The paisley is elaborated to visualise leadership learning

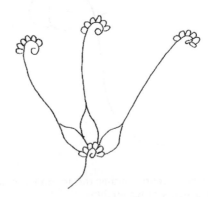

Figure 5.5 New spirals represent new directions and new learning

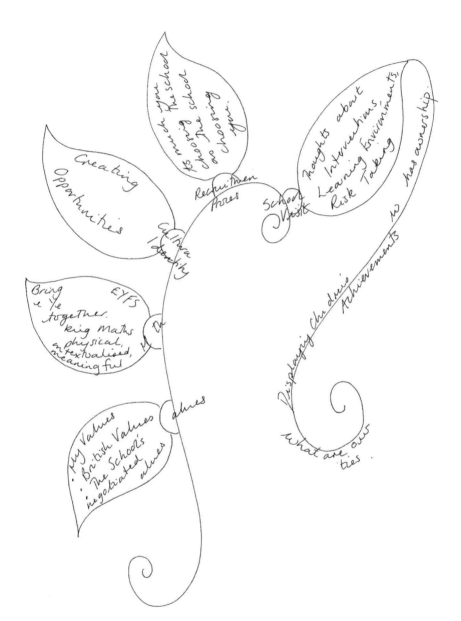

Figure 5.6 'Our learning'

the components of a representation of the research process applying the rich pattern-making prevalent in the Pakistani heritage community. The paisley design originates from Iran and symbolises the tree of life (Edwards, 2009). It travelled to India in the eighteenth century and became popular in Regency England and Scotland. The name change originated from the Scottish town of Paisley where fine woollen and silk fabrics were produced. The paisley design has a contemporary resonance as it is a popular design for both eastern and western designers. The design is recognisable in the mehndi patterns, which are temporary designs drawn on women's feet and hands during Islamic, Hindu and Sikh marriage and religious ceremonies. Girls attending one of the school's chat groups taught me how to draw one design which has enabled me to incorporate these images into the visualisation of the research process. I have asked myself if I am making my 'theory making' fit lines, shapes, patterns and constructs because I want to make them fit, or do they truly make sense of the theory and connected processes. It is my opinion that these configurations illuminate and enrich theory making.

There is resonance with other global heritages that have taken symbolic representations to facilitate visualisation. For example, in the Te Whariki Early Childhood Curriculum in New Zealand the principles and strands of the curriculum are demonstrated through the application of the Maori woven mat (Ministry of Education, New Zealand, 1996). The paisley design has been used to invite responses from peers during the process of research dissemination as a symbol of the Pakistani heritage community but at the same time acknowledging that the design has a rich global dimension. I begin with the learning spiral, as shown in Figure 5.1.

In Figure 5.2 are the 'bumps,' which can be representative of groups of action learners, research themes and aspects of leadership.

Next in Figure 5.3 the paisleys represent learning, lines of inquiry, emergent themes and recurring themes and new theories.

Each paisley can be elaborated further, as depicted in Figure 5.4 to visualise learning.

Discursive learning generates plans for new directions, new learning and ways to strengthen the learning community, this is represented by new spirals that are added in Figure 5.5.

The value of this visualisation is that every piece is unique and different. There is no one model or design. It facilitates the sense of the theory making. I continue to apply this design when facilitating learning sessions with adults. Figure 5.6 is illustrative of how learning has been visualised by a group of student teachers.

To illustrate this chapter I have used my visualisation to conceptualise the themes I consider (Figure 5.7). The spiral is entitled 'living life as a learning leader.' Each theme has a 'bump' and the content is represented by a paisley.

I return to the visualisation at the end of this chapter to illustrate the connecting themes discussed in this leadership book.

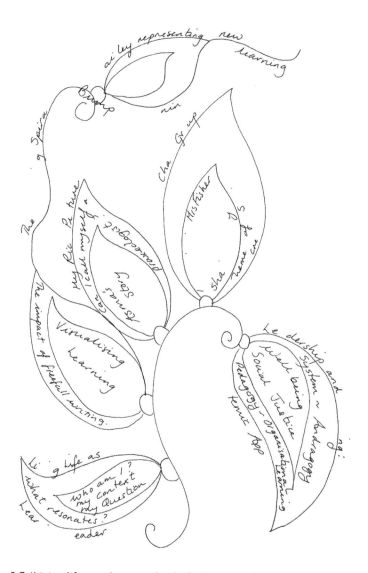

Figure 5.7 'Living life as a learning leader': themes and content

My rich picture (Figure 5.8)

I pause, observe, reflect on this moment in my leadership narrative. I unpick the whole to reveal the detail. At one of the PhD sessions Margy suggested that I map my perception of my school leadership. The image I created encapsulated all aspects of my practice, theory and research. This rich picture is the

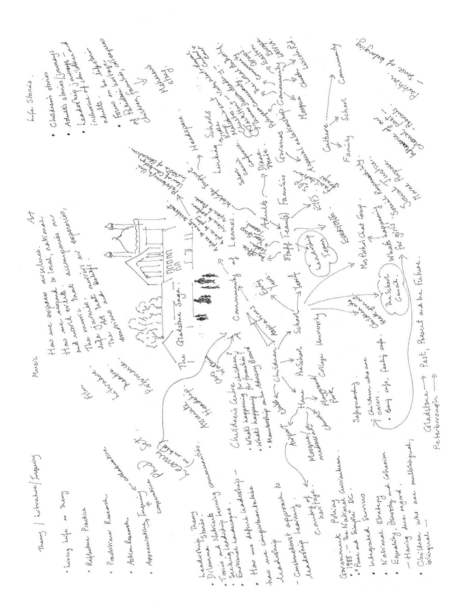

Figure 5.8 My rich picture: a community of learners

recording of ideas and connections. It was at this point, this aha! moment that I saw myself as a leader who has emerged as a praxeologist with a systemic approach to school leadership. This rich picture represented my perception of my role as a practitioner, a leader and a researcher at a given moment in time. It is illustrative of a process of reflection, identification and acknowledgement of the value of a systemic approach to school leadership. My starting point was to draw an image in the centre of the paper. This image includes the church building located in the school grounds, the mosque that is central to the Muslim community and the school building which is significant to the community, not only as a place for children to learn but also as an intergenerational meeting place. Developing an understanding of local community and heritage is an aspect of school leadership that is at risk of falling by the wayside in our current times of extreme pressures to produce academic results. In my rich picture, I identify the different communities I engaged with. I recognise the complexities of these relationships.

The political aspect of leadership can feel like a distraction, even an irritant. Are we preparing children and young people to be politicised, by which I mean to question, show curiosity, to seek political solutions to what concerns us today in society? Do we create safe spaces for open dialogue? Or are we allowing personalities and outmoded ideas of leadership to create barriers to honest political debate?

Can I call myself a praxeologist?

I can see in my rich picture that I reveal myself as a praxeologist. "Can I call myself a praxeologist?" was a genuine question I asked Margy in one of many PhD tutorials. My rich picture shows how I spontaneously refer to my pedagogical and andragogical practice and underpinning theory and research knowledge. This rich picture is illustrative of a systemic view of school leadership (Senge, 2006; Whitaker, 2009). There is recognition of systems consciousness in that the different networks are identified and in the notion of developing personal mastery through the acknowledgement of the need for the practitioner/leader to refer to the research literature. The themes of my thesis emerged alongside the acknowledgement of the 'life stories' or research through narrative.

Since becoming a nursery lead in 1986 I have struggled with the varied viewpoints of early years and school leadership. There continues to be an expectation that as a designated leader you should lead from the front. There are times as a designated leader you do need to show you can take that level of responsibility especially through difficult times. However, this notion of dependency on one person does not sit well with the realities of organisational learning. Leadership as a concept needs to be broader and deeper. I have reflected on definitions and I like the idea of a leader being a person who is seeking and finding a way through a dilemma. All learners have the potential to lead in their own learning and all leaders have the potential to learn in their own leadership.

What appeals is the idea of everyone within an organisation being supported to realise their potential as learners and leaders; to recognise that everyone has these responsibilities. The School Council quotation reverberates for me: "We all have responsibilities therefore we are all potential leaders." Therefore, ideas of a systemic approach to early years and school leadership allows for individual specialisms to impact overall, an acknowledgement of an organisation's political, social, historical, cultural and economic context as well as a research-based approach to development and improvement.

Asma's story

I recognised that I had insufficient knowledge of the children's families and the community. I needed to know more. A local authority funded project, 'Connecting Communities' provided the opportunity for Robina and I to work with children and their parents. We learnt with an artist, Husnain, with the aim to find a way to graphically represent the local community. Husnain facilitated an exploration of the locality. The participants were five families represented by six parents and ten children from Years One and Six and myself. The aim was to learn more about our perceptions of the locality and belonging, finding ways of representing our ideas. Asma was one of the parents who engaged in this local authority funded project with two of her children aged 6 years and 11 years.

In one session facilitators and participants brought physical props to support their dialogue about their ideas of community and belonging. Asma's daughters Nafeesa and Aleesha were keen to show their items. Nafeesa had brought a pair of sunglasses that she had bought in Pakistan. Asma explained, "It was the first time she went and she really liked it. She went with my mum." Aleesha had brought her baby blanket. She informed us, "This is my blanket. My mum told me she wrapped me in this."

Asma told us that she and her family did not live in the catchment area of the school but that she was happy to bring her children to the school each day, it was her choice. I began to understand how important the locality was to Asma when she produced the object she had brought to show us. Asma's object was a front door key. She held up the door key. Asma's action was strong and defining. This simple object represented her sense of belonging to a community she had physically moved away from but her heart and soul remained. As Asma held the front door key up, she explained,

> This is the key to my old house – it's ten years of memories. It's in this area. It's the people. It's the environment. I'll never get the same neighbours, local mosque, shops and school. We got a new gas cooker, we're getting rid of the old one so everything is fading away. It's like when my children change classes, I feel for Aleesha.

Asma's expression of her emotional connection with the neighbourhood, where she no longer lives, demonstrated to us all the strength of her feelings and emotional ties. The Connecting Communities project had provided the opportunity for her to give voice to her loves and concerns. Sitting attentively listening to Asma and her children tell their stories of belonging was a powerful moment in my school leadership life. Asma had told her story about the significance of her old front door key (Figure 5.9).

In a later session, Asma created a graphic representation of the locality (Figure 5.10). Her love and attachment to the area did not deter her from confronting the realities of drug abuse, physical attacks, hate crimes and burglaries as well as the positive aspects of a diverse community. This engagement with the children's families enabled a deepening of my understanding and knowledge of life in the locality. Intergenerational learning is powerful and is as relevant in the primary and secondary phases of education as it has proven to be

Figure 5.9 Asma holds up her front door key, illustrative of her bond with her community and the locality

Figure 5.10 Asma graphically represents the school's locality identifying the factors that concern her as well as those that nourish her

in the early years (Whalley, 1994). If practitioners had the resource to capture these family Learning Stories how much better they would be informed.

The girls' chat group

When I reflected on my rich picture I acknowledged the learning communities I had engaged within my roles as a designated school leader and academic researcher. There was one learning community that above all others was to have a profound effect on me and thus I have sought opportunities to actively share our story, the story of the girls' chat group.

During one Autumn Term three girls, Aamina, Zarah and Shazia were involved in a racist incident. They were the initiators. The victim was an adult employed in a partner organisation. It was necessary to take serious action and discuss the incident with the girls' parents. The girls were given time out of class to reflect on their actions and were then carefully reintroduced to the normal school day. They wrote letters of apology and personally apologised to the adult they had offended.

The actions had been so concerning that it was decided that Aamina, Zarah and Shazia would become members of a girls' chat group. The original purpose of the girls' chat group was to facilitate dialogue and inquiry, discuss any subject the girls chose and follow identified lines of inquiry. The school learning community had identified that overall girls' academic achievements fell behind that of boys'. Collectively we were concerned that older girls were losing the confidence they had shown in the earlier years of schooling. Aamina, Zarah and Shazia would be expected to meet once every week, during a lunchtime, to discuss and reflect on what racism means and its connection with bullying.

Anti-discriminatory practice has been developed in schools in England. It was in the 1980s that the idea of multicultural education gained some prominence, especially in English cities where diverse ethnic communities lived (Alexander, 2010). Elton-Chalcraft (2009) identifies five general categories of stances children took towards diversity issues arising from her research in four schools engaging with Year Five children.

> Same but not identical. Many children, in different ways, expressed the concept of all humans being the same but not identical. People from different cultures may have different outward appearances, different customs and beliefs but nevertheless inside they are still human.
>
> Politically correct. Some children expressed politically correct opinions, for example they did not use sexist or racist language or gestures.
>
> White privilege. The general assumption is that white western culture is normal and that all other cultures are different from the norm, thus implying inferiority.
>
> Important to be nice. What was important to many children was whether people are nice, moral, kind etc. This was given far more emphasis than their colour or cultural roots.
>
> Knowledge leads to harmony, ignorance leads to conflict. Numerous children said that they thought it was important to learn about other cultures: some believed that knowledge is important to dispel fear and ignorance which often led to racist incidents and conflict.
>
> (Elton-Chalcraft, 2009, pp. 81–82)

For the three girls, it wasn't only necessary to create a safe space it was also essential to create the time. This was not a task to be completed in one day or one week or one term. I was ambitious for the girls and I wanted the girls to reflect and change their attitudes for the long term. The girls' chat group met regularly throughout the school year. The girls wrote reflective journals, created a mind map to answer the question 'What is racism?' and conducted a semi-structured interview with a member of the staff.

At the first meeting, each girl was given a reflective journal. It was explained that they could write whatever they liked in their journals and could bring them to the meetings to support the process of reflection. The reflective journals provided a place where the girls could write with honesty and candour and this is evidenced in Shazia's story. Tears were shed as they reflected on their own actions and the impact of their words.

Following the first meeting of the girls' chat group it was decided that the girls would consider the line of inquiry, 'What is racism?' in a space where they would not be judged and they could articulate their ideas freely. At the second girls' chat group meeting the girls were invited to define racism. The question was written in the centre of their poster. Their task was to consider and interpret this line of inquiry in their own words.

Aamina, Shazia and Zahra engaged in active and critical dialogue, and revealed their perceptions. Aamina, Shazia and Zahra identified how people are different from one another. The identification of differences provides the opportunity to tease or bully and has the potential to evolve into racism (Richardson & Miles, 2008). Their ideas ranged from concepts of nationality and religion to individual traits including physical features such as hair colour.

Allowing the time for the discourse was important. I listened and the dialogic process was honoured. My role was to identify the children's theories about their perceptions of racism and bullying. The girls' dialogue provided evidence of their collaborative approach. They supported each other to formulate their ideas and theories. They co-constructed meaning together. For example:

Aamina: Yeah, that is kind of right but why don't we do this one when some people are playing in the park and they are a different colour or race and you say you're not allowed to come in.
Zahra: Their relation. . . .
Shazia: Relationship with someone?

The girls continued to co-construct meaning concerning perceptions of personal weaknesses. They recognised that some people struggle with aspects of literacy. The girls were clear that they did not want to consider what they perceived as an intellectual failing. They said, "We wouldn't want to write someone is not clever enough." During this discourse Aamina took the lead in creating a pause and a moment of reflection. She identified a dilemma in that they had difficulty in identifying the appropriate terminology. She said, "We get the ideas right but we need to think about how to word them." Zahra brought their focus back to a consideration of 'race.' What would happen to the end product became important to Zahra. She asked, "After we've done this, where's it gonna go?" This was the first time it was considered that the girls' findings would be shared. This identification of the need to communicate the girls' ideas to a wider audience indicated an awareness of systems consciousness and their need to contribute to organisational learning.

The racist incident had been directed at a woman of Black Afro-Caribbean heritage. However, the notion of 'being Black' was not identified as a potential target for racism in this discourse between the three girls although reference had been made to skin colour. It was suggested that the girls invite a member of the office team who was of Black Afro-Caribbean heritage to one of the girls' chat group sessions. It was considered reasonable that the team member would be able to respond to any question the girls would ask.

Interviewing Mrs Fisher

Aamina, Shazia and Zahra interviewed a member of staff to find out about her past experiences as a child. The member of staff's heritage was Jamaican. The girls wanted to know more about her perceptions of racism in relation to her personal experiences. From the researcher's perspective, the purpose of the meeting was to develop the girls' insight and therefore their systems consciousness.

The first part of the discourse illustrated the value of the creation of a space to ask what children and adults genuinely want to ask, both the personal and the social (Formosinho & Oliveira-Formosinho, 2012). Shazia asked Mrs Fisher, "Do you feel uncomfortable here in school?" By the tone of her voice, Mrs Fisher expressed shock that a child would perceive her position in this way. She responded by saying, "No, I like it here, why?. . . . My little brother came here and my big brother." Mrs Fisher's reference to her brothers having attended the school reflected her thinking. Underlying her vocalisation were the thoughts, 'why would you think that? I have a long association with this school.'

Mrs Fisher's response prompted Aamina's question, "How did it feel growing up here in England as a Black child?" Mrs Fisher hesitated and then expressed the perception that she did not think about being a person of Black Afro-Caribbean heritage. She explained, "It's never bothered me because I was born in London and then from an early age I've lived in this city." At this point Mrs Fisher began to relate her story. She informed the girls that she grew up in the locality of the school. She finished this story by reaffirming that, "I've never thought about being Black. It's never something I consciously think about. I just think about myself as a person not any particular type of person." Aamina valued Mrs Fisher's response and thanked her for her answer.

The discourse between the three girls and Mrs Fisher enabled the children to revisit their theory making about life as a Black person in the UK. Mrs Fisher challenged the girls' personal theories about Black culture and the Black community. Mrs Fisher continued to present herself positively. She articulated her perceptions and feelings and these contradicted the girls' expectations. The following quotation is illustrative of the discourse.

Zahra: How do you feel now?
Mrs Fisher: About myself?
Zahra: About yourself and feelings.
Mrs Fisher: I'm quite comfortable inside my skin. I like the person I am.

Zahra responded by saying, "I thought you were going to say, 'Now I feel okay but first I felt worried.'" She anticipated that Mrs Fisher's ethnicity would create a 'worry' for her. Mrs Fisher reaffirmed by responding, "I've never felt worried because I never thought about being Black as a thing I needed to worry about." Elton-Chalcraft (2009) maintains that children are less aware of the wider political picture of perceptions of race. The children's perceptions of identity are based on their personal experience within their families and school. They create their own theories, which are partly formed by the knowledge and understanding acquired at school.

Aamina brought the discussion back to the children's perceived dilemma of growing up as a Black child in England. She asked Mrs Fisher, "Were you friends with any white children?" Mrs Fisher's initial reaction conveyed her shock at this line of inquiry. She stuttered. Each sentence was interspersed with hesitation. Mrs Fisher confirmed the notion that friendships are not about only relating to people from either your ethnic or cultural group, which the girls had assumed based on their personal experience. She explained that,

> I had, and even now I have, a broad circle of friends. They're not necessarily all black or all white. My best friend is Italian. Another one of my friends is Asian. I have lots of different friends. They're my friends because of the people they are not because of what their cultures are.

Mrs Fisher continually reaffirmed that she was a confident individual, that her wellbeing was good and that she was positive regarding her position in society. Zahra continued to pursue the notion that Mrs Fisher's experiences had created "problems and issues." Mrs Fisher's confidence and ability to articulate her views presented a perspective Zahra had not anticipated. At this point Mrs Fisher put the question back to the girls. She wanted to pursue a line of inquiry about their sense of identity and sense of self. She asked, "Do you guys like how you are? Would you change anything?" However, this did not gain the response she sought. Aamina affirmed that she liked who she was with a solitary, "Yes." Zahra moved the dialogue on by deepening the girls' line of inquiry with, "Why do you like how you are?" Mrs Fisher's response was:

Mrs Fisher: I suppose because as you grow up you have lots of experiences and sometimes they're good ones and sometimes they're not so good. The experiences you have in life change you and I'm more tolerant of people.

Mrs Fisher continued to provide frank responses. She revealed that there have been times in her life when she has not been so tolerant of some people. Mrs Fisher checked with Zahra that she had understood her explanation. Wellbeing had come to the fore. The presentation of Mrs Fisher's narrative provided a place for reflection and a space for a reconsideration of shared understanding.

Shazia developed the discourse further by asking a 'What if?' question. "What if you were bullied?" Mrs Fisher explained that if she experienced a situation where she felt threatened and troubled she would seek advice and support from another person.

Aamina moved the dialogue along with what was perceived by the two adults as a startling line of inquiry, "Could you go to the same school as white children?" However, children's perceptions of time and history are not fully developed and in Aamina's thinking what happened historically in the school's locality could reflect apartheid in South Africa. Mrs Fisher's response, which was to laugh and say, "Yes it wasn't the dark ages," saw her making light of the question. Aamina's line of inquiry provided Mrs Fisher with the opportunity to revisit the city's recent history and acknowledge the different communities that have arrived at different times.

After 12 minutes of discourse Mrs Fisher recalled an incident of racial discrimination. She narrated to the group,

> My mum came here in 1962 and there were a lot of West Indian people in the city. They all lived around here and that was because this was the only area where they could find rooms to rent. They weren't allowed to live anywhere else. There were signs in the window where they weren't allowed to live.

Mrs Fisher described discriminatory practice. She confirmed that the situation did change and that "People became more tolerant." She continued, "This is a multicultural country so people accept peoples' differences." I sought confirmation that there were localities where the immigrant Black population were discouraged from living. Mrs Fisher confirmed but then reaffirmed, "We all grew up together." Was Mrs Fisher shocked by her own revelation? She continued by stating where she had attended school and reaffirmed that she had not personally suffered from discrimination. The dialogue continued to confirm the value of telling stories.

The honesty and trust created after 13 minutes of dialogue gave Zahra the confidence to ask a question that, in the way she spoke, acknowledged her doubt in asking it. She took time to formulate her inquiry and her speech was peppered with pauses and hesitation. Mrs Fisher admitted that she did not understand. Zahra's theory was that the Black community does not have equity in the same way that the white community does. The full transcript is recorded below.

Zahra: How would you feel if a prime minister or someone came up to your manager or someone came up to you and said that umm . . . or the king . . . came to you.

Mrs Fisher: So, someone really high up.

Zahra: They came to you and they said they came to you . . . black people . . . and they said um . . . I'm going to change a rule and um . . . you people are no longer . . . the blacks . . . and you . . . um . . . you are equally free with the whites. How would you feel then?

Mrs Fisher: I don't really understand what you're trying to ask me.

Zahra continued to have difficulty shaping her thoughts. Again, she was hesitant. Did Zahra feel intimidated? Or was she questioning her own assumptions? She struggled with her perceptions. She imagined a scenario where it was asked "Do all Blacks have to live here?" Zahra had asked Mrs Fisher to imagine a scenario where Black people are restricted to living in specific locations. Zahra had had the confidence to ask. She was a child trying to define her world and how the wider world works. Mrs Fisher sought clarification by restating, "A bit like in South Africa where there was distinct segregation where white people lived in one part and Black people lived in another part."

The transcript provides evidence of the value of creating opportunities for adults and children to engage in open, honest and thought-provoking discourse. It is evident that these opportunities are powerful and healthy. The child was learning from the adult and the adult was learning from the child. Mutual respect was evident. The focus was on the shared learning and development of shared understanding.

It was not long before the girls wanted to share what they were saying and learning with other children in a school assembly. They identified a need for anti-racist and anti-bullying champions. These champions would be children who had shown that they had been proactive in anti-discriminatory practice and had demonstrated this to others.

The girls' chat group and the School Council formulated a plan to launch the One World project. The girls designed a One World badge which depicted a globe with two clasped hands encircling the world, one Black and one white. Children were to be selected having met their identified criteria. The criteria were based on anti-bullying and anti-racist strategies. The girls' chat group teamed up with other children from Year Six. They planned and prepared a One World assembly to disseminate to other primary schools in the local authority. This included the presentation of a box of badges and certificates so that the One World project could extend beyond the school.

Shazia's story

Shazia gave permission for her journal to be used as fieldwork data. She had made the commitment to write in her journal daily and her story illustrates her leadership learning and her role as a learning leader and leading learner. Shazia benefitted from the opportunity to write openly about her experiences and what she had done. She wrote: "*I am feeling very angry because of the silly things that I did in school and I can't get it out of my head.*" Shazia expressed her emotions and her developing awareness of the impact of her actions on others. She continued: "*I am feeling very pleased because I am slowly starting to hate myself for doing the things I have done in the past.*" Shazia used powerful words to describe her emotions. The notion of being 'happy' because you are 'hating' yourself is a challenge for me to comprehend. Shazia was telling her tale and illustrated the power of narrative and autobiographical discourse (Rosen, 1998). Shazia reflected on her past words and actions. She articulated that she has hurt the feelings of others.

Shazia clarified her thoughts and her need for others to trust her. She wrote, "People will start to trust me again." Shazia developed her sense of systems consciousness and social justice. She wrote, "There will be no bullying in our school." Shazia's interpretation of bullying related to the notion of 'making fun' of another person due to a specific personal characteristic. These characteristics related to a person's skin colour, their learning, their name, their facial features and their weight. Shazia wrote in the second person applying the phrase "when you make fun of." There was an openness and honesty communicated. Shazia's perception was one where bullying could be an isolated incident rather than a persistent and recurrent act. There is no acknowledgement that Shazia could be a victim herself.

Shazia continued to develop her systems consciousness through the process of reflective journaling. She wanted to have a positive impact on others. This is evidence of the power of reflection (Schön, 1983). Over the period of a week she wrote:

> "I think I can improve this behaviour by setting a good example for the youngers."
> "I feel excited that it is Eid tomorrow and we can celebrate with our familys."
> "I feel happy because I have had an excellent Eid and I got £90 for my Eid money."
> "I am feeling really happy because I don't do bullying anymore."
> "I feel happy because the girls' chat room has helped me to improve my behaviour."

In four of these five extracts, Shazia starts with her feelings. I adopted this phraseology in my reflective journaling in challenging times, when freefall writing was not productive.

Figure 5.11 is the first of two images from Shazia's reflective journal to be presented here. It confirms Shazia's need to gain trust from everyone at school. Shazia's story illustrates connectivity with her real-life experiences. Her narrative presents evidence of relief and release. Shazia found strength in her faith and cultural heritage. Her learning connects with her emergent sense of identity, place and belonging (Charlton et al., 2011; Wyse et al., 2010). Shazia identified the characteristics of a good friend to be a person who fights for you and that they need to be loving, good, honest and helpful.

Shazia continued her journaling, reflecting on aspects of her daily life. Empathy was an emergent theme. For the first time Shazia considered the notion that she could be a victim and how that could make her feel. She wrote:

> "If people bullied me because I was a different colour I would feel left out and like nobody cares about me."
> "I walk home with my friends, my brother and his friend we talk as a group and so everybody is equal."

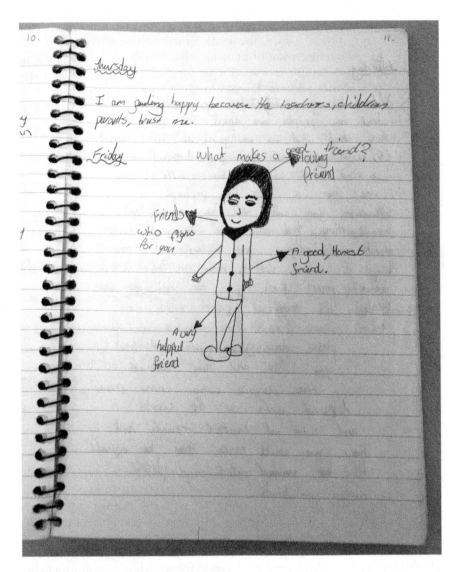

Figure 5.11 What makes a good friend?

Shazia stated her perception that the learning community was an organisation where equity was undeniable. "*I feel happy in school because everyone is treated equally.*" She conveyed a sense of determination: "*I feel happy because the bullying in school will stop.*" Shazia wrote stories about overcoming bullying and racism in school based on her personal experience, retold in the third person and so a change in voice was evident. She was coming to terms with her actions and a demonstration of inquiry through narrative and the power of narration in a search for clarity and strength.

There was once three girls who were best of friends and had always been, they played and chatted. The next day they did something, it was bad and not caring. They got in lots of trouble and instead of learning came trouble. The headteacher explained to them not everyone likes what you like. The three girls were worried. They went home and thought and thought about it. The next day they started the day fresh and everybody was happy and so were the teachers in the Primary School.

Figure 5.12 is further evidence of Shazia's preoccupation with bullying. She tells of a girl being bullied by a group of boys.

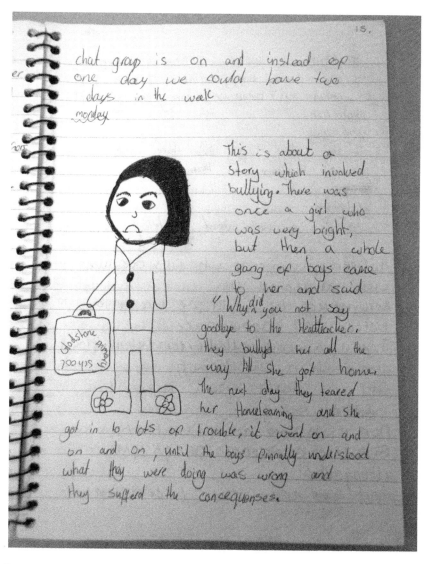

Figure 5.12 Shazia tells a story

Shazia acknowledged people who care for her and revealed that she sensed she was now trusted by others. This is indicative of her developing systems consciousness. She wrote: "*I am feeling happy because the teachers and children are starting to trust us once again. And we can stop thinking about the past. And start to think about the future.*"

Shazia began to use her reflective journal as a place to test out her script for a school assembly. Shazia applied the conventions of a school assembly by introducing the theme of the assembly, preparing her audience for what they might expect and inviting the audience to reflect for a moment by bowing their heads and closing their eyes. Shazia's dialogue became increasingly directed towards the audience. Her use of language becomes increasingly refined. Here is Shazia's final version.

> *Today we are going to think about bullying and racism and why it should stop. Bullying and racism is a sign of disrespect to the people that surround you and community you live in. Bullying can happen in many different ways for example if you are fat, if you are short, if you are tall and many other ways.* BUT BULLYING CAN STOP. *But of course with the help of adults and together we will all work together as a team. We would like people to be treated equally in our city.*

Shazia's journaling evidenced and acknowledged the notion that taking responsibility for our actions can impact on how a child behaves as a learner. Shazia wanted to put the past behind her. "I am feeling happy because we have forgotten the PAST and just thinking about the FUTURE." Shazia applies capital letters for emphasis. Shazia's use of recurring phrases appeared to be her security and prompt for further reflections. This repetition of statements is a reminder of how followers of faith repeat prayers in their worship. For example, in Islam there are special prayers for daily routines and in Christianity the Lord's Prayer is always spoken at a service.

In conclusion, the implications of not creating this opportunity was that Shazia would have continued to hurt the feelings of others, become increasingly confused and potentially become a victim herself when she transferred to a secondary school where she would be in a minority. Journaling provided Shazia with the opportunity to state how she felt, how sorry she was and her need for forgiveness.

Shazia's story confirmed that children benefit from the opportunity to reflect on social justice. They require the time and space to articulate thoughts to develop understanding. Shazia's dialogue highlights how active dialogue about a traumatic situation became a place for changing attitudes, for developing systems consciousness to the extent which Shazia became a school leader in her drive for social justice and equality. The implications are that in learning communities these opportunities have to be created to develop every child's capacity to articulate and explore serious issues and dilemmas.

I now articulate the theoretical underpinning that has influenced my leadership learning.

Leadership and Learning: A Systemic Approach

There has been a period of extensive, rapid change and development in primary school education in England over the last 25 years. One consequence of this is that school leadership has diversified, become more complex and a focus for educational research (Gronn, 2010). With an increasingly performance-oriented educational landscape (Watkins, 2005), the need to address and improve school leadership is imperative. Leadership theory serves its purpose in provoking leaders to reconsider and reflect on their roles and responsibilities. Designated leaders are reminded that they do not hold the exclusive rights to leadership. Everyone benefits from identifying leaderfulness within a learning organisation. It is evident that different leadership theorists favour specific perspectives on leadership, however what is also evident is that there are many connections and networks to be identified between the theories. Leithwood and Levin devised a framework to illuminate the connectivity between a school leader's "learning experiences, their practices and their effect on student learning" (Leithwood & Levin, 2004). They maintain that it is not possible to claim an improvement in school development on one aspect of school life such as designated leadership but identified ten variables that have the potential to impact on student learning. Their theory supports a systemic approach to research in education where these variables are recognised and taken into consideration. Leaders, whether designated or not, have a rich resource to inform, influence and facilitate their leadership learning. Within the context of the research project I have touched upon here, the selected theories that have influenced my praxeological inquiry are pedagogical leadership (NCSL, 2004), andragogical leadership (John, 2011) and the notion of a systemic approach to school leadership.

The Leadership Development Web emerged and evolved during my PhD studies as shown in the 'Leadership and Learning: A Systemic Approach' diagram (Figure 5.13). The essence of Whitaker's ideas remains (2009) but the processes of co-construction benefit from taking account of the research evidence and the influence of other theorists including Fullan (2005), Robinson (2012) and Marshall (2004). I finally identified the following as the six aspects of 'Leadership and Learning: A Systemic Approach':

- Systems consciousness
- Andragogical leadership and learning
- Pedagogical leadership and learning
- Wellbeing
- Social justice
- Organisational learning

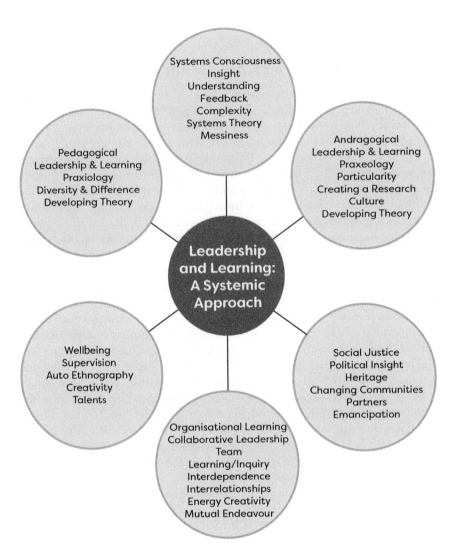

Figure 5.13 Leadership and Learning: A Systemic Approach

A systemic approach values processes of networking, working in collaboration and a constructivist approach to developing processes, ways of thinking and acting (Whitaker, 2009). For the purposes of my PhD research project a systemic approach to school leadership is defined as one that develops everyone's ability to identify process, acknowledge the value of seeing the whole and the patterns established by the parts within. It recognises the dynamic nature of the relationships between the parts and focuses on how things work together rather than with what they are like. A systemic approach to school leadership values and focuses on the interrelatedness and the interdependence of all phenomena. It values integration and autonomy.

I acknowledge the interconnectivity between leadership and learning and in this process of theory making I recognise an emergent systemic approach to leadership and learning. The notion of 'systems consciousness' is identified as an aspect of this systemic approach. Insight, understanding, feedback, complexity, the theoretical underpinning and messiness are key constructs to a systemic approach to organisational leadership.

Both pedagogy and andragogy in terms of leadership and learning are identified as key aspects of a systemic approach. Child learning processes and adult learning processes are connected but are valued for their distinctiveness and they invite different approaches. Within 'pedagogical leadership and learning' and 'andragogical leadership and learning' resides an acknowledgement of praxeological processes (Pascal & Bertram, 2012) to support and develop organisational inquiry and the emergence of new perspectives on theory. I have struggled with Whitaker's constructs, for example, the separation of 'theory and practice' from research and therefore a praxeological approach is favoured (Whitaker, 2009).

Within pedagogical leadership and learning, 'diversity and difference' are identified to recognise the necessity for the learning community to be active in building its knowledge and understanding of the contextualisation of its locality and demography. Within andragogical leadership and learning, *particularity* is included in recognition of the value of attention to detail alongside that systemic view of the bigger picture. The aspect of andragogical leadership embraces the notion of creating a research culture.

Cooperative and collaborative inquiry are located well within the concept of organisational learning and provide the starting point for professional development through action research methods and methodology. These are strong strategies, which create sustainable organisational improvement, as each member of the school learning community takes responsibility and is accountable for their learning and their contribution to the whole organisation. The aspect of organisational learning subsumes interdependence and interrelationships, the generation of energy and creativity in striving for mutual endeavour.

There are two more aspects of 'Leadership and Learning: A Systemic Approach' to be considered. As shown in Figure 5.13, these are wellbeing and social justice.

Wellbeing has emerged as significant for the learning community I worked in. Due regard for a person's wellbeing is recognised as the way adults and children can build their resilience to meet life's challenges. Supervision is identified as the strategy for supporting adults in the learning community. Opportunities for engagement in auto-ethnography, including the creation of leadership narratives, have been shown to further enrich a person's wellbeing and confidence to take on their responsibilities, whether a child or an adult. The identification of what nourishes us as human beings is recognised and encourages us to pursue ways to feed our creativity and acknowledge our talents.

The aspect of social justice had a resonance throughout the research process. I suggest that we cannot be afraid to ask difficult and challenging questions of ourselves and of others. To be empowered to follow challenging lines of inquiry for the development of political insight is essential. This, combined with deepening knowledge and understanding of heritage, our changing communities and our community partners, generates the motivation to make a difference, connects with action research methodology and the goal of emancipation.

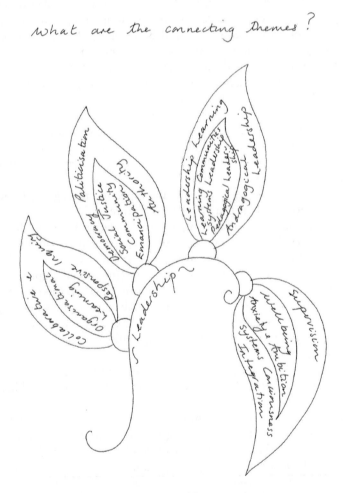

Figure 5.14 Our connecting leadership and learning themes

I acquired the resource to research, to explore and discover and ultimately present a critique on leadership theory and represent that theory considering my findings. It is now a part of me. I cannot separate the personal and the professional and I continue to revisit, refine, develop and disseminate.

To develop a resilient, sustainable and responsive paradigm in school education, I advocate collaborative approaches to organisational development. It takes longer but the difference made is more effective and deeper.

If it is true and genuine that education professionals and government officers want to embed the idea of a formal education system that is underpinned by a moral purpose then there is an onus on all involved, children and adults, to create safe places for open dialogue. However, practitioners need properly funded supervision to support these dialogic processes concerning all aspects of their work with children and young people. It is my hope that this chapter will inform learning communities in their future interactions, reflections and commitment to act. In my final visualisation and to conclude my contribution, I illustrate the connecting themes of this leadership book (Figure 5.14).

Note

1   Gladstone Primary School Council, Peterborough, 2010.

References

Alexander, R. (ed) (2010) *Children, Their World, Their Education. Final Report and Recommendations of the Cambridge Primary Review*. London: Routledge.

Boog, B. (2014) Examplarian action research: ethics and methodology. Seminar Held at the Pen Green Research, Corby, 3rd & 4th April 2014.

Charlton, E., Wyse, D., Cliff Hodges, G., Nikolajeva, M., Pointon, P. & Taylor, L. (2011) Place-related identities through texts: from interdisciplinary theory to research agenda in *British Journal of Educational Studies*. Vol. 59, No. 1, March 2011, 63–74.

Edwards, C. (2009) *How to Read Pattern*. London: Herbert Press.

Elton-Chalcraft, S. (2009) *'It's Not Just About Black and White, Miss' Children's Awareness of Race*. Stoke on Trent, UK: Trentham Books.

Formosinho, J. & Oliveira-Formosinho, J. (2012) Towards a social science of the social: the contribution of praxeological research in *European Early Childhood Education Research Journal: Special Issue: Praxeological Research in Early Childhood: A Contribution to a Social Science of the Social*. Vol. 20, No. 4, December 2012.

Fullan, M. (2005) *Leadership and Sustainability. Systems Thinkers in Action*. London: Sage.

Gronn, P. (2010) Leadership: its genealogy, configuration and trajectory in *Journal of Educational Administration and History*. Vol. 42, No. 4, November 2010, 405–435.

John, K. (2011) Theoretical underpinnings of the NPQICL: inspiration and grounding. In Trodd, L. & Chivers, L. (eds) *Interprofessional Working in Practice: Learning and Working Together for Children and Their Families*. Maidenhead, UK: McGraw-Hill, Open University Press.

Leithwood, K. & Levin, B. (2004) Approaches to the evaluation of leadership programs and leadership effects. Prepared for England's Department for Education and Skills, February 2004.

Marshall, J. (1999) Living life as inquiry in *Systemic Practice and Action Research. Vol. 12, No. 2, 155–171.*

Marshall, J. (2001) Self-reflective inquiry practices. In Reason, P. & Bradbury, H. (eds) *Handbook of Action Research: Participative Inquiry and Practice.* London: Sage, pp. 433–439.

Marshall, J. (2004) Living systemic thinking: exploring quality in first-person action research in *Action Research.* Vol. 2, No. 3, 309–329.

Marshall, J. (2007) Finding form in writing for action research. In Reason, P. & Bradbury, H. (eds) *Handbook of Action Research* (2nd Edition). London: Sage.

Ministry of Education New Zealand. (1996) *Te Whariki. Early Childhood Curriculum.* Wellington: Learning Media.

NCSL. (2004) *National Professional Qualification for Integrated Centre Leadership (NPQICL) Participants' Guide 5. Leadership Concepts and Tools.* Nottingham, UK: National College for School Leadership (NCSL).

Pascal, C. & Bertram, T. (2012) Praxis, ethics and power: developing praxeology as a participatory paradigm for early childhood research in *European Early Childhood Education Research Journal: Special Issue: Praxeological Research in Early Childhood: A Contribution to a Social Science of the Social.* Vol. 20, No. 4, December 2012.

Richardson, R. & Miles, B. (2008) *Racist Incidents and Bullying in Schools.* Stoke on Trent, UK: Trentham Books.

Robinson, S. (2012) *School and System Leadership. Changing Roles for Primary Headteachers.* London: Continuum.

Rosen, H. (1998) *Speaking from Memory. A Guide to Autobiographical Acts and Practices.* Stoke on Trent: Trentham Books.

Schön, D. (1983) *The Reflective Practitioner. How Professionals Think in Action.* Farnham: Ashgate.

Senge, P. (2006) *The Fifth Discipline. The Art and Practice of the Learning Organisation* (2nd Edition). London: Random House.

Sharp, P. (2001) *Nurturing Emotional Literacy: A Practical Guide for Teachers, Parents and those in the Caring Professions.* Abingdon: David Fulton Publishers.

Watkins, C. (2005) *Classrooms as Learning Communities.* What's in It for Schools? Oxon, UK: Routledge.

Whalley, M. (1994) *Learning to be Strong: Setting Up a Neighbourhood Service for Under-Fives and Their Families.* London: Hodder & Stoughton.

Whitaker, P. (2009) *Applying Systems Theory to Leadership in Services for Children, Families and Schools – A Critical Review, with Suggestions for Future Developments.* Corby, UK: Pen Green Research.

Wyse, D. (2014) *Creativity and the Curriculum.* London: Institute of Education Press.

Wyse, D., Nikolajeva, M., Charlton, E., Cliff Hodges, G., Pointon, P. & Taylor, L. (2010) *Place-Related Identities Through Texts: An Interdisciplinary Analysis of Transculturality.* Cambridge, UK: University of Cambridge, Faculty of Education.

Chapter 6

Working together or pulling apart? How early years leaders and practitioners can encourage collaborative practice to flourish

Julie Vaggers

Introduction

Early, effective and integrated public service responses to the needs of children and families continue to be a cornerstone of National Policy. Leadership is known to be the key to successful collaboration, bringing together people who have not worked together before. This chapter aims to explore the challenges of leading and supporting people from different professional backgrounds to work together collaboratively.

As a headteacher, tutor and children's centre leader I was fascinated by the development of integrated early years services. My experience was that most attempts to collaborate stuttered, faltered or failed. I frequently observed tension and resistance when services were asked to work together to support families.

I strongly believe that families deserve the best from their public services. When professionals pull together, the services they offer are responsive, resilient and consistent. They can then mirror the stability, sensitivity and coherence expected of families. Successful collaborations can increase capacity and resources, share the risks and create opportunities for learning (Sandfort & Milward, 2010, p. 148). In practice rather than seizing the *collaborative advantage* too often *collaborative inertia* sets in (Huxham & Vangen, 2006). This inertia is mired in difficulties, in communicating and gaining agreement to act, differences between parties on organisational purpose, procedures and structures, professional languages, accountabilities and power. "Collaborative inertia captures what happens very frequently in practice: the output from a collaborative arrangement is negligible, the rate of output is extremely slow, or stories of pain and hard grind are integral to successes achieved" (ibid., p. 60).

I decided to research and explore with a number of my colleagues why *collaborative inertia* happens and consider ways to enable *collaborative advantage* within a *complex adaptive system* (Lichtenstein et al., 2006). My doctoral studies as part of a Community Learning Group at Pen Green Research Base gave me an opportunity to better understand how to create a climate where everyone felt part of a shared endeavour, pulling together rather than pulling apart. This research discovered useful and creative responses to the barriers and tensions of *collaborative inertia* and *turf wars* (Raham, 1998). We developed practical leadership strategies in order to maximise any opportunities, so that cultural and professional differences could be better understood, respected and protected. As leaders we explored new approaches and made professional connections which enabled us to travel across the borderlands between interprofessional cultures. I was better able to support colleagues in their leadership of integrated settings

In collaboration with ten other heads of early years settings, I focussed on researching *how* leaders can best lead the development of integrated services, considering both process and context. As James Spillane and colleagues (2004) point out in their work on the distribution of school leadership, there is very little data that illustrates the "how" of leadership, "that is knowledge of the ways in which school leaders develop and sustain those conditions and processes believed necessary for innovation" (p. 4).

In this chapter I discuss:

A   Who are the potential collaborators in an early years setting? What are the barriers to working together effectively? What does working together for *collaborative advantage* look like?

B   I shall provide a range of practical activities (Boundary Objects) for use in group exercises with professional partners and organisations, including building trust to compare compatibilities and explore social processes (Jenkins & Jenkins, 2006), a mythical cultures map (CMPS, 2002), a conceptual model of integration represented as an ongoing journey with three stages: Emerging, Developing, Secure and a values contract (Vaggers, 2014).

C   I will share four leadership processes that can be used for personal reflection. I also explore thoughtful actions called borderlands to help us navigate between new professional worlds and hopefully encourage integrated working to flourish. In a constantly evolving and moving landscape, understanding these leadership processes with overlapping borderlands can be helpful when travelling through unfamiliar interprofessional service paradigms. These processes or criteria could help leaders practice their craft and create the climate in which integrated working can flourish. They are:

1   **Systemic thinking** and the reactions that occur through personal interactions need to be considered with intent. There is a need for early years leaders to think systemically with insight and a deep understanding of complexity (Whitaker, 2009; Senge, 1990; Wheatley, 2007). Integration can be viewed as a continuum that shifts from

loose to *tight*. Interactional shifts at the right moment can develop this continuum from an emerging integrative position into more secure practice. The borderland between systemic thinking and relationships is: *interactions*. Consider sharing our interconnected struggles and difficulties, identifying patterns that undermine team communications, as well as considering our own generative and degenerative behaviours, helping build successful collaborative practice.

2   **Build and rebuild relationships** constantly. Colleagues come and go so this work must never stop. Leaders must champion relational practice, promote feminine values and the importance of relationships (Ancona et al., 2007; Fletcher, 2001; Putnam, 2000; Anning et al., 2010). When building relationships appears difficult, there may be leverage points that when recognised can shift deeply entrenched professional roles and identities to build new ways of working together. Making deliberate and practical attempts to establish, nourish and grow relationships across professional divides may help leaders to embed an approach that can be revisited when new personnel arrive and staffing changes occur. Collaboration and a shared commitment take time. Andrea Wild and Geoffrey Meads (2005) write in their research into health and social care interprofessional collaboration, real roots are required to embed collaborations: "Collaboration is the tortoise to the hare of competition" (p. 153). Building trusting relationships requires integrity, authenticity and honest curiosity. In order to be a relational champion individual integrity and fairness are critical. The borderland between building relationships and self-actualisation is *integrity*. This is defined by constancy, congruity, reliability and builds trust (Bennis, 2009). Expecting this of oneself and others leads the collaborative process in a nourishing manner and encourages humble inquiry.

3   **Self-actualisation** is a continual process of working to one's full potential, being aware of one's own identity and with a strong sense of personal authority and moral responsibility (Goldstein, 1934; Maslow, 1943; Rogers, 1995). With a strong sense of self it is possible to immerse oneself in the process of working together with others, to become fully involved and enjoy the process. Self-actualisation requires encouraging realism, having the courage to be imperfect; being realistic about what is achievable and accepting responsibility for one's humanity. This releases energy and *flow* (Csikszentmihalyi, 2002), the borderland across which one must travel to develop new problem-solving approaches, and a creative response to building shared meanings and potential connections.

4   **Alternative approaches to solving complex problems** may be hard to find if organisations are unable to embrace research and professional development. Encouraging people to work together requires

everyone to strive to make sense of collaborative endeavours through stimulating research that embraces paradox. Early years settings could utilise knowledge of inter-organisational relations and the theory and practice of collaborative advantage better. Exploring new domains enhances one's own understanding. If this is carried out with *sensitivity* it can help to develop multiple perspectives and make the imagined real. It is necessary to interpret and translate visions and values. Leaders can help to facilitate understanding across and between agencies. Ros Tennyson (2005), co-director of both the Partnering Initiative and of the Partnership Brokers Accreditation Scheme, describes how the leadership role has shifted from figurehead to catalyst with new non-traditional leaders needing the: "capacity to create clarity in the midst of our complex, information-rich, rapidly moving, politically unstable and economically unequal world" (p. 9).

To conclude, this chapter will identify practical ideas and approaches to deliberately surface answers as to how to develop a culture of working together to serve families and children rather than pulling apart and creating a public disservice.

A: Who is working together?

Early years practitioners and leaders are frequently asked to collaborate with other services to improve a child's life chances. Figure 6.1 demonstrates the range of professionals who may be asked to work together to support a family. In addition to those depicted there may also be relationships with the justice and crime prevention system, youth services, sport and culture, housing, employment services and the private and voluntary sector.

What does working together for collaborative advantage look like?

Collaborative advantage is: "a world in which it is possible to feel inspired" (Huxham & Vangen, 2006, p. 3). It creates energy, access to resources, a shared risk, efficiency, co-ordination and seamlessness; it prevents repetition, omission, divergence, conflicting activities. It creates opportunities for learning, dissemination and addresses moral issues that will only be alleviated through a multi-organisational response, (ibid., p. 7). This was described by research participants as a *secure approach* to working together. *Collaborative inertia* was described as a *loose approach*.

The best way to describe these approaches to working together in the early years is to give two contrasting examples.

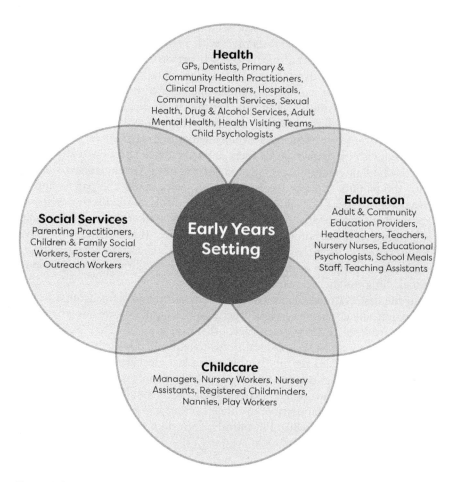

Figure 6.1 Potential partners in the early years

The first example represents a *loose approach* with a likely outcome of *collaborative inertia*.

A child psychologist is running a service for families with children under 2 in the local area. His manager wants him to run this service in a local childcare setting. He pops in to the early years setting and arranges to see clients there and agrees to give the clients a copy of the setting's leaflet and timetable. He will meet with staff at the centre individually for one-off meetings if they want to discuss their professional practice. He does not attend meetings in the centre or have an office space there. The setting does not know who the psychologist is working with.

The second example explains how the professionals might work more effectively with the child and family and achieve *collaborative advantage*.

The managers of both services meet with their staff teams and discuss the best way to maximise the impact of each person's professional expertise in order to achieve positive long-term outcomes for the children and families. A child psychologist works on a one-to-one basis with a parent identified as having parenting issues. It is agreed that the child psychologist also attends a weekly group for all these parents and their children and works with an early years practitioner to share and explore parenting experiences. The child is provided with up to two days a week childcare. Each child has a key worker. Parent-child interactions are videoed for the child psychologist to explore with the parents and key worker. The key worker and the parent and the psychologist meet to develop shared goals, and this also helps to develop the key worker's professional development. The key worker shares how the child is learning with the family. The psychologist gives the staff training. Where appropriate specific fathers' sessions are delivered. Each family receives eighteen weeks of support; at the end of this time the family and the professionals discuss progress and agree on the next steps.

In the first example the motivation is one-sided and stems from a need to geographically co-locate services. The second example shows how the professionals are keen to learn from each other's perspective. They put both the child's learning and psychological needs together in a holistic way to benefit the child, family and setting. In this example a great deal of time, planning and resources has gone into making a shared commitment to collaborate in reality. Huxham and Vangen (2006) advise against collaborating unless the potential for real collaborative advantage is clear; it is generally best, if there is a choice, to avoid it (p. 80). Put bluntly, don't do it unless you must.

The barriers that prevent people from working together

Historically in Britain silos of practice developed. Education, health and social care developed their own professional standards and therefore unique traditions and went on to develop separate cultures, systems, qualifications, beliefs about practice, terminology, funding sources, benefactors, budgets, departments, unions, legislation and inspection. The historical development of these professional silos is important to understand. The barriers to integrated working created by these silos can be immense and problematic, as Devita and Hillman (2006) describe in their work on the political, sociological and political barriers to medical emergency team implementation:

Teaching the various health professionals exclusively their own profession creates a tendency towards cultural and intellectual isolation. . . . The intellectual and role isolationism sets up a system of ownership, competition and egocentricism, and is perhaps the foundation for blame when things go wrong.

(p. 93)

Early years leaders raised the following issues as barriers to integrated working:

- Recruitment delays
- Different visions/perceptions from professionals of what an integrated service was
- Lack of time
- Resistance to change
- Preference for old ways of working
- No opportunities to develop new skills for a new way of working
- Juggling numerous roles and responsibilities
- Lack of experience

My research found that when services were brought together to work on new initiatives very little time was given to building up a clear vision and framework for these collaborations. Implementation was frequently rushed and there were few if any opportunities to build a shared commitment to working together and to explore new professional paradigms.

If people cannot have the time to discuss whether working together is better than working separately, joint working is likely to fail. There has to be an agreement that sharing expertise will be more productive and benefit all parties. There have to be clear outcomes that are recognised by all parties. If this is not the case then why collaborate in the first place? Leaders must influence other leaders to give their teams time and resources for joint planning and team building. Research by Professor Colin Eden, in collaboration with Chris Huxham and Siv Vangen (1989) has confirmed that the process of agreeing upon collaborative goals between organisations can be extremely difficult because of the variety of goals and constraints that different organisations and their individual representatives bring to a negotiating table. They conclude that those involved therefore often have to take action without clear specification of what the endpoint should be.

B: A range of practical activities (boundary objects) for group exercises with professional partners and organisations' boundary objects

As a research group we developed a range of practical activities to be used whenever there was an opportunity to meet with professionals from other services.

The following examples maximise opportunities to discuss the complexities of working together and develop shared ownership and outcomes. They surface the individual's capacity to work collaboratively. They have been designed to be used as interactive activities at meetings, training sessions or any shared discussions to increase understanding and build trust. They are also known as *boundary objects* that help people to map new professional territories and cross into unfamiliar lands.

The creation of boundary experiences, boundary groups and organisations, boundary object creation and their use is discussed by Barbara Crosby and John Bryson (2010) from Minnesota University. They explored integrative leadership and the creation and maintenance of cross-sector collaborations. They concluded that collaborative exercises such as mapping and navigating relationships support the cognitive, social and behavioural complexity required in integrative leadership, especially since cross-sector collaborations are more likely to form in turbulent times. Boundary objects: "are typically important in helping people create shared meaning. Boundary objects are physical objects that enable people to understand others' perspectives. Beyond that, boundary objects can facilitate the transformation of diverse views into shared knowledge and understanding" (ibid., p. 220).

Trevor Chandler (2006) identified that the ability of professionals to work together was impacted by the many variables which affected their capacity to engage in the integrative process.

> For any worker, whether they are an educationalist, health worker, social worker or volunteer, there are three levels that will influence their practice within multi-disciplinary teams and external agencies:
>
> 1. Their personal life history and what has motivated them to work in their chosen profession.
> 2. Their professional background, training and experience.
> 3. The agency in which they work and what the beliefs, values, aims and objectives of the agency are.
>
> (p. 142)

These activities are designed to allow thoughtful action and to build trust. Building trust requires a shared commitment to getting to know and understand each other's life history, professional experience and heritage. Discussing the questions in the examples below begin this critical process.

Activity 1: exploring compatibilities and building trust

Building a trust triangle was designed to compare compatibilities and explore social processes. It was based on the work of Jon and Maureen Jenkins (2006) and their work on the disciplines of a facilitator. They identified nine disciplines of effective facilitators: Detachment, Engagement, Focus, Awareness, Action, Presence, Interior Council, Intentionality and a Sense of Wonder.

These were then aligned to three paths of development: Regarding Others (Detachment, Engagement and Focus), Regarding Life (Awareness, Action and Presence) and Regarding Oneself (Interior Council, Intentionality and a Sense of Wonder). I have adapted this to reflect the questions that early years professionals and partners could ask one another (Figure 6.2).

These questions are designed to build trust, knowledge and understanding. Creating long-lasting change requires a level of trust being built over time and a building of relationships. Warren Bennis identified in his book *Becoming a Leader* (2009) four critical ingredients that generate and sustain trust. They are constancy, congruity, reliability and integrity. He goes on to quote Francis Hesselbein, credited with turning around the Girl Scouts movement in America, "Short term thinking is the societal disease of our time" (p. 152). Collaborative inertia is peppered with short-term thinking, leadership challenges and changes, inconsistency and competition.

Andrea Wild and Geoffrey Meads (2005) write in their research into health and social care interprofessional collaboration, real roots are required to embed collaborations: "Collaboration is the tortoise to the hare of competition" (p. 153).

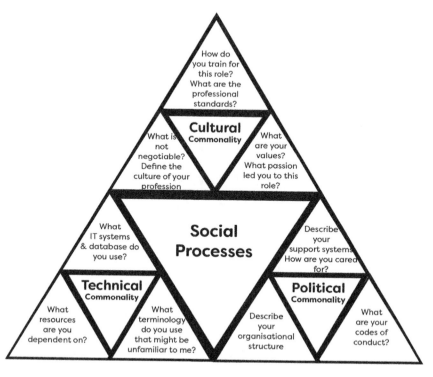

Figure 6.2 Social processes

Activity 2: exploring myths

Another exercise designed to grow roots and explore professional cultures and myths is the Mythical Culture Map. This exercise offers a deliberate intent to make explicit organisational rituals, routines, dynamics and stories. It was based on the work of Cranfield School of Management (CMPS, 2002) and an Organisational Culture Web. These components reflect the current culture of an organisation and also indicate the aspects of an organisation that must be changed. In other words these are the cultural change levers. These questions can surface many interesting stories and build relationships between professional partners (Figure 6.3).

Activity 3: exploring where we are on the journey towards the integration of services

The next example gives people who are working together an opportunity to audit the state of the integrative process at play. It can be helpful viewing working together as an ongoing journey. This helps those involved to recognise the ups and downs and ongoing nourishment that is required to keep the process going. Table 6.1 shows a conceptual model of integration with three

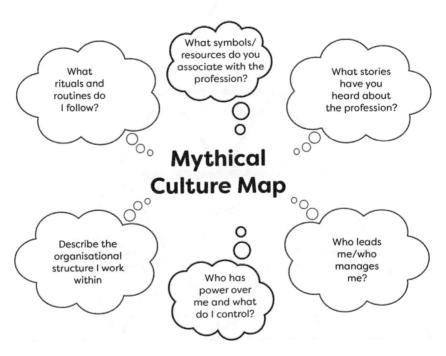

Figure 6.3 Mythical Culture Map

Table 6.1a Factors that support integrated working – a matrix

	Emerging	Conditions for growth	Developing	Shifts in my leadership	Confident
Relational nourishment	**The relationship between people is poor, inconsistent, lacking in trust and transparency with little contact.**	Recognise the need to be introduced. Choosing and being involved in the decision to work together. Understand the motivation to work together. Both parties feeling wanted and needed. Constant personnel: a regular familiar physical presence over time. Arrangements in place for two-way honest feedback. Having regular contact. Shared training. Shared Induction Learning together. Having opportunities for being more than your role: offering insights and other skills and strengths.	**Talking has started and relationships are developing.**	Openly acknowledging one's own ignorance about another service. Remaining open minded about change. Being generous. Being honest. Valuing everyone's expertise and knowledge. Being a listener. Being curious. Wanting to know about the person. Being open and friendly.	**The relationships have commonality, parity, breadth, multiplexity, continuity and directness.**

Table 6.1b Factors that support integrated working – a matrix

	Emerging	Conditions for growth	Developing	Shifts in my leadership	Confident
Strategic and structural robustness	**Information and knowledge about each other's services and its potential is unknown. No process is known to exist to develop collaborative vision building. Personnel may attend meetings but there is no resulting action, no proactive engagement.**	Multi agency delivery is planned in from the start. There is a deliberate intention to create a vision that is clear to all. Strategic managers involved from the start. Time given to building a shared vision. There is a vision and commitment to maintaining consistent personnel. A commitment to joint training. Shared budgets. Shared supervision. An understanding that changes in personnel will affect services and that resources will have to be front loaded to start developing a shared understanding and commitment each time personnel change.	**There is a shared commitment to shared planning of services but barriers exist, e.g. recruitment. Short-term pilot projects in place. Developing some protocols, in the process of developing a local forum for decision making.**	Everyone is being seen as a learner. Experimenting and trying it out for a while and reviewing how things are going. Establishing the time to discuss role expectations and limitations. Recognising the impact of the change process and being able to manage this. Developing shared aspirations. Developing a shared commitment to being creative and fearless.	**Services are planned collaboratively, shared vision building, and shared aims are clearly defined.**

Table 6.1c Factors that support integrated working – a matrix

	Emerging	Conditions for growth	Developing	Shifts in my leadership	Confident
Operational cohesion	**Each service keeps to its own remit. Neither party reaches out. There are no familiar ways of contacting one another.**	Clear lines of accountability for all aspects of the work. Input from all involved to develop the potential of a shared service. Being involved in recruitment from the start. Multi agency team meetings which ask and seek feedback – what is working well? Not so well? What would be better? Agreeing over time which meetings and training sessions to attend together. Lots of opportunities for two-way flow of communication. Shared goals for working together. Shared database. Useful and effective information sharing.	**Developing some protocols, working together when there is a joint plan for a family or child. Short-term pilot project. Occasional sharing of information.**	Questioning each other and asking is this good enough? Being flexible within transparent ethical boundaries. Having the courage to step out of traditional expectations of the role.	**Flexibility of response, joint case work, shared caseloads, shared planning, seamless flow of communication.**

Table 6.1d Factors that support integrated working – a matrix

	Emerging	Conditions for growth	Developing	Shifts in my leadership	Confident
Geographical synchronicity	**Rarely present in setting or no presence.**	Co-location. Synchronised sessions well-advertised locally. Connecting similar services on the same day. Connecting meetings on the same day as services. Establishing a shared system of knowing where each other are; when in and out of the centre. Being available. Co-creating a shared perspective into the needs of the local families and community; gaining deeper insights together. Training together. Close proximity: shared office space, working in close proximity. Co-located within the systems in the setting.	**Some synchronisation of services in locality.**	Acknowledging and addressing tensions, e.g. split line management arrangements.	**Co-located, close by – pram pushing distance.**

stages: emerging, developing and secure. It covers four areas considered key to working together:

A **Relational nourishment:** knowing one another well, building trusting relationships
B **Strategic and structural robustness:** building the systems for a shared vision and commitment
C **Operational cohesion:** building the infrastructure for shared policies and procedures
D **Geographical synchronicity:** avoiding the repetition, dilution, confliction of services in a locality

It also considers that if conditions are only beginning to emerge for working together what would help this improve (conditions for growth) and what the leaders can do to shift this even further (shifts in my leadership).

Through the use of these boundary objects a shared commitment to working together can emerge. Processes that embed these commitments can be formalised in a values contract such as the example below.

Activity 4: a values contract

These activities or boundary objects hopefully provide simple opportunities to help people striving to work together to clarify their ideas and help leaders guide, stabilise and steer these complex interactions.

This is an important part of the trust-building process. Chris Huxham and Siv Vangen (2010) describe this as the *Trust Building Loop*:

> Two factors are critical to building trust. The first is about the expectations of partners and formalising future potential together and agreeing aims. The second is about risk taking which requires enough trust to create a platform for future more ambitious collaboration.
>
> (p. 77)

A list of the benefits of joint working, such as in the example shown in Table 6.2 makes the value of working together explicit. These values can then be underpinned with processes that make these values overt and unambiguous.

Table 6.2 What I value in joint working and what might support this

I value that:	Processes we could put in place to support these values
You share information with me and keep me informed.	
We work together as part of a team.	

(Continued)

Table 6.2 (Continued)

I value that:	Processes we could put in place to support these values
You share your professional expertise. **You teach me new skills.** **You allow me to contact you for advice and ideas.** **You listen to me.** **You reassure me when I need a helping hand.**	

C: Four leadership processes for personal reflection

When it is not possible to shift thinking about working together in collaboration with others the only alternative may be self reflection and personal action. The research participants identified four themes and connected borderlands that might help provide insights into facilitating integrative processes (see Figure 6.4). Reflecting on this model might enable a more effective and secure platform for working together and developing collaborative advantage.

C.1 Systemic thinking

Take time to think about the forces and relationships that are shaping your behaviour and the behaviour of others as you attempt to work together.

This research illustrated the need for early years professionals to think systemically and reflect on the inter-related nature of integrated working. Peter Senge (1990), a senior lecturer in leadership and sustainability at the MIT Sloan School of Management, defined *systems thinking* as a key discipline for a learning organisation. Senge (1992) describes how this helps us understand the subtlest shifts occurring within our settings:

> At the heart of a learning organisation is a shift of mind – from seeing ourselves as separate from the world to connected to the world, from seeing problems as caused by someone or something "out there" to seeing how our own actions create the problems we experience. A learning organisation is a place where people are continually discovering how they create their reality, and how they can change it.
>
> (p. 12)

Senge believed that systems thinking would lead to a better understanding of how to make effective change and to be in tune with the natural and economic world.

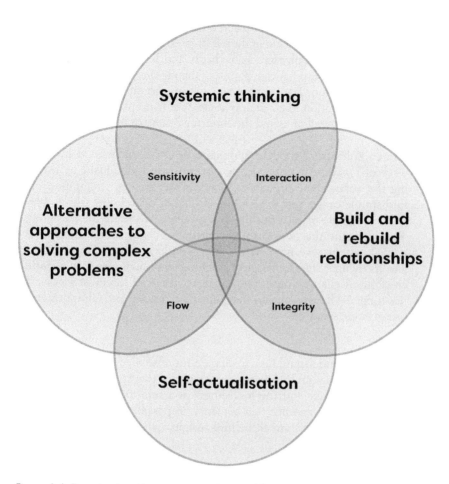

Figure 6.4 Four leadership processes that enable integrated working to flourish and four borderlands that connect these processes

Business and other human endeavours are also systems. They, too, are bound by invisible fabrics of interrelated actions which often take years to fully play out their effects on each other. Since we are part of that lacework ourselves, it's doubly hard to see the whole pattern of change. Instead, we tend to focus on snapshots of isolated parts of the system, and wonder why our deepest problems never seem to get solved. Systems' thinking is a conceptual framework, a body of knowledge and tools that has been developed over the past fifty years, to make the full patterns clearer and to help us to see how to change them effectively.

(p. 9)

Margaret Wheatley (2007), an organisational consultant and researcher, explored the connections between leadership and organisational change with the natural world even further. She believed in the self-organising capacity of *complex systems*. By looking at quantum physics, chaos theory and biology she challenged conventional thinking about leadership. Rather than traditional western approaches of control, imposition, fear, scarcity and self-interest she advocated creativity, learning and adaptation, the certainty cycles, the triumph of order over chaos, the innate artistry in all of us and the enduring beauty of the human spirit.

> The complexity of modern systems cannot be understood by our old ways of separating problems, or scapegoating individuals, or rearranging the boxes on an org chart. In a complex system, it is impossible to find simple causes that explain our problems or to know who to blame. A messy tangle of relationships has given rise to these unending crises. To understand this new world of continuous change and intimately connected systems, we need new ways of understanding. Fortunately, life and its living systems offer great teachings on how to work in a world of continuous change and boundless creativity. And foremost among life's teachings is the recognition that human creativity and commitment are our greatest resources.
>
> (p. 76)

When trying to understand how to create a more secure approach to working together, tuning into and thinking about systems theory might help. Accepting chaos, democracy and the foolishness of assumptions, recognising that individuals need one another, that control is impossible and that systems contain their own solutions are all helpful insights when creating a climate for integrated working.

> We need less reverence for the plan as an object and much more attention to the processes we use for planning and measuring. It is attention to the process, more than the product that enables us to weave an organisation as flexible and resilient as a spider's web.
>
> (Wheatley, 2007, p. 112)

The borderland to remember in this model is interactions. Research participants suggested that when interacting with potential partners it was helpful to reflect, log, consider and practice the following:

- Recognise the need to keep practicing; working together is a process not an end state
- Have conversations to explore why people think in the way that they do
- Prioritise building a shared vision

- Facilitate dialogues that identify patterns of team behaviours that can undermine learning
- Explore beneath the invisible dynamics of interrelated actions. Ask yourself: What's really going on here? Who is upset and why? What are they losing, gaining? What do I need to make explicit?
- Think about our interconnectedness to the difficulties we experience: Why is this hard for me? What is an achievable short-term goal? Can we make time for a coffee and a chat? Can I go to their place of work and walk a day in their shoes?

C.2 Build and rebuild relationships

All the participants in this research said that building relationships was critical for successful integrated working. This suggests that greater attention should be paid to the development of nourishing relationships.

Lord Laming, a former probation officer and social worker, in his report into the protection of children in England wrote: "Relationships are crucial; it's not about structures, it's about making it work out there for children" (2009, p. 36).

Deborah Ancona and her colleagues (2007) describe recent shifts in thinking about relational leadership:

> Traditional images of leadership didn't assign much value to relating. Flawless leaders shouldn't need to seek counsel from anyone outside their tight inner circle, the thinking went, and they were expected to issue edicts rather than connect on an emotional level. Times have changed, of course, and in this era of networks, being able to build trusting relationships is a requirement of effective leadership.
>
> (p. 3)

She advocated three ways to do this namely through:

1. Inquiring
2. Advocating
3. Connecting

Joyce Fletcher's work (2001) on leadership and the interaction of gender and power in the workplace and relational practice is particularly relevant to early years settings because it describes the relationship practice required for organisational transformation such as building webs of connections, teamwork, collaboration, partnership and learning. Fletcher's research study of female design engineers described how certain feminine relational practices such as mutuality, empowerment, empathy, vulnerability and growth-in-connection were often *disappeared* not because they were ineffective but because of gender and power issues:

> The disappearing dynamic helps us to see that there are powerful, gender-linked forces that silence and suppress relational challenges to organisational norms. The result is that behaviours such as relational practice are not merely difficult to encourage in organisations, they are systematically disappeared through a process in which they are coded as private-sphere (feminine) activities that stand outside the public-sphere (masculine) definition of work and competence.
>
> (2001, p. 116)

Fletcher (ibid.) argued that relational interactions have the power to affect change through mutual engagement and co-influence. Relational skills such as paying attention to emotional data, sensitivity to others' emotional realities, self reflection and fluid expertise have the potential to transform organisations. However her research identified that:

> People who engage in these practices are not simply unrewarded but instead are often misunderstood, exploited, or suffer negative career consequences for engaging in these activities. Those who enable others are likely to be characterised by co-workers as helpful or nice people rather than competent workers who are contributing to organisational learning.
>
> (p. 114)

Her research also showed that women were motivated to enact relational practice because of three underlying forces:

1   *Expectations*: The expectation that they will act relationally
2   *Skills*: The skill set to do so
3   *Beliefs*: A belief in a relational model of effectiveness

(p. 118)

It is through relationships that people develop attachments and make the connections that inspire a feeling of responsibility, rather than an obligation, towards common goals and objectives. Leaders could utilise Fletcher's four practical pushing strategies (naming, norming, negotiating and networking) to push back on the disappearing dynamic and make relational practice explicit and valued.

Building on the work of Robert Putnam (2000) about social capital and the need to bond as social groups and bridge across social divides in order to create community action and engagement, Dr George Otero from the Centre for Relational Learning (New Mexico) worked with the National College for

School Leadership to produce a leadership development programme called Better Together (2004–2007). He concluded that:

> Building and nurturing trustworthy relationships now becomes a pivotal leadership function. Developing such relationships gives rise to community. Community is the vessel and capacitor for working in multiagency settings to transform people's lives. Integrated interventions will depend on funding ways of working with people that transcend but include professional technique and language.
>
> (2009, p. 2)

The programme's fundamental theme was the centrality and importance of social capital:

> Human relationships are fundamental to educational and social development, and learning is a social process; communities only exist and thrive to the extent to which they develop the quality of human relationships.
>
> (Otero, 2009, p. 2)

Working together successfully acknowledges the existence of relationships without bounds, a relationship of mutuality and reciprocity as described by Buber (1970), an Austrian-born Israeli philosopher, as I and Thou (Kaufman, 1996). It also requires emotional intelligence. Daniel Goleman (1996) in his seminal work on emotional intelligence described five components of emotional intelligence including social skills that build networks, relationships, an ability to find common ground and persuasiveness. Kate Skinner (2010), an independent consultant in health and social care writing about leadership in social care, said: "The most likely path to success in collaborative working lies in the use of strong interpersonal skills" (p. 50).

Vincent Waldron (2000) reframed emotion at work as a relational phenomenon. During his studies into emotions at work he looked at the ways employees communicate during emotional, stressful or risky work situations. Organisational relationships cause intense emotion because they are governed by informal rules and expectations (unlike personal liaisons). At work, relationship difficulties often occur in public view and can quickly be communicated across an organisation. Relationships at work are part of many dynamics, including power, loyalty, betrayal, that can lead to true emotions being hidden and this can lead to resentment and fury. Often an unwritten code of relational ethics emerges for relational morality and emotional rights and obligations at work. Waldron suggests that relationship maintenance is crucial and is what most people do most of the time, and that most jobs require: "a kind of interpersonal emotional savvy if they are to be performed well" (p. 80).

Angela Anning, a research professor at the University of Leeds and a principal investigator at Birkbeck College, London, for the national evaluation of Sure Start, and her colleagues (2010) stressed the importance to create and maintain a sense of teamwork, casual coffee and corridor chats: "All these activities took time and yet seemed an essential part of creating a team that could function" (p. 48). Time spent on team nurturing and maintenance helped to build mutual respect and understanding. Professor Angela Anning, in her paper "Knowing Who I Am and What I Know" (2001), suggested that the destabilising of professional identities needed to be confronted and skilfully managed as new versions of knowledge were exemplified in new kinds of activities in integrated service settings. She went on to suggest that:

> Little attention has been given to two significant aspects of operationalising integrated services. The first is the challenge for workers of creating new professional identities in the emergent communities of practice (who I am). The second is for workers to articulate and share their personal and professional knowledge in order to create new versions of knowledge (what I know) for new ways of working.
>
> (p. 9)

The interconnected borderland between relational practice and the next theme of self-actualisation is integrity. The following suggestions for self reflection by the research participants require honesty and strong moral principles.

- Be hospitable, champion and nourish relationships.
- Facilitate relational co-ordination with cross functional teams. The more diverse the team is the more potential there is for alternative perspectives and solutions.
- Make humble enquiries. "Humble inquiry is the art of drawing someone out, of asking questions to which you do not already know the answer, of building a relationship based on curiosity and interest in the other person" (Schein, 2013, p. 2).
- Enable people to know one another as people and what they do.
- Analyse and respect heterogeneity. Appreciate the benefits of working with a diverse group of people with different backgrounds.
- Bask in continuity. If you have consistent personnel you don't have to keep starting to build networks, values and relationships over and over again.
- Make new connections when continuity is lacking. Always make the effort to build bridges with new personnel and apply the knowledge you have gained in how to do this.
- Give time, attention and communicate openly.

Asking questions and being curious is utilising a useful platform to tentatively develop relationships between professional groups.

Early years practitioners are part of many networks of relationships that are complex, changing, intersecting and fluid. An understanding of relational practice and an ability to champion both informal encounters and formal systems can help build social networks across agencies, develop reciprocity and interdependence.

The authors also identified conditions that promoted dialogue. These were:

1   Hospitality
2   Participation
3   Mindfulness
4   Humility
5   Mutuality
6   Deliberation
7   Appreciation
8   Hope
9   Autonomy

(West-Burnham, Farrar & Otero, 2007, p. 95)

Building relationships honestly and openly requires integrity. This is the borderland through which practitioners need to travel to the third theme of self-actualisation.

C.3 Self-actualisation

Early years practitioners can help enable integrated working to flourish by nourishing a stable and meaningful perception of self-actualisation. Self-actualisation means a continual process of working to one's full potential, being aware of one's own identity and with a strong sense of personal author-ity and moral responsibility (Goldstein, 1934; Maslow, 1943; Rogers, 1995). This approach may help settings manage in the face of constant change and in the current landscape of early years provision. Government policy is con-tinually shifting, often conflicting and changing at a rapid pace. Inspection demands are often perverse, conflicting and inconsistent. Phil Goss, senior lecturer in counselling and psychotherapy at the University of Central Lan-caster, illustrates this well in a letter in the Times Educational Supplement (31/05/13), in response to a number of letters from headteachers about the current pressure they are experiencing:

> The continuing lack of suitable candidates for school leadership posts remains no surprise while principals are being asked to put their careers on the line each time they are visited by England's school inspectorate

Ofsted. This debate would benefit from insights from depth psychology, as there are powerful unconscious influences at work here.

His argument is that leaders have come to embody society's aspirations for successful lives and hopes for a happier society. These leaders supposedly have the power and authority to make this happen by raising aspirations and ensuring student success. In this sense society is projecting on to leaders the "ideal parent figure". He continues, "We should stop seeing the school as the panacea for all that is faulty or inadequate about society, and therefore the repository for our own inadequacies when they do not live up to our unrealistic expectations". Leaders need to be consciously aware of these demands in order to be able to rationalise them.

It helps to be aware of the impact that degenerative changes have on self-actualisation and to ensure that we strive to maintain a way of being that is credible and trustworthy in such an emotive arena. An external view through the use of external supervision can be helpful in order to recognise absurd demands and rationalise adverse pressures. External supervision, that is a supervisor who does not have a line management role and is outside of the authority or governance of the organisation, can be helpful in gaining an external perspective. It may help to seek supervision from a professional in a different field. Sirpa Laitinen-Väänänen, a principal lecturer at the Teacher Education College in the JAMK University of Applied Sciences, Jyväskylä, Finland has carried out research that suggests that when the supervision is carried out by someone outside of the profession it provides more opportunities for enhancing critical thinking, reflective practice and self-directedness and does not get dominated by management tasks and expectations (Laitinen-Vaaananen, Talvitie & Luukka, 2007).

An external supervisor from a different professional body was seen as helpful by Lucy Chipchase and colleagues (2012). They suggest in their research on inter-professional supervision in an intercultural context that:

> In the inter-professional context, supervision from educators whose profession differs from that of the students can be a beneficial and rewarding experience for students. Characteristics of supervisors deemed important by students included being supportive, sensitive and realistic about what could be achieved, in addition to having prior inter-professional experience.
>
> (p. 469)

This Australian health research study reported that students and supervisors would have preferred to have a supervisor from each of the professions to be in attendance throughout the placement and that supervision from one's own profession was also needed as well. Local authorities, centre leaders and organisations managing children's centres may want to consider what inter-professional opportunities could be put in place that would complement profession-specific supervision. This could include discussion groups across agencies looking at current critical early years' issues such as free-birthing and herd immunity levels. This would provide opportunities to see early years work through the different professional lenses.

Trusting your own judgement and that of others is a critical leadership process. All professionals leave an impression in all their day-to-day encounters; they need to nourish and maintain a stable and resilient sense of self in order to nourish and build the confidence of the people around them. As Maya Angelou, American author and poet, wrote: "People will forget what you said. People will forget what you did. But people will never forget how you made them feel" (Kelly, 2003, p. 263). If professional partners are left with the feeling of being trusted and seen as capable this will leave a lasting impression. Carl Rogers (1995), American psychologist and one of the founders of the humanistic approach (or client-centred approach) to psychology, described the fundamentals of person-centred learning in his book *A Way of Being*. He described as a fundamental precondition:

> The leaders, or persons who are perceived as authority figures in the situation, are sufficiently secure within themselves and in their relationships to others that they experience an essential trust in the capacity of others to think for themselves, to learn for themselves.
>
> (p. 299)

He argued that when leaders are able to promote a person-centred approach, this led to a growth-promoting climate for mutual learning, which was deeper, more rapid and more pervasive.

A sense of good authority is also a critical leadership process for self-actualisation and a growth-promoting learning environment. Dr Karen John, a consultant psychologist and psychotherapist, describes good authority as:

> Claiming our "good authority" requires understanding our own and others' needs. . . . Being clear about our beliefs, values and boundaries, and about the requirements of those involved in a range of situations. . . . Confidence to be responsible for – and take and stick to decisions on behalf of others – sharing considerations with, and consulting with them when reasonable to do so. Ultimately, our sense of belonging and self-authority are emotionally felt, rather than known, and therefore, parents/leaders who doubt their belonging, worth and self-authority invariably have children/staff/citizens who also lack these essential feelings.
>
> (2012, p. 108)

To remain aware of your own identity, to be able to reflect on your role and responsibilities and remain grounded, the research participants suggested the following points to consider:

- Keep a balance in life and work to remain composed.
- Develop self awareness. Examine at various points of the day how you are feeling, take regular breaks, consider if you feel you have control, that you count, can connect and have courage (Lew & Bettner, 1990).
- Persist in being authentic. Are your words and actions congruent?
- Seek and external perspective. Supervision from someone outside of your professional background may be helpful.
- Develop your moral purpose. How do you uphold your current vision and values and what is your hope for the future?
- Tune into your emotions and trust your feelings.
- Act with integrity.
- Claim your good authority.
- Be open to new experiences.
- Be able to adjust and change.
- Look for new challenges and experiences.
- Be surprised and follow sparks of interest everyday.

Energy flows when fully immersed and involved in the process of working to your full potential. This is the third borderland to travel through that of flow. Csikszentmihalyi (2002) defined "flow" as a state of mind achieved when someone is fully immersed in a task, full of energy, fully involved and enjoying the process. This is the borderland that takes the children's centre leader from self-actualisation into the fourth leadership process in this study, that of creativity through the cultivation of flow.

C.4 Alternative approaches to solving complex problems

Looking outwards and exploring research from alternative paradigms can help leaders reframe the difficulties they encounter when developing integrated working processes. Chris Huxham and Siv Vangen (2006) point out: "It is far from straightforward to translate mainstream theories of leadership to collaborative settings" (p. 202). They describe the messiness, contradictions, tensions, dilemmas, multiple views, dynamics and frustrations of intention in collaborative work, and they go on to say: "For those involved in complex multi-party, multi location, interacting social collaborations, the complexity will be obvious, and the message here is about learning to love it and manage it" (p. 253).

Steve Cropper, professor of management at Keele University, and colleagues (2010) write that inter-organisational relations (IOR) research:

focuses on the property and overall pattern of relations between and among organisations that are pursuing a mutual interest while remaining independent and autonomous, thus retaining separate interests. For all IOR researchers, the aim is to understand the antecedents, content, patterns, forms, processes, management, or outcomes of relations between or among organisations.

(p. 9)

There is much that can be learnt from this field. It has a defined language and vocabulary that could be very useful in integrated centres. Table 6.3 presents the commonly used names, descriptors and acts used to describe inter-organisational entities which serve as a useful discussion document to help collaborators clarify their ideas and help leaders to guide, stabilise and steer these complex interactions. This is an important part of the trust-building process, described by Chris Huxham and Siv Vangen (2010) as the *Trust Building Loop*:

Two factors are critical to building trust. The first is about the expectations of partners and formalising future potential together and agreeing aims. The second is about risk taking which requires enough trust to create a platform for future more ambitious collaboration.

(p. 77)

Inertia is identified by Cropper and Palmer (2010) in their accounts of IOR dynamics. They identified the following barriers to collaborative working:

- **Threat-rigidity theory**

    A rigidity in established routines and responses means that IORs may avoid change, even when environmental pressures suggest that change

Table 6.3 Commonly used inter-organisational relations language

Names for inter-organisational entities

An alliance	An association	A cluster	A coalition
A collaboration	A consortium	A constellation	A cooperation
A federation	A joint venture	A network	A one stop shop
A partnership	A relationship	A strategic alliance	A zone

Descriptors for inter-organisational entities

Collaborative	Cooperative	Coordinated	Interlocking
Multi-organisational	Inter-professional	Joined up	Joint
Multi agency	Multi-party	Multi-organisational	Multiplex
Trans-organisational	Virtual		

Names for inter-organisational acts

Bridging	Collaboration	Contracting	Co-operation
Franchising	Networking	Outsourcing	Partnering
Working together			

Source: Cropper and Palmer (2010, p. 5).

is needed. Under threat or pressure managers become rigid in their thinking.

- **Learning disabled theory**

  IORs may fail to evolve as they become trapped by their own success, which inhibits them from responding appropriately to new conditions that emerge.

- **Stability theory**

  Forces for change are counter-balanced by forces which reinforce stability. IOR responsiveness may be inhibited where stability forces, embedded in IOR practices and routines, outweigh change forces. Familiar risk averse social networks may inhibit innovation (Cropper & Palmer, 2010, p. 649).

What these forces have in common is a resistance to change, resulting in inertia. Barbara Gray (2010), professor of organisational behaviour at Pennsylvania State University, describes eight intervention tasks and techniques which may exert some leverage over how partners are interacting and shifting a state of inertia. These include: visioning, convening, reflective intervening, process managing, problem structuring, brokering, conflict handling and institutional entrepreneurship.

Gray's elaborated description of tasks and techniques that help facilitators to shift inertia is similar to that of boundary spanning and networking which Anning and her colleagues (2010) identified in their research into children's centre leadership. They describe these leaders as being at the "cutting edge of practice development" (Anning et al., 2010, p. 93).

Chris Skelcher, professor of public governance at the Institute of Local Government Studies, and colleagues (2004) in their work on effective partnership and good governance, also identified the importance of boundary spanning:

> We identified a number of "boundary spanning" individuals who operated as entrepreneurs in creating new solutions to public policy problems. They had well-developed skills at mobilising political, financial and technical resources from a range of sources and bringing these to bear on particular needs and issues . . . these individuals start from the problem rather than the procedures. They are adept at managing the procedures, but only because this is necessary in order to gain access to resources that will deliver their objective.
>
> (p. 4)

The creation of boundary experiences, boundary groups and organisations, boundary object creation and their use is discussed by Barbara Crosby and

John Bryson (2010) from Minnesota University when they explore integrative leadership and the creation and maintenance of cross-sector collaborations. Collaborative exercises such as mapping and navigating relationships support the cognitive, social and behavioural complexity required in integrative leadership, especially since they argue that cross-sector collaborations are more likely to form in turbulent times. They define cross boundary groups as

> collections of actors who are drawn together from different ways of knowing or bases of experience for the purpose of coproducing cross boundary actions. . . . Adeptly designed forums allow boundary groups to have boundary experiences, defined as shared or joint activities that create a sense of community and an ability to transcend boundaries amongst participants.
>
> (p. 220)

Boundary objects: "are typically important in helping people create shared meaning. Boundary objects are physical objects that enable people to understand others' perspectives. Beyond that, boundary objects can facilitate the transformation of diverse views into shared knowledge and understanding" (p. 220). They conclude by saying: "The normal expectation ought to be that success will be very difficult to achieve in cross-sector collaborations, regardless of leadership effectiveness" (p. 227).

There is a great deal of pertinent knowledge and approaches in the IOR literature that is relevant to the leaders of children's centres. Its focus on the relationships between organisations and the processes that can be employed to encourage collaborative advantage is significant. Using this knowledge could support the facilitation of the climate required to develop a shared commitment to integrated working that will benefit children and their families. Michael Beyerlein, a professor for organisational leadership and supervision at Purdue University Indiana, and colleagues (2004) add that participation in collaborative activities often brings an intrinsic satisfaction, especially when things go well. The fun, playfulness and pleasure did not come from extrinsic motivation but from meeting complex challenges, performing effectively and deriving satisfaction from the success of these efforts: "in other words, fun is not the cause of their success; it is a by-product of their successful efforts. Therefore, by focussing on the other factors, the fun will be likely to follow" (p. 23).

Creative approaches can help bring professionals together and develop a better understanding of each other's cultural heritage. This requires a sensitive approach which is the fourth borderland between the themes. Professionals who want to work together need to be sensitive to difference, empathetic and ethical.

The following suggestions were made by the research group:

• Encourage joy as the optimal learning environment
• Make connections and appreciate the connectivity

- Visualise complexity through map making
- Build relationships through sense making
- Use boundary objects to bridge cultures and span boundaries
- Generate shared meaning
- Find innovative solutions
- Explore and understand identities and social experiences
- Make the imagined real
- Help people feel safe to explore new possibilities
- Develop multiple perspectives and multivocality (many or different meanings of equal validity)

Summary

In this chapter I have discussed collaborative inertia and the barriers to successfully working together across the professions. I have shared practical activities for groups and for individual personal reflection that have resulted from my doctoral studies work with a group of early years leaders.

Encouraging professions to work together to provide coherent services in the early years can be difficult. There is no simple linear pathway to follow. It requires a sophisticated, subtle and sensitive approach. It demands heightened levels of self awareness and self reflection. Hopefully some of these ideas, practical activities and self reflective exercises may help.

When working together goes well it is transformative. All the participants in the research experienced positive shifts in the development of collaborative advantage. They took advantage of every opportunity to shift their thinking, start conversations and construct thoughtful actions with other professionals.

I shall finish with the words of a research participant:

> Being part of the Leadership Research group had a huge impact on me at that time in my career. I sadly left the borough following voluntary redundancy shortly after the Leadership research sessions. However I took a new self-reflective approach to my leadership as I developed in new leadership posts in a new Local Authority. The most powerful aspect was the understanding that the importance of multi-agency working takes time and most importantly that time is well worth investing in, as effective relationships are vital to ensure successful outcomes for all children. I have a deeper respect for other professionals as I take more time to really listen and as a result I have gone on to develop stronger relationships across agencies.
>
> (March 2014)

References

Ancona, D., Malone, T.W., Orlikowski, W.J. & Senge, P.M. (2007) In praise of the incomplete leader. *Harvard Business Review*, 85(2), 92–100. Reprint R0702E (p. 1–9).

Anning, A. (2001) Knowing who I am and what I know: Developing new versions of professional knowledge in integrated service settings British educational research association annual conference, University of Leeds, 13–15 September 2001.

Anning, A., Cottrell, D., Frost, N., Green, J. & Robinson, M. (2010) *Developing Multi-professional Teamwork for Integrated Children's Services*. Berkshire: Open University Press.

Bennis, W. (2009) *On Becoming a Leader*. New York: Perseus Books.

Beyerlein, M., Johnson, D. & Bayerlein, S. (eds) (2004) Complex collaborations building the capabilities for working across boundaries. In *Advances in Interdisciplinary Studies of Work Teams*, Vol. 10. Oxford, UK: Emerald Group Publishing Limited.

Chandler, T. (2006) Working in multidisciplinary teams. In G. Pugh and B. Duffy (eds), *Contemporary Issues in the Early Years* (4th edition). London: Sage.

Chipchase, L., Allen, S., Eley, D., McAllister, L. & Strong, J. (11/2012) Interprofessional supervision in an intercultural context: A qualitative study. *Journal of Interprofessional Care* (Impact Factor: 1.48), 26(6), 465–471.

CMPS, Civil Service College Directorate (2002) *Navigating Change a Practitioners Guide for Delivering Change Successfully Within Public Services*. London: Cabinet Office.

Cropper, S., Ebers, M., Huxham, C. & Smith Ring, P. (2010) *The Oxford Handbook of Inter-Organisational Relations*. New York: Oxford University Press.

Cropper, S. & Palmer, I. (2010) Change, dynamics, and temporality in inter-organisational relationships. In S. Cropper, M. Ebers, C. Huxham and P. Smith Ring (eds), *The Oxford Handbook of Inter-Organisational Relations*. New York: Oxford University Press.

Crosby, B.C. & Bryson, J.M. (2010) Integrative leadership and the creation and maintenance of cross-sector collaborations. *The Leadership Quarterly*, 21, 211–30.

Csikszentmihalyi, M. (2002). *Flow the Classic Work on How to Achieve Happiness*. London: Random House.

Devita, M. & Hillman, K. (2006) In M. DeVita, K. Hillman & R. Bellomo (eds), *Medical Emergency Teams: Implementation and Outcome Measurement*. New York: Springer.

Eden, C. (1989) Using cognitive mapping for strategic options development and analysis (SODA). In J. Rosenhead (ed), *Rational Analysis in a Problematic World*, pp. 21–42. Chichester: John Wiley & Sons.

Fletcher, J.K. (2001) *Disappearing Acts Gender, Power and Relational Practice at Work*. Cambridge, MA: Massachusetts Institute of Technology.

Goldstein, K. (1934) *The Organism: A Holistic Approach to Biology Derived from Pathological Data in Man*. New York: Zone Books.

Goleman, D. (1996). *Emotional Intelligence*. London: Bloomsbury Publishing.

Goss, P. (2013) Who Wants to Step Forward and Lead? Anyone? *Times Educational Supplement*, 31.05.13.

Gray, B. (2010) Intervening to improve inter-organisational partnerships. In S. Cropper, M. Ebers, C. Huxham and P. Smith Ring (eds), *The Oxford Handbook of Inter-Organisational Relations*. New York: Oxford University Press.

Huxham, C. & Vangen, S. (2006) *Managing to Collaborate the Theory and Practice of Collaborative Advantage*. London: Routledge.

Huxham, C. & Vangen, S. (2010) Doing things collaboratively realising the advantage or succumbing to inertia? In Z. Van Zwanenberg (ed), *Leadership in Social Care, Research Highlights*. London: Jessica Kingsley.

Jenkins, J. & Jenkins, M. (2006) *The 9 Disciplines of a Facilitator: Leading Groups by Transforming Yourself*. San Francisco, CA: Jossey-Bass.

John, K. (2012) A case study of efforts to lead democratically when good authority is undermined. In *UK Adlerian Year Book 19th Volume* (2014 issue). London: Adlerian Society Institute For Individual Psychology.

Kaufman, W. (1996) *I and Thou Martin Buber*. New York: Simon & Schuster.

Kelly, B. (2003) *Worth Repeating: More Than 5,000 Classic and Contemporary Quotes*. Knoxville, TN: Kregel Academic & Professional.

Laitinen-Vaaananen, S., Talvitie, U. & Lukka, M.R. (2007) Clinical supervision as an interaction between the clinical educator and the student. *Physiotherapy, Theory and Practice*, 23, 95–103.

Lew, A. & Bettner, B. (1990) *A Parent's Guide to Understanding and Motivating Children*. Media, PA: Connexions Press.

Lord, L. (2009) *The Protection of Children in England: A Progress Report*. London: HMSO.

Lichtenstein, B., Uhl-Bien, M., Marion, R., Seers, A., Orton, J. & Schreiber, C. (2006) Complexity leadership theory: An interactive perspective on leading in complex adaptive systems. *Emergence: Complexity and Organization*, 8(4), 2–12.

Maslow, A.H. (1943) A theory of human motivation. *Psychological Review*, 50(4), 370–396.

Meads, G., Ashcroft, J., Barr, H., Scott, R. & Wild, A. (2005) *The Case for Interprofessional Collaboration in Health & Social Care (CAPIE)*. Hoboken: Blackwell Publishing.

Otero, G. (2009) *Unpublished Thinkpeice for National College of School Leadership*. Nottingham, UK: NCSL Better Together Handbook 2004–2007.

Putnam, R. (2000) *Bowling Alone: The Collapse and Revival of American Community*. New York: Simon & Schuster.

Raham, H. (1998) Full service schools. *School Business Affairs*, 64(6), 24–28.

Rogers, C. (1995) *A Way of Being*. New York: Houghton Mifflin Company.

Sandfort, J. & Milward, H.B. (2010) Collaborative service provision in the public sector. In S. Cropper, M. Ebers, C. Huxham and P. Smith-Ring (eds), *Oxford Handbook of Inter-Organisational Relationships*, pp. 147–174. New York: Oxford University Press.

Schein, E.H. (2013) *Humble Inquiry: The Gentle Art of Asking Instead of Telling*. San Francisco, CA: Berrett-Koehler.

Senge, P. (1992). *The Fifth Discipline the Art and Practice of the Learning Organisation*. London: Century Business.

Skelcher, D., Mathur, N. & Smith, M. (2004) *Effective Partnership and Good Governance: Lessons for Policy and Practice*. Birmingham: INLOGOV.

Skinner, K. (2010) Supervision, management and leadership think piece. In Z. Van Zwanenberg (ed), *Leadership in Social Care, Research Highlights*. London: Jessica Kingsley.

Spillane, J., Halverson, R. & Diamond, J. (2004) Towards a theory of leadership practice: A distributed perspective. *Journal of Curriculum Studies*, 36(1), 3–34.

Tennyson, R. (2005) *The Brokering Guidebook*. The International Business Leaders Forum (BLF) Cambridge University, The Partnering Initiative, Cambridge.

Vaggers, J. (2014) *How Can Children's Centre Leaders Best Enable Integrated Working to Flourish?* Unpublished Thesis, University of Leicester. Available at https://lra.le.ac.uk/bitstream/2381/32454/1/2015VAGGERSJPHD.pdf

Waldron, V. (2000) Relational experiences and emotions at work. In R. Vincent (eds), *Emotion in Organizations* (2nd edition). London: Sage.

West-Burnham, J., Farrar, M. & Otero, G. (2007) *Schools and Communities: Working Together to Transform Children's Lives*. London: Bloomsbury Publishing.

Wheatley, M. (2007) *Finding Our Way Leadership for an Uncertain Time*. San Francisco, CA: Berrett-Koehler.

Whitaker, P. (2009) *Applying Systems Theory to Leadership in Services for Children, Families and Schools – A Critical Review, with Suggestions for Future Developments*. Corby, UK: Pen Green Research (unpublished).

Index

Note: Page numbers in *italics* indicate figures or boxes on the corresponding page and page numbers in **bold** indicate tables on the corresponding page.

Abraham, K. 59
action inquirers 126
action research (collaborative inquiry): developing leadership and 121–123; emancipation and 31–33; impact on outcomes 123–125; journaling and 141–142; leader-researcher role in 129–136; overview of 7; praxeology and 151–152; rich picture depicting 149–151, *150*; stages of research 126–129; visualisation of 144, *145, 146, 147*, 148, *149*
activism: developing leadership via 109–113, *111*; parents/carers/ grandparents and 92–93
actualizing tendency 54–55
Adler, A.: on equality 5; on good authority 74–75; Individual Psychology 52–53, 63–66, 122; on social embeddedness 47
Ancona, D. 189
andragogy: approach to leadership 165, *166*, 167; model of learning 4
Angelou, M. 195
Anning, A. 192, 198
anti-discriminatory practice 154–160
Apple, M. 33
art, learning and 144, *145, 146, 147*, 148, *149*
Ashby, R. 15, 17
Asma's story 152–154, *153, 154*
Assessment for Learning: Early Childhood Exemplars (Carr) 118
authoritarian/autocratic parenting 45
authoritative/democratic parenting 45
Authority and the Individual (Russell) 75

basic-assumption-groups 49
basic needs, in theory of human motivation 6
Bateson, G. 17
Baumrind, D. 45
Becoming a Leader (Bennis) 179
Benn, T. 87–113
Bennis, W. 42, 179
Bentley, T. 104
Bertalanffy, L. von 15, 16–17
Better Together programme 190–191
Bettner, B.L. 50
Beyerlein, M. 199
biased apperceptions 65
Bion, W. 49, 62–63
Blaffer Hrdy, S. 92, 93
Boldt, R. 133
Boog, B. 25–26, 32, 143
Boulding, K. 17
Boulton, J.C. 131
boundary objects: building trust triangle 178–179; exploring myths 180, *180*; importance of 177–178, 199; supporting integrated working 180, **181–184**, 185; values contract 185, **185–186**
boundary spanning 198–199
Boyle, D. 109
brain, IPNB definition *43*
Braun, V. 127
Bronfenbrenner, U. 77
Bryson, J. 178, 198–199
Buber, M. 191
bullying 160–165

Cahn, E, 90
capable, to feel 50, *51*
Capra, F. 15–16

carers, activism and 92–93
Carr, M. 118
Centre Inquiry Group 120, 126–127
Centres of Innovation 118
Chandler, T. 178
chaos theory 18–19
chat group, girls' 154–157
Children's Centre programme 95–96,
    98–99
Chipchase, L. 194
Churchman, C.W. 17
Clarke, V. 127
climbing frame of opportunity *97*
co-construction, at Pen Green 107, 109
collaborative advantage 176
collaborative endeavours: barriers to
    176–177, 197–198; boundary objects
    and 177–180, 185; building relationships
    and 189–193; potential partners in
    175; reframing difficulties 196–200;
    secure vs. loose approach 174–176; self-
    actualisation and 193–196; systemic
    thinking and 30–31, 186–189, *187*
collaborative inertia 171–172, 174, *175*,
    197–198
collaborative inquiry *see* action research
    (collaborative inquiry)
collective unconscious 54
community: developing leadership in
    109–113; development/action of 7–8;
    good authority and 75–77, **76**
competition, systems theory and 25
complexity, of integrated Children's
    Centres 4
complexity theory 18–19, 131
complex system 16, *16*
confirmation, in good authority 67
connectedness 50, *51*
Connecting Communities project 152–153
conscious experience (qualia) 32–33
containment 62–63, *64*, 68
continuity, in good authority 67
courage *51*, 51–52
Coyne, I.T. 131
Cropper, S. 196–197
Crosby, B. 178, 198–199
cross boundary groups 199
Crucial Cs (psychological needs) 49–52, *51*
Csikszentmihalyi, M. 196
*Curious Incident of the Dog in the Night-
    Time, The* (Haddon) 120

democracy 4–5, *46*
Democracy in America (de Tocqueville) 75
democratising leadership: challenges of
    integrated provision *39–40*, 39–41;
    leadership and management in 41–44;
    overview of 9, 38–39; parenting parallels
    44–46, *46*; psychological understandings
    of *see* psychology of leadership
denigration of past, systems theory and 24
depressive position 61
depth psychologies, NPQICL and 6
development/formative function, of
    supervision 70–71, *71*
Devita, M. 176–177
Dewey, J. 4
discriminatory behaviour: interview
    regarding 157–160; Shazia's story
    160–165, *162*, *163*
Doctoral Study Group 132–133
double hermeneutic process 33
Dreikurs, R.: on belonging 131; on courage
    66; on democracy 38, 75; on emotions
    130; goals of misbehaviour 52; on
    inferiority feelings 133; on parenting 45
Dweck, C.S. 133

Early Childhood Education and Care
    settings (ECEC): activism in 92–93,
    109–113; as integrated centre 87–88;
    leadership programme for 100–107
Early Excellence Centres (EECs) 1–2, 39,
    77, 94–95
Early Years Foundation Stage Framework
    (EYFS) 116
Eden, C. 177
ego development 52–53, 56, **57–58**
ego ideal 60
ego strength 53, **53**
Elton-Chalcraft, S. 155, 158
emancipation, in systems approach 31–33
emotion, at work 191
emotional contagion 68–69
endosymbiotic theory 17
Erikson, E. 53, **53**
European Early Childhood Education
    Research Association (EECERA)
    conference 142
existential dilemma 59
experience-based learning 7
expressive arts, leadership and 141–142
external supervision 194

Fairbairn, R. 59
Fairhurst, G.T. 133
false self 62
family systems theory 52
feedback 25, 122, 132–133
feeling, containment and 63, *64*
Ferenczi, S. 59
Ferguson, E.D. 75
Fifth Discipline, The (Senge) 19–20, 22
first person action inquiry 126; *see also*
    action research (collaborative inquiry)
Fletcher, C. 3
Fletcher, J. 189–190
flow, defined 196
Focus Group Discussion Reports 127–128
Fonagy, P. 44
Forest School 125, *125*
Formosinho, J. 46
fractal geometry 18
freefall writing 142–144
Freire, P. 7, 31, 109
Freud, A. 53
Freud, S. 47–48, 59–60
Fromm, E. 56, 58–59
Fullan, M. 22, 165
funding, for early years education 1–2

Gaia Hypothesis 19
gender, power and 189–190
geographical synchronicity, integrated
    working and **184**, 185
Giddens, A. 135
girls' chat group 154–157
Glaser, B.G. 131
Goals of Misbehaviour (Dreikurs) 52
Goleman, D. 44, 191
good authority: ecological systems
    promoting 74–77, **76**; functions of
    67–68; leadership and 195; seeking
    feedback and 123; undermining of
    77–81, *79*
Good Regulator Theorem 17
Gopnik, A. 93
Goss, P. 193–194
government, good authority and 75–77, **76**
grandparents, activism and 92–93
grand strategy, systems theory and 24
Gray, B. 198
group dynamics 48–49
groupthink 24–25
guardianship, at Pen Green 107–109, *108*

Haddock, L. 88
Haddon, M. 120
Hall, V. 41
Hamlin, R. 45
Hargreaves, A. 101
Harris, M. 109
Hartmann, H. 53
Hawkins, P. 70
Heisenberg, W. 16
Heron, J. 123, 126
Hesselbein, F. 179
hierarchy of needs *55*, 55–56
Hillfields Centre 3
Hillman, K. 176–177
Hitler, A. 49
Hodge, M. 100
holding environment 62
holism 63
holons, in systems theory 15
Horney, K. 56, 58
humanistic psychology 5–6, 54
Human Relations (journal) 49
Human Side of Enterprise, The
    (McGregor) 31
Hume, J. 24
Huxham, C. 176, 177, 185, 196, 197

iceberg theory 47–49, *48*
incompatibility, systems theory and 23
individual-client interface tensions *71*, *72*
individual-management interface tensions
    71, *72*
Individual Psychology 52–53, 122
individuals, good authority and **76**, 76–77
individuation 50, 53–54
inferiority *65*, 65–66, *67*
inquiry, living life as 140–142; *see also* action
    research (collaborative inquiry)
integration, IPNB definition *43*
integrative services for children: 1996–2006
    developments 94–99; guardianship at
    Pen Green 107–109, *108*; leadership
    programme for 100–107, *101*, *103*; at
    Pen Green 87–88
integrity, building relationships and 173
inter-organisational relations (IOR)
    196–198, **197**
interpersonal dynamics theories 56, 58–59
Interpersonal Neurobiology (IPNB)
    42–43, *43*
interview, regarding racism 157–160

Jaworski, J. 115
Jenkins, J. 178
Jenkins, M. 178
John, K. 3, 8, 38–81, 134, 195
Jones, E. 60
journaling: as freefall writing 142–144; reflective 155, 160–165, *162*, *163*; value of 141–142
Jung, C. 53–54

Kadushin, A. 70
Kauffman, S. 18
Kegan, R. 66
Klavins, E. 115–136
Klein, M. 59–62
Knowing Who I Am and What I Know (Anning) 192
Koestler, A. 15
Koru symbolism 117–118
Kraemer, S. 93, 111–112
Kuhn, T. 20

Labour Early Years Task Force 94
Laitinen-Väänänen, S. 194
Lambert, L. 112, 132, 136
Laming, L. 189
lateral brain function 41–42
Law of Requisite Variety 17
Layard, R. 6
leadership: approaches to problems 173–174; awakening conscious 115–119; building relationships and 173; in co-operative practice research 129–136; in democracies *46*; democratising *see* democratising leadership; expressive arts and 141–142; as inquiry 122–123; management and 41–44; political aspect of 151; as praxeology 151–152; rich picture depicting 149–151, *150*; self-actualisation and 173; slow/visible 144; styles of 45; systemic approach to 165–169, *166*, 172–173; untangling democratic 119–121
leadership development: applying systems theory to 19–22; building relationships and 189–193; initiatives in 27–36; Pen Green programme 100–107; PhD studies in 8; reframing difficulties 196–200; self-actualisation and 193–196; systemic thinking and 186–189, *187*; systems theory inconsistencies in 22–26; web illustrating *29*
Leadership Development Web 165

learning: art and 144, *145*, *146*, *147*, 148, *149*; leadership and 165–169
learning disabled theory 198
learning organisations 21
Learning Stories approach 118–119
Learning to be Strong: Setting Up a Neighbourhood Service for Under-Fives and Their Families (Whalley) 89
Le Bon, G. 49
Lew, A. 50
Lewin, K. 4, 18, 45, 49
line management supervision 70
Loevinger, J. 56, **57–58**
Lofland, J. 128
Lofland, L. 128

Macy Conferences 18
Mahler, M. 50
management 19–22, 41–44
management-client interface tensions *71*, 72
management/normative function, of supervision 70–71, *71*
Margulis, L. 17
Marshall, J. 119, 123, 131, 140–142, 165
Maslow, A. 6, 54, *55*, 55–56
Maturana, H. 18
McGilchrist, I. 41–42
McGregor, D. 31, 134
McMillan, M. 95
McNiff, J. 24
Meads, G. 173, 179
Mendelbrot, B. 18
Mezirow, J. 6, 122, 132, 134
mind, IPNB definition *43*
mindsight 44
mirror neuron system 42
Mitchell, J. 60
Mosak, H. 133
Moss, P. 89
Mythical Culture Map 180, *180*

National Children's Centre Network 102
National College for School Leadership (NCSL) 14, 26–27, 38, 190–191
National Professional Qualification in Integrated Centre Leadership (NPQICL): development 2–3, 100–107, *101*; philosophy 3–4; pilot programme participation 117–118; theoretical underpinnings 4–8
National Reference Group 102
Neighbourhood Nurseries Programme 95
neuroscience research 41, 47

object relations theory 59–62
Ofsted Inspection 124–125
Oliveira-Formosinho, J. 46
operational cohesion, in integrated working **183**, 185
organic networks 35
organisation, in systems theory *29*, 35
Otero, G. 190–191
outcome focus 23

paisley design 144, *145*, *146*, *147*, 148, *149*
Pakistani heritage community 144, 148
Palmer, I. 197
paranoid position 61
parenting: activism in 92–93, 99; as educators 98; as leaders 44–46, *46*
Parker, C. 139–169
participative/democratic parenting 45, *46*
Pearce-McCall, D. 42, 43
pedagogical leadership 165, *166*, 167
pedagogy of activism 92
Peeters, J. 110
Pen Green Centre: 1996–2006 developments 94–99; community development of 89–92, *90*; guardianship at 107–109, *108*; as integrative 87–88; leadership programme 100–107; leadership qualification 2–3; as learning organisation *97*, 98
permissive parenting 45
person-centred therapy 55, 195
PhD Learning Group 140
philosophy, of NPQICL 3–4
Pickett, K. 5
pleasure principle 59–60
political aspect, of leadership 151
political imperative, systems theory and 23
poverty 96
practice-based research: acting upon feedback in 121–123; developing systemic leadership 129–136; impact on outcomes 123–125; research methods overview 126–129; struggle towards 119–121; vision of 119
praxeology 151–152, *166*, 167
predictability, systems theory and 25–26
Prigogine, I. 18
problem solving strategies 196–200
Proctor, B. 70
professional silos 176–177
Psychogenesis of Manic-Depressive States, The (Klein) 60
psychological needs (Crucial Cs) 49–52, *51*

psychology of leadership: family systems theory 52; fundamental needs 49–52; group development 49; group dynamics 48–49; iceberg theory 47–48, *48*; neuroscience research and 47
psychosocial developmental stages 52–53, **53**
Pugh, G. 89
Putnam, R. 190

qualia (conscious experience) 32–33
qualitative research 34

racism: interview 157–160; reflection on 154–157; Shazia's story 160–165, *162*, *163*
randomness, systems theory and 26
Rapaport, A. 17
rapprochement 50
Reason, P. 119, 126, 131
reflective practice 33–34, 154–157
regression 6, 56
relational nourishment **181**, 185
relationships: building/rebuilding 189–193; gender and 190; IPNB definition *43*; leadership and 173
Repositioning Leadership in Early Years Contexts (Klavins) 119
research practice, in systems approach *29*, 34
Robinson, S. 165
Rogers, C. 5–6, 54–55, 195
rule of optimism 68–69
Russell, B. 75

safeguarding the self 58, 68
Sawyer, J. 45
Schön, D. 33, 119
second person action inquiry 126
self-actualisation 5–6, 54, 173, 193–196
self-integration 63
self-preoccupation *65*, 65–66, *67*
Senge, P. 19–22, 24, 31, 186
Sergiovanni, T.J. 136
service landscape 23–24
'Seven strong claims about successful school leadership' (Leithwood) 27
Shohet, R. 70
Siegel, D. 42, 43, 44
Sigmoid Curve 34
Skelcher, C. 198
Skinner, K. 191
social equality, stability and 4–5

Social Equality: The Challenge of Today (Dreikurs) 38, 75
social justice *166*, 168
society, good authority and 75–77, **76**
Spillane, J. 172
Spirit Level, The: Why Equality Is Better for Everyone (Wilkinson & Pickett) 5
stability theory 198
standardisation, systems theory and 26, 28
strategic/structural robustness **182**, 185
superego 60
superiority *65*, 65–66, *67*
supervisees' responsibilities 72
supervision/supervisors: effective 69–70; functions of 70–72, *71*; models of 70; promoting wellbeing 74; responsibilities of 72; skills 73, *73–74*; supportive 67–68
supportive/restorative function, of supervision 70–72, *71*
Sure Start Children's Centres (SSCCs) 1–2, 39, 77–81, 95
systemic approach: collaborative advantage and 186–189; leadership and 172–173; to leadership/learning 165–169, *166*
Systemic Leadership (Marshall) 123
systems consciousness *29*, 29–30, *166*, 167
systems theory: collaboration and *29*, 30–31; confusion of terms 15; development of 15–16; emancipation in *29*, 31–33; inconsistencies 22–26; leadership development and 19–22, 27–29, *29*; organisation in *29*, 35–36; overview of 8–9, 14–15; pioneers 16–19; research practice in *29*, 34; systems consciousness and *29*, 29–30; theory and practice *29*, 33–34
systems thinking 26, 160–165
systems, use of term 25

Tennyson, R. 174
tensions, workplace *71*, 72
theory and practice, in systems approach *29*, 33–34
theory of human motivation 6

theory of self organisation 19
thinking, containment and 63, *64*
Thorpe, S. 3
threat-rigidity theory 197–198
Tocqueville, A. de 75
Torbert, B. 122
transcendence, individuation and 53–54
transformational learning 6, 132
triangle of wellbeing *43*
Trotter, W. 49
true self 62
Trust Building Loop 185, 197
trust triangle 178–179
Tuckman, B. 49
Tuckman's Group Stages 49

unconscious, the 47–48

Vaggers, J. 171–200
Valera, F. 17–18
Vandenbroeck, M. 110
Vangen, S. 176, 177, 185, 196, 197

Waldron, V. 191
Way of Being, A (Rogers) 195
wellbeing *166*, 167–168
Whalley, M.: founding Pen Green 2, 3; on leadership 41, 43, 87–113; PhD studies in learning 8
Wheatley, M. 188
Whitaker, P.: on applying systems theory 14–36; developing NPQICL 3; leadership and management 36n1, 41; studies in learning 8, 136; theory and practice 165, 167
White, R. 53
Whitehead, J. 24
Wild, A. 173, 179
Wilkinson, R. 5
Winnicott, D. 62
Woolf, V. 142
workplace tensions *71*, 72
Wyse, D. 143

Zoller, H.M. 133